THE

LAST AMERICAN FRONTIER

BY

FREDERIC LOGAN PAXSON

JUNIOR PROFESSOR OF AMERICAN HISTORY
IN THE UNIVERSITY OF WISCONSIN

THE PRAIRIE SCHOONER

From an oil painting made in 1856 and owned by the University of Michigan.

THE

LAST AMERICAN FRONTIER

BY

FREDERIC LOGAN PAXSON

JUNIOR PROFESSOR OF AMERICAN HISTORY
IN THE UNIVERSITY OF WISCONSIN

COOPER SQUARE PUBLISHERS, INC.
NEW YORK
1970

Originally Published 1910
Published by Cooper Square Publishers, Inc.
59 Fourth Avenue, New York, N. Y. 10003
Standard Book Number 8154-0324-0
Library of Congress Catalog Card No. 75-115693

PREFACE

I HAVE told here the story of the last frontier within the United States, trying at once to preserve the picturesque atmosphere which has given to the "Far West" a definite and well-understood meaning, and to indicate those forces which have shaped the history of the country beyond the Mississippi. In doing it I have had to rely largely upon my own investigations among sources little used and relatively inaccessible. The exact citations of authority, with which I might have crowded my pages, would have been out of place in a book not primarily intended for the use of scholars. But I hope, before many years, to exploit in a larger and more elaborate form the mass of detailed information upon which this sketch is based.

My greatest debts are to the owners of the originals from which the illustrations for this book have been made; to Claude H. Van Tyne, who has repeatedly aided me with his friendly criticism; and to my wife, whose careful readings have saved me from many blunders in my text.

FREDERIC L. PAXSON.

ANN ARBOR, August 7, 1909.

v

CONTENTS

CONTENTS

CHAPTER XXI

CHAPTER XXII

CHAPTER XXIII

THE LAST AMERICAN FRONTIER

CHAPTER I

THE WESTWARD MOVEMENT

THE story of the United States is that of a series of frontiers which the hand of man has reclaimed from nature and the savage, and which courage and foresight have gradually transformed from desert waste to virile commonwealth. It is the story of one long struggle, fought over different lands and by different generations, yet ever repeating the conditions and episodes of the last period in the next. The winning of the first frontier established in America its first white settlements. Later struggles added the frontiers of the Alleghanies and the Ohio, of the Mississippi and the Missouri. The winning of the last frontier completed the conquest of the continent.

The greatest of American problems has been the problem of the West. For four centuries after the discovery there existed here vast areas of fertile lands which beckoned to the colonist and invited him to migration. On the boundary between the settlements and the wilderness stretched an indefinite line that advanced westward from year to year.

Hardy pioneers were ever to be found ahead of it, blazing the trails and clearing in the valleys. The advance line of the farmsteads was never far behind it. And out of this shifting frontier between man and nature have come the problems that have occupied and directed American governments since their beginning, as well as the men who have solved them. The portion of the population residing in the frontier has always been insignificant in number, yet it has well-nigh controlled the nation. The dominant problems in politics and morals, in economic development and social organization, have in most instances originated near the frontier or been precipitated by some shifting of the frontier interest.

The controlling influence of the frontier in shaping American problems has been possible because of the construction of civilized governments in a new area, unhampered by institutions of the past or conservative prejudices of the present. Each commonwealth has built from the foundation. An institution, to exist, has had to justify itself again and again. No force of tradition has kept the outlawed fact alive. The settled lands behind have in each generation been forced to remodel their older selves upon the newer growths beyond.

Individuals as well as problems have emerged from the line of the frontier as it has advanced across a continent. In the conflict with the wilderness, birth, education, wealth, and social standing have counted for little in comparison with strength, vigor, and aggressive courage. The life there has always been hard, killing off the weaklings or driving them back to the settlements, and leaving as a result a picked population not noteworthy for its culture or its refinements, but eminent in qualities of positive force for good or bad. The bad man has been quite as typical of the frontier as the hero, but both have possessed its dominant virtues of self-confidence, vigor, and initiative. Thus it has been that the men of the frontiers have exerted an influence upon national affairs far out of proportion to their strength in numbers.

The influence of the frontier has been the strongest single factor in American history, exerting its power from the first days of the earliest settlements down to the last years of the nineteenth century, when the frontier left the map. No other force has been continuous in its influence throughout four centuries. Men still live whose characters have developed under its pressure. The colonists of New England were not too early for its shaping.

The earliest American frontier was in fact a European frontier, separated by an ocean from the life at home and meeting a wilderness in every extension. English commercial interests, stimulated by the successes of Spain and Portugal, began the organization of corporations and the planting of trading depots before the sixteenth century ended. The accident that the Atlantic seaboard had no exploitable products at once made the American commercial trading company of little profit and translated its depots into resident colonies. The first instalments of colonists had little intention to turn pioneer, but when religious and political quarrels in the mother country made merry England a melancholy place for Puritans, a motive was born which produced a generation of voluntary frontiersmen. Their scattered outposts made a line of contact between England and the American wilderness which by 1700 extended along the Atlantic from Maine to Carolina. Until the middle of the eighteenth century the frontier kept within striking distance of the sea. Its course of advance was then, as always, determined by nature and geographic fact. Pioneers followed the line of least resistance. The river valley was the natural communicating link, since along its waters the vessel could be advanced, while along its banks rough trails could most easily develop into highways. The extent and distribution of this colonial frontier was determined by the contour of the seaboard along which it lay.

Running into the sea, with courses nearly parallel, the Atlantic rivers kept the colonies separated. Each colony met its own problems in its own way. England was quite as accessible as some of the neighboring colonies. No natural routes invited communication among the settlements, and an English policy deliberately discouraged attempts on the part of man to bring the colonies together. Hence it was that the various settlements developed as island frontiers, touching the river mouths, not advancing much along the shore line, but penetrating into the country as far as the rivers themselves offered easy access.

For varying distances, all the important rivers of the seaboard are navigable; but all are broken by falls at the points where they emerge upon the level plains of the coast from the hilly courses of the foothills of the Appalachians. Connecting these various waterfalls a line can be drawn roughly parallel to the coast and marking at once the western limit of the earliest colonies and the line of the second frontier. The first frontier was the seacoast itself. The second was reached at the falls line shortly after 1700.

Within these island colonies of the first frontier American life began. English institutions were transplanted in the new soil and shaped in growth by the quality of their nourishment. They came to meet the needs of their dependent populations, but they ceased to be English in the process. The facts of similarity among the institutions of Massachusetts and Pennsylvania, or Virginia, or Georgia, point clearly to the similar stocks of ideas imported with the colonists, and the similar problems attending upon the winning of the first frontier. Already, before the next frontier at the falls line had been reached, the older settlements had begun to develop a spirit of conservatism plainly different from the attitude of the old frontier.

The falls line was passed long before the colonial period came to an end, and pioneers were working their way from clearing to clearing, up into the mountains, by the early eighteenth century. As they approached the summit of the eastern divide, leaving the falls behind, the essential isolation of the provinces began to weaken under the combined forces of geographic influence and common need. The valley routes of communication which determined the lines of advance run parallel, across the first frontier, but have a tendency to converge among the mountains and to stand on common ground at the summit. Every reader of Francis Parkman knows how in the years from 1745 to 1756 the pioneers of the more aggressive colonies crossed the Alleghanies and meeting on the summit found that there they must make common cause against the French, or recede. The gateways of the West converge where the headwaters of the Tennessee and Cumberland and Ohio approach the Potomac and its neighbors. There the colonists first came to have common associations and common problems. Thus it was that the years in which the frontier line reached the forks of the Ohio were filled with talk of colonial union along the seaboard. The frontier problem was already influencing the life of the East and impelling a closer union than had been known before.

The line of the frontier was generally parallel to the coast in 1700. By 1800 it had assumed the form of a wedge, with its apex advancing down the rivers of the Mississippi Valley and its sides sloping backward to north and south. The French war of 1756–1763 saw the apex at the forks of the Ohio. In the seventies it started down the Cumberland as pioneers filled up the valleys of eastern Kentucky and Tennessee. North and south the advance was slower. No other river valleys could aid as did the Ohio, Cumberland, and Tennessee, and population must always follow the line of least resistance. On both sides of the main advance, powerful Indian confederacies contested the ground, opposing the entry of the whites. The centres of Indian strength were along the Lakes and north of the Gulf. Intermediate was the strip of "dark and bloody ground," fought over and hunted over by all, but occupied by none; and inviting white approach through the three valleys that opened it to the Atlantic.

The war for independence occurred just as the extreme frontier started down the western rivers. Campaigns inspired by the West and directed by its leaders saw to it that when the independence was achieved the boundary of the United States should not be where England had placed it in 1763, on the summit of the Alleghanies, but at the Mississippi itself, at which the lines of settlement were shortly to arrive. The new nation felt the influence of this frontier in the very negotiations which made it free. The development of its policies and its parties felt the frontier pressure from the start.

Steadily after 1789 the wedge-shaped frontier advanced. New states appeared in Kentucky and Tennessee as concrete evidences of its advance, while before the century ended, the campaign of Mad Anthony Wayne at the Fallen Timbers had allowed the northern flank of the wedge to cross Ohio and include Detroit. At the turn of the century Ohio entered the Union in 1803, filled with a population tempted to meet the trying experiences of the frontier by the call of lands easier to till than those in New England, from which it came. The old eastern communities still retained the traditions of colonial isolation; but across the mountains there was none of this. Here state lines were artificial and convenient, not representing facts of barrier or interest. The emigrants from varying sources passed over single routes, through single gateways, into a valley which knew little of itself as state but was deeply impressed with its national bearings. A second war with England gave voice to this newer nationality of the newer states.

The war with England in its immediate consequences was a bad investment. It ended with the government nearly bankrupt, its military reputation redeemed only by a victory fought after the peace was signed, its naval strength crushed after heroic resistance. The eastern population, whose war had been forced upon it by the West, was bankrupt too. And by 1814 began the Hegira. For five years the immediate result of the struggle was a suffering

East. A new state for every year was the western accompaniment.

The westward movement has been continuous in America since the beginning. Bad roads, dense forests, and Indian obstructers have never succeeded in stifling the call of the West. A steady procession of pioneers has marched up the slopes of the Appalachians, across the trails of the summits, and down the various approaches to the Mississippi Valley. When times have been hard in the East, the stream has swollen to flood proportions. In the five years which followed the English war the accelerated current moved more rapidly than ever before; while never since has its speed been equalled save in the years following similar catastrophes, as the panics of 1837 and 1857, or in the years under the direct inspiration of the gold fields.

Five new states between 1815 and 1821 carried the area of settlement down the Ohio to the Mississippi, and even up the Missouri to its junction with the Kansas. The whole eastern side was filled with states, well populated along the rivers, but sparsely settled to north and south. The frontier wedge, noticeable by 1776, was even more apparent, now that the apex had crossed the Mississippi and ascended the Missouri to its bend, while the wings dragged back, just including New Orleans at the south, and hardly touching Detroit at the north. The river valleys controlled the distribution of population, and as yet it was easier and simpler to follow the valleys farther west than to strike out across country for lands nearer home but lacking the convenience of the natural route.

For the pioneer advancing westward the route lay direct from the summit of the Alleghanies to the bend of the Missouri. The course of the Ohio facilitated his advance, while the Missouri River, for two hundred and fifty miles above its mouth, runs so nearly east and west as to afford a natural continuation of the route. But at the mouth of the Kansas the Missouri bends. Its course changes to north and south and it ceases to be a highway for the western traveller. Beyond the bend an overland journey must commence. The Platte and Kansas and Arkansas all continue the general direction, but none is easily navigable. The emigrant must leave the boat near the bend of the Missouri and proceed by foot or wagon if he desire to continue westward. With the admission of Missouri in 1821 the apex of the frontier had touched the great bend of the river, beyond which it could not advance with continued ease. Population followed still the line of easiest access, but now it was simpler to condense the settlements farther east, or to broaden out to north or south, than to go farther west. The flanks of the wedge began to move. The southwest cotton states received their influx of population. The country around the northern lakes began to fill up. The opening of the Erie Canal in 1825 made easier the advancing of the northern frontier line, with Michigan, Wisconsin, and even Iowa and Minnesota to be colonized. And while these flanks were filling out, the apex remained at the bend of the Missouri, whither it had arrived in 1821.

There was more to hold the frontier line at the bend of the Missouri than the ending of the water route. In those very months when pioneers were clearing plots near the mouth of the Kaw, or Kansas, a major of the United States army was collecting data upon which to build a tradition of a great American desert; while the Indian difficulty, steadily increasing as the line of contact between the races grew longer, acted as a vigorous deterrent.

Schoolboys of the thirties, forties, and fifties were told that from the bend of the Missouri to the Stony Mountains stretched an American desert. The makers of their geography books drew the desert upon their maps, coloring its brown with the speckled aspect that connotes Sahara or Arabia, with camels, oases, and sand dunes. The legend was founded upon the fact that rainfall becomes more scanty as the slopes approach the Rockies, and upon the observation of Major Stephen H. Long, who traversed the country in 1819–1820. Long reported that it could never support an agricultural population. The standard weekly journal of the day thought of it as "covered with sand, gravel, pebbles, etc." A writer in the forties told of its "utter destitution of timber, the sterility of its sandy soil," and believed that at "this point the

Creator seems to have said to the tribes of emigration that are annually rolling toward the west, 'Thus far shalt thou go, and no farther.'" Thus it came about that the frontier remained fixed for many years near the bend of the Missouri. Difficulty of route, danger from Indians, and a great and erroneous belief in the existence of a sandy desert, all served to barricade the way. The flanks advanced across the states of the old Northwest, and into Louisiana and Arkansas, but the western outpost remained for half a century at the point which it had reached in the days of Stephen Long and the admission of Missouri.

By 1821 many frontiers had been created and crossed in the westward march; the seaboard, the falls line, the crest of the Alleghanies, the Ohio Valley, the Mississippi and the Missouri, had been passed in turn. Until this last frontier at the bend of the Missouri had been reached nothing had ever checked the steady progress. But at this point the nature of the advance changed. The obstacles of the American desert and the Rockies refused to yield to the "heel-and-toe" methods which had been successful in the past. The slavery quarrel, the Mexican War, even the Civil War, came and passed with the area beyond this frontier scarcely changed. It had been crossed and recrossed; new centres of life had grown up beyond it on the Pacific coast; Texas had acquired an identity and a population; but the so-called desert with its doubtful soils, its lack of easy highways and its Indian inhabitants, threatened to become a constant quantity.

From 1821 to 1885 extends, in one form or another, the struggle for the last frontier. The imperative demands from the frontier are heard continually throughout the period, its leaders in long succession are filling the high places in national affairs, but the problem remains in its same territorial location. Connected with its phases appear the questions of the middle of the century. The destiny of the Indian tribes is suggested by the long line of contact and the impossibility of maintaining a savage and a civilized life together and at once. A call from the farther West leads to more thorough exploration of the lands beyond the great frontier, bringing into existence the continental trails, producing problems of long-distance government, and intensifying the troubles of the Indians. The final struggle for the control of the desert and the elimination of the frontier draws out the tracks of the Pacific railways, changes and reshapes the Indian policies again, and brings into existence, at the end of the period, the great West. But the struggle is one of half a century, repeating the events of all the earlier struggles, and ever more bitter as it is larger and more difficult. It summons the aid of the nation, as such, before it is concluded, but when it is ended the first era in American history has been closed.

CHAPTER II

A LENGTHENING frontier made more difficult the maintenance of friendly relations between the two races involved in the struggle for the continent. It increased the area of danger by its extension, while its advance inland pushed the Indian tribes away from their old home lands, concentrating their numbers along its margin and thereby aggravating their situation. Colonial negotiations for lands as they were needed had been relatively easy, since the Indians and whites were nearly enough equal in strength to have a mutual respect for their agreements and a fear of violation. But the white population doubled itself every twenty-five years, while the Indians close enough to resist were never more than 300,000, and have remained near that figure or under it until to-day. The stronger race could afford to indulge the contempt that its superior civilization engendered, while its individual members along the line of contact became less orderly and governable as the years advanced. An increasing willingness to override on the part of the white governments and an increasing personal hatred and contempt on the part of individual pioneers, account easily for the danger

14

to life along the frontier. The savage, at his best, was not responsive to the motives of civilization; at his worst, his injuries, real or imaginary, — and too often they were real, — made him the most dangerous of all the wild beasts that harassed the advancing frontier. The problem of his treatment vexed all the colonial governments and endured after the Revolution and the Constitution. It first approached a systematic policy in the years of Monroe and Adams and Jackson, but never attained form and shape until the ideal which it represented had been outlawed by the march of civilization into the West.

The conflict between the Indian tribes and the whites could not have ended in any other way than that which has come to pass. A handful of savages, knowing little of agriculture or manufacture or trade among themselves, having no conception of private ownership of land, possessing social ideals and standards of life based upon the chase, could not and should not have remained unaltered at the expense of a higher form of life. The farmer must always have right of way against the hunter, and the trader against the pilferer, and law against self-help and private war. In the end, by whatever route, the Indian must have given up his hunting grounds and contented himself with progress into civilized life. The route was not one which he could ever have determined for himself. The stronger race had to determine it for him. Under ideal conditions it might have been determined

without loss of life and health, without promoting
a bitter race hostility that invited extinction for the
inferior race, without prostituting national honor
or corrupting individual moral standards. The
Indians needed maintenance, education, discipline,
and guardianship until the older ones should have
died and the younger accepted the new order, and
all these might conceivably have been provided.
But democratic government has never developed a
powerful and centralized authority competent to
administer a task such as this, with its incidents of
checking trade, punishing citizens, and maintaining
rigorously a standard of conduct not acceptable to
those upon whom it is to be enforced.

The acts by which the United States formulated
and carried out its responsibilities towards the
Indian tribes were far from the ideal. In theory
the disposition of the government was generally
benevolent, but the scheme was badly conceived,
while human frailty among officers of the law and
citizens as well rendered execution short of such ideal
as there was.

For thirty years the government under the Constitution had no Indian policy. In these years it
acquired the habit of dealing with the tribes as
independent — "domestic dependent nations," Justice Marshall later called them — by means of
formal treaties. Europe thought of chiefs as kings
and tribes as nations. The practice of making
treaties was based on this delusion. After a century

of practice it was finally learned that nomadic savages have no idea of sovereign government or legal obligation, and that the assumption of the existence of such knowledge can lead only to misconception and disappointment.

As the frontier moved down the Ohio, individual wars were fought and individual treaties were made as occasion offered. At times the tribes yielded readily to white occupation; occasionally they struggled bitterly to save their lands; but the result was always the same. The right bank of the river, long known as the Indian Shore, was contested in a series of wars lasting nearly until 1800, and became available for white colonization only after John Jay had, through his treaty of 1794, removed the British encouragement to the Indians, and General Wayne had administered to them a decisive defeat. Isolated attacks were frequent, but Tecumseh's war of 1811 was the next serious conflict, while, after General Harrison brought this war to an end at Tippecanoe, there was comparative peace along the northwest frontier until the time of Black Hawk and his uprising of 1832.

The left bank of the river was opened with less formal resistance, admitting Kentucky and Tennessee before the Indian Shore was a safe habitation for whites. South of Tennessee lay the great southern confederacies, somewhat out of the line of early western progress, and hence not plunged into struggles until the War of 1812 was over. But as Wayne

c

and Harrison had opened the Northwest, so Jackson cleared the way for white advance into Alabama and Mississippi. By 1821 new states touched the Mississippi River along its whole course between New Orleans and the lead mines of upper Illinois.

In the advance of the frontier to the bend of the Missouri some of the tribes were pushed back, while others were passed and swallowed up by the invading population. Experience showed that the two races could not well live in adjacent lands. The conditions which made for Indian welfare could not be kept up in the neighborhood of white settlements, for the more lawless of the whites were ever ready, through illicit trade, deceit, and worse, to provoke the most dangerous excesses of the savage. The Indian was demoralized, the white became steadily more intolerant.

Although the ingenious Jefferson had anticipated him in the idea, the first positive policy which looked toward giving to the Indian a permanent home and the sort of guardianship which he needed until he could become reconciled to civilized life was the suggestion of President Monroe. At the end of his presidency, Georgia was angrily demanding the removal of the Cherokee from her limits, and was ready to violate law and the Constitution in her desire to accomplish her end. Monroe was prepared to meet the demand. He submitted to Congress, on January 27, 1825, a report from Calhoun, then Secretary of War, upon the numbers of the tribes, the area of their lands, and the area of available destinations for them. He recommended that as rapidly as agreements could be made with them they be removed to country lying westward and northwestward, — to the further limits of the Louisiana Purchase, which lay beyond the line of the western frontier.

Already, when this message was sent to Congress, individual steps had been taken in the direction which it pointed out. A few tribes had agreed to cross the Mississippi, and had been allotted lands in Missouri and Arkansas. But Missouri, just admitted, and Arkansas, now opening up, were no more hospitable to Indian wards than Georgia and Ohio had been. The Indian frontier must be at some point still farther west, towards the vast plains overrun by the Osage[1] and Kansa tribes, the Pawnee and the Sioux. There had been few dealings with the Indians beyond the Mississippi before Monroe advanced his policy. Lieutenant Pike had visited the head of the Mississippi in 1805 and had treated with the Sioux for a reserve at St. Paul. Subsequent agreements farther south brought the Osage tribes within the treaty arrangements. The year 1825 saw the notable treaties which prepared the way for peace among the western tribes, and the reception by these tribes of the eastern nations.

[1] My usage in spelling tribal names follows the list agreed upon by the bureaus of Indian Affairs and American Ethnology, and printed in C. J. Kappler, Indian Affairs, Laws and Treaties, 57th Cong., 1st Sess., Sen. Doc. 452, Serial 4253, p. 1021.

Five weeks after the special message Congress authorized a negotiation with the Kansa and Osage nations. These tribes roamed over a vast country extending from the Platte River to the Red, and west as far as the lower slopes of the Rocky Mountains. Their limits had never been definitely stated, although the Osage had already surrendered claim to lands fronting on the Mississippi between the mouths of the Missouri and the Arkansas. Not only was it now desirable to limit them more closely in order to make room for Indian immigrants, but these tribes had already begun to worry traders going overland to the Southwest. As soon as the frontier reached the bend of the Missouri, the profits of the Santa Fé trade had begun to tempt caravans up the Arkansas valley and across the plains. To preserve peace along the Santa Fé trail was now as important as to acquire grounds. Governor Clark negotiated the treaties at St. Louis. On June 2, 1825, he persuaded the Osage chiefs to surrender all their lands except a strip fifty miles wide, beginning at White Hair's village on the Neosho, and running indefinitely west. The Kaw or Kansa tribe was a day later in its agreement, and reserved a thirty-mile strip running west along the Kansas River. The two treaties at once secured rights of transit and pledges of peace for traders to Santa Fé, and gave the United States title to ample lands west of the frontier on which to plant new Indian colonies.

The autumn of 1825 witnessed at Prairie du Chien

the first step towards peace and condensation along the northern frontier. The Erie Canal, not yet opened, had not begun to drain the population of the East into the Northwest, and Indians were in peaceful possession of the lake shores nearly to Fort Wayne. West of Lake Michigan were constant tribal wars. The Potawatomi, Menominee, and Chippewa, first, then Winnebago, and Sauk and Foxes, and finally the various bands of Sioux around the Mississippi and upper Missouri, enjoyed still their traditional hostility and the chase. Governor Clark again, and Lewis Cass, met the tribes at the old trading post on the Mississippi to persuade them to bury the tomahawk among themselves. The treaty, signed August 19, 1825, defined the boundaries of the different nations by lines of which the most important was between the Sioux and Sauk and Foxes, which was later to be known as the Neutral Line, across northern Iowa. The basis of this treaty of Prairie du Chien was temporary at best. Before it was much more than ratified the white influx began, Fort Dearborn at the head of Lake Michigan blossomed out into Chicago, and squatters penetrating to Rock Island in the Mississippi had provoked the war of 1832, in which Black Hawk made the last stand of the Indians in the old Northwest. In the thirties the policy of removal completed the opening of Illinois and Wisconsin to the whites.

The policy of removal and colonization urged by

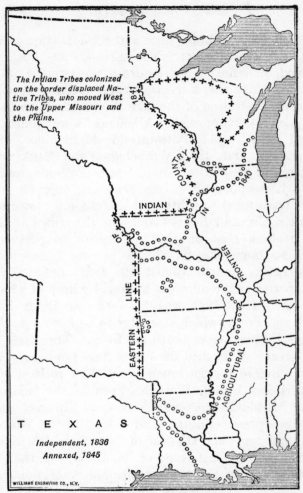

The Indian Tribes colonized on the border displaced Native Tribes, who moved West to the Upper Missouri and the Plains.

INDIAN COUNTRY
IN
FRONTIER
AGRICULTURAL
1841
1840
EASTERN LINE OF INDIAN

T E X A S

Independent, 1836
Annexed, 1845

WILLIAMS ENGRAVING CO., N.Y.

INDIAN COUNTRY AND AGRICULTURAL FRONTIER, 1840–1841

Showing the solid line of reservation lands extending from the Red River to Green Bay, and the agricultural frontier of more than six inhabitants per square mile.

22

Monroe and Calhoun was supported by Congress and succeeding Presidents, and carried out during the next fifteen years. It required two transactions, the acquisition by the United States of western titles, and the persuasion of eastern tribes to accept the new lands thus available. It was based upon an assumption that the frontier had reached its final resting place. Beyond Missouri, which had been admitted in 1821, lay a narrow strip of good lands, merging soon into the American desert. Few sane Americans thought of converting this land into states as had been the process farther east. At the bend of the Missouri the frontier had arrived; there it was to stay, and along the lines of its receding flanks the Indians could be settled with pledges of permanent security and growth. Here they could never again impede the western movement in its creation of new communities and states. Here it would be possible, in the words of Lewis Cass, to "leave their fate to the common God of the white man and the Indian."

The five years following the treaty of Prairie du Chien were filled with active negotiation and migration in the lands beyond the Missouri. First came the Shawnee to what was promised as a final residence. From Pennsylvania, into Ohio, and on into Missouri, this tribe had already been pushed by the advancing frontier. Now its ever shrinking lands were cut down to a strip with a twenty-five-mile frontage on the Missouri line and an extension

west for one hundred and twenty-five miles along
the south bank of the Kansas River and the south
line of the Kaw reserve.   Its old neighbors, the Delawares, became its new neighbors in 1829, accepting
the north bank of the Kansas, with a Missouri
River frontage as far north as the new Fort Leavenworth, and a ten-mile outlet to the buffalo country,
along the northern line of the Kaw reserve.   Later
the Kickapoo and other minor tribes were colonized
yet farther to the north.   The chase was still to be
the chief reliance of the Indian population.   Un-
limited supplies of game along the plains were to
supply his larder, with only occasional aid from
presents of other food supplies.   In the long run
agriculture was to be encouraged.   Farmers and
blacksmiths and teachers were to be provided in
various ways, but until the longed-for civilization
should arrive, the red man must hunt to live.   The
new Indian frontier was thus started by the colonization of the Shawnee and Delawares just beyond
the bend of the Missouri on the old possessions of
the Kaw.

The northern flank of the Indian frontier, as it
came to be established, ran along the line of the
frontier of white settlements, from the bend of the
Missouri, northeasterly towards the upper lakes.
Before the final line of the reservations could be
determined the Erie Canal had begun to shape the
Northwest.   Its stream of population was filling the
northern halves of Ohio, Indiana, and Illinois, and

working up into Michigan and Wisconsin. Black Hawk's War marked the last struggle for the fertile plains of upper Illinois, and made possible an Indian line which should leave most of Wisconsin and part of Iowa open to the whites.

Before Black Hawk's War occurred, the great peace treaty of Prairie du Chien had been followed, in 1830, by a second treaty at the same place, at which Governor Clark and Colonel Morgan re-enforced the guarantees of peace. The Omaha tribe now agreed to stay west of the Missouri, its neighbors being the Yankton Sioux above, and the Oto and Missouri below; a half-breed tract was reserved between the Great and Little Nemahas, while the neutral line across Iowa became a neutral strip forty miles wide from the Mississippi River to the Des Moines. Chronic warfare between the Sioux and Sauk and Foxes had threatened the extinction of the latter as well as the peace of the frontier, so now each tribe surrendered twenty miles of its land along the neutral line. Had the latter tribes been willing to stay beyond the Mississippi, where they had agreed to remain, and where they had clear and recognized title to their lands, the war of 1832 might have been avoided. But they continued to occupy a part of Illinois, and when squatters jumped their cornfields near Rock Island, the pacific counsels of old Keokuk were less acceptable than the warlike promises of the able brave Black Hawk. The resulting war, fought over the country between the Rock and Wisconsin rivers, threw the frontier into a state of panic out of all proportion to the danger threatening. Volunteers of Illinois and Michigan, and regulars from eastern posts under General Winfield Scott, produced a peace after a campaign of doubtful triumph. Near Fort Armstrong, on Rock Island, a new territorial arrangement was agreed upon. As the price of their resistance, the Sauk and Foxes, who were already located west of the Mississippi, between Missouri and the Neutral Strip, surrendered to the United States a belt of land some forty miles wide along the west bank of the Mississippi, thus putting a buffer between themselves and Illinois and making way for Iowa. The Winnebago consented, about this time, to move west of the Mississippi and occupy a portion of the Neutral Strip.

The completion of the Indian frontier to the upper lakes was the work of the early thirties. The purchase at Fort Armstrong had made the line follow the north boundary of Missouri and run along the west line of this Black Hawk purchase to the Neutral Strip. A second Black Hawk purchase in 1837 reduced their lands by a million and a quarter acres just west of the purchase of 1832. Other agreements with the Potawatomi, the Sioux, the Menominee, and the Chippewa established a final line. Of these four nations, one was removed and the others forced back within their former territories. The Potawatomi, more correctly known as the Chippewa,

Ottawa, and Potawatomi, since the tribe consisted of Indians related by marriage but representing these three stocks, had occupied the west shore of Lake Michigan from Chicago to Milwaukee. After a great council at Chicago in 1833 they agreed to cross the Mississippi and take up lands west of the Sauk and Foxes and east of the Missouri, in present Iowa. The Menominee, their neighbors to the north, with a shore line from Milwaukee to the Menominee River, gave up their lake front during these years, agreeing in 1836 to live on diminished lands west of Green Bay and including the left bank of the Wisconsin River.

The Sioux and Chippewa receded to the north. Always hereditary enemies, they had accepted a common but ineffectual demarcation line at the old treaty of Prairie du Chien in 1825. In 1837 both tribes made further cessions, introducing between themselves the greater portion of Wisconsin. The Sioux acknowledged the Mississippi as their future eastern boundary, while the Chippewa accepted a new line which left the Mississippi at its junction with the Crow Wing, ran north of Lake St. Croix, and extended thence to the north side of the Menominee country. With trifling exceptions, the north flank of the Indian frontier had been completed by 1837. It lay beyond the farthest line of white occupation, and extended unbroken from the bend of the Missouri to Green Bay.

While the north flank of the Indian frontier was

being established beyond the probable limits of
white advance, its south flank was extended in an
unbroken series of reservations from the bend of the
Missouri to the Texas line.   The old Spanish boundary of the Sabine River and the hundredth meridian
remained in 1840 the western limit of the United
States.   Farther west the Comanche and the plains
Indians roamed indiscriminately over Texas and the
United States.   The Caddo, in 1835, were persuaded to leave Louisiana and cross the Sabine into
Texas; while the quieting of the Osage title in 1825
had freed the country north of the Red River from
native occupants and opened the way for the
colonizing policy.

The southern part of the Indian Country was early
set aside as the new home of the eastern confederacies lying near the Gulf of Mexico.   The Creeks,
Cherokee, Choctaw, Chickasaw, and Seminole had
in the twenties begun to feel the pressure of the
southern states.   Jackson's campaigns had weakened them even before the cession of Florida to
the United States removed their place of refuge.
Georgia was demanding their removal when Monroe
announced his policy.

A new home for the Choctaw was provided in the
extreme Southwest in 1830.   Ten years before, this
nation had been given a home in Arkansas territory,
but now, at Dancing Rabbit Creek, it received a new
eastern limit in a line drawn from Fort Smith on the
Arkansas due south to the Red River.   Arkansas

had originally reached from the Mississippi to the hundredth meridian, but it was, after this Choctaw cession, cut down to the new Choctaw line, which remains its boundary to-day. From Fort Smith the new boundary was run northerly to the southwest corner of Missouri.

The Creeks and Cherokee promised in 1833 to go into the Indian Country, west of Arkansas and north of the Choctaw. The Creeks became the neighbors of the Choctaw, separated from them by the Canadian River, while the Cherokee adjoined the Creeks on the north and east. With small exceptions the whole of the present state of Oklahoma was thus assigned to these three nations. The migrations from their old homes came deliberately in the thirties and forties. The Chickasaw in 1837 purchased from the Choctaw the right to occupy the western end of their strip between the Red and Canadian. The Seminole had acquired similar rights among the Creeks, but were so reluctant to keep the pledge to emigrate that their removal taxed the ability of the United States army for several years.

Between the southern portion of the Indian Country and the Missouri bend minor tribes were colonized in profusion. The Quapaw and United Seneca and Shawnee nations were put into the triangle between the Neosho and Missouri. The Cherokee received an extra grant in the "Cherokee Neutral Strip," between the Osage line of 1825 and

the Missouri line. Next to the north was made a
reserve for the New York Indians, which they refused to occupy. The new Miami home came
next, along the Missouri line; while north of this
were little reserves for individual bands of Ottawa
and Chippewa, for the Piankashaw and Wea, the
Kaskaskia and Peoria, the last of which adjoined
the Shawnee line of 1825 upon the south.

The Indian frontier, determined upon in 1825,
had by 1840 been carried into fact, and existed unbroken from the Red River and Texas to the Lakes.
The exodus from the old homes to the new had in
many instances been nearly completed. The tribes
were more easily persuaded to promise than to act,
and the wrench was often hard enough to produce
sullenness or even war when the moment of departure arrived. A few isolated bands had not even
agreed to go. But the figures of the migrations,
published from year to year during the thirties,
show that all of the more important nations east of
the new frontier had ceded their lands, and that by
1840 the migration was substantially over.

President Monroe had urged as an essential part
of the removal policy that when the Indians had
been transferred and colonized they should be carefully educated into civilization, and guarded from
contamination by the whites. Congress, in various
laws, tried to do these things. The policy of removal, which had been only administrative at the
start, was confirmed by law in 1830. A formal

Bureau of Indian Affairs was created in 1832, under the supervision of a commissioner. In 1834 was passed the Indian Intercourse Act, which remained the fundamental law for half a century.

The various treaties of migration had contained the pledge that never again should the Indians be removed without their consent, that whites should be excluded from the Indian Country, and that their lands should never be included within the limits of any organized territory or state. To these guarantees the Intercourse Act attempted to give force. The Indian Country was divided into superintendencies, agencies, and sub-agencies, into which white entry, without license, was prohibited by law. As the tribes were colonized, agents and schools and blacksmiths were furnished to them in what was a real attempt to fulfil the terms of the pledge. The tribes had gone beyond the limits of probable extension of the United States, and there they were to settle down and stay. By 1835 it was possible for President Jackson to announce to Congress that the plan approached its consummation: "All preceding experiments for the improvement of the Indians" had failed; but now "no one can doubt the moral duty of the Government of the United States to protect and if possible to preserve and perpetuate the scattered remnants of this race which are left within our borders. . . . The pledge of the United States," he continued, "has been given by Congress that the country destined for the residence of this people shall be forever 'secured and guaranteed to them.' . . . No political communities can be formed in that extensive region. . . . A barrier has thus been raised for their protection against the encroachment of our citizens." And now, he concluded, "they ought to be left to the progress of events."

The policy of the United States towards the wards was generally benevolent. Here, it was sincere, whether wise or not. As it turned out, however, the new Indian frontier had to contend with movements of population, resistless and unforeseen. No Joshua, no Canute, could hold it back. The result was inevitable. The Indian, wrote one of the frontiersmen in a later day, speaking in the language of the West, "is a savage, noxious animal, and his actions are those of a ferocious beast of prey, unsoftened by any touch of pity or mercy. For them he is to be blamed exactly as the wolf or tiger is blamed." But by 1840 an Indian frontier had been erected, coterminous with the agricultural frontier, and beyond what was believed to be the limit of expansion. The American desert and the Indian frontier, beyond the bend of the Missouri, were forever to be the western boundary of the United States.

CHAPTER III

In the end of the thirties the "right wing" of the frontier, as a colonel of dragoons described it, extended northeasterly from the bend of the Missouri to Green Bay. It was an irregular line beyond which lay the Indian tribes, and behind which was a population constantly becoming more restless and aggressive. That it should have been a permanent boundary is not conceivable; yet Congress professed to regard it as such, and had in 1836 ordered the survey and construction of a military road from the mouth of the St. Peter's to the Red River. The maintenance of the southern half of the frontier was perhaps practicable, since the tradition of the American desert was long to block migration beyond the limits of Missouri and Arkansas, but north and east of Fort Leavenworth were lands too alluring to be safe in the control of the new Indian Bureau. And already before the thirties were over the upper Mississippi country had become a factor in the westward movement.

A few years after the English war the United States had erected a fort at the junction of the St. Peter's and the Mississippi, near the present city of

D 33

St. Paul. In 1805, Zebulon Montgomery Pike had treated with the Sioux tribes at this point, and by 1824 the new post had received the name Fort Snelling, which it was to retain until after the admission of Minnesota as a state. Pike and his followers had worked their way up the Mississippi from St. Louis or Prairie du Chien in skiffs or keelboats, and had found little of consequence in the way of white occupation save a few fur-trading posts and the lead mines of Du Buque. Until after the English war, indeed, and the admission of Illinois, there had been little interest in the country up the river; but during the early twenties the lead deposits around Du Buque's old claim became the centre of a business that soon made new treaty negotiations with the northern Indians necessary.

On both sides of the Mississippi, between the mouths of the Wisconsin and the Rock, lie the extensive lead fields which attracted Du Buque in the days of the Spanish rule, and which now in the twenties induced an American immigration. The ease with which these diggings could be worked and the demand of a growing frontier population for lead, brought miners into the borderland of Illinois, Wisconsin, and Iowa long before either of the last states had acquired name or boundary or the Indian possessors of the soil had been satisfied and removed. The nations of Winnebago, Sauk and Foxes, and Potawatomi were most interested in this new white invasion, while all were reluctant to

yield the lands to the incoming pioneers. The
Sauk and Foxes had given up their claim to nearly
all the lead country in 1804 ; the Potawatomi ceded
portions of it in 1829; and the Winnebago in the
same year made agreements covering the mines
within the present state of Wisconsin.

Gradually in the later twenties the pioneer miners
came in, one by one. From St. Louis they came up
the great river, or from Lake Michigan they crossed
the old portage of the Fox and Wisconsin. The
southern reënforcements looked much to Fort Armstrong on Rock Island for protection. The northern, after they had left Fort Howard at Green Bay,
were out of touch until they arrived near the
old trading post at Prairie du Chien. War with
the Winnebago in 1827 was followed in 1828 by
the erection of another United States fort, — at the
portage, and known as Fort Winnebago. Thus the
United States built forts to defend a colonization
which it prohibited by law and treaty.

The individual pioneers differed much in their
morals and their cultural antecedents, but were uni-
form in their determination to enjoy the profits for
which they had risked the dangers of the wilderness.
Notable among them, and typical of their highest
virtues, was Henry Dodge, later governor of Wisconsin, and representative and senator for his state
in Congress, but now merely one of the first in the
frontier movement. It is related of him that in
1806 he had been interested in the filibustering ex-

pedition of Aaron Burr, and had gone as far as New
Madrid, to join the party, before he learned that
it was called treason. He turned back in disgust.
"On reaching St. Genevieve," his chronicler con-
tinues, "they found themselves indicted for treason
by the grand jury then in session. Dodge surrendered himself, and gave bail for his appearance;
but feeling outraged by the action of the grand jury
he pulled off his coat, rolled up his sleeves, and whipt
nine of the jurors; and would have whipt the rest,
if they had not run away." With such men to deal
with, it was always difficult to enforce unpopular
laws upon the frontier. Dodge had no hesitation
in settling upon his lead diggings in the mineral
country and in defying the Indian agents, who did
their best to persuade him to leave the forbidden
country. On the west bank of the Mississippi
federal authority was successful in holding off the
miners, but the east bank was settled between
Galena and Mineral Point before either the Indian
title had been fully quieted, or the lands had been
surveyed and opened to purchase by the United
States.

The Indian war of 1827, the erection of Fort Winnebago in 1828, the cession of their mineral lands by
the Winnebago Indians in 1829, are the events most
important in the development of the first settlements
in the new Northwest. In 1829 and 1830 pioneers
came up the Mississippi to the diggings in increasing
numbers, while farmers began to cast covetous eyes

upon the prairies lying between Lake Michigan and the Mississippi. These were the lands which the Sauk and Fox tribes had surrendered in 1804, but over which they still retained rights of occupation and the chase until Congress should sell them. The entry of every American farmer was a violation of good faith and law, and so the Indians regarded it. Their largest city and the graves of their ancestors were in the peninsula between the Rock and the Mississippi, and as the invaders seized the lands, their resentment passed beyond control. The Black Hawk War was the forlorn attempt to save the lands. When it ended in crushing defeat, the United States exercised its rights of conquest to compel a revision of the treaty limits.

The great treaties of 1832 and 1833 not only removed all Indian obstruction from Illinois, but prepared the way for further settlement in both Wisconsin and Iowa. The Winnebago agreed to migrate to the Neutral Strip in Iowa, the Potawatomi accepted a reserve near the Missouri River, while the Black Hawk purchase from the offending Sauk and Foxes opened a strip some forty miles wide along the west bank of the Mississippi. These Indian movements were a part of the general concentrating policy made in the belief that a permanent Indian frontier could be established. After the Black Hawk War came the creation of the Indian Bureau, the ordering of the great western road, and the erection of a frontier police. Henry Dodge was one of the few individuals to emerge from the war with real glory. His reward came when Congress formed a regiment of dragoons for frontier police, and made him its colonel. In his regiment he operated up and down the long frontier for three years, making expeditions beyond the line to hold Pawnee conferences and meetings with the tribes of the great plains, and resigning his command only in time to be the first governor of the new territory of Wisconsin, in 1836. He knew how little dependence could be placed on the permanency of the right wing of the frontier. "Nor let gentlemen forget," he reminded his colleagues in Congress a few years later, "that we are to have continually the same course of settlements going on upon our border. They are perpetually advancing westward. They will reach, they will cross, the Rocky Mountains, and never stop till they have reached the shores of the Pacific. Distance is nothing to our people. . . . [They will] turn the whole region into the happy dwellings of a free and enlightened people."

The Black Hawk War and its resulting treaties at once quieted the Indian title and gave ample advertisement to the new Northwest. As yet there had been no large migration to the West beyond Lake Michigan. The pioneers who had provoked the war had been few in number and far from their base upon the frontier. Mere access to the country had been difficult until after the opening of the Erie Canal, and even then steamships did not run regularly on Lake Michigan until after 1832. But notoriety now tempted an increasing wave of settlers. Congress woke up to the need of some territorial adjustment for the new country.

Ever since Illinois had been admitted in 1818, Michigan had been the one remaining territory of the old Northwest, including the whole area north of Ohio, Indiana, and Illinois, and extending from Lake Huron to the Mississippi River. Her huge size was admittedly temporary, but as no large centre of population existed outside of Detroit, it was convenient to simplify the federal jurisdiction in this fashion. The lead mines on the Mississippi produced a secondary centre of population in the late twenties and pointed to an early division of Michigan. But before this could be accomplished the Black Hawk purchase had carried the Mississippi centre of population to the right bank of the river. The American possessions on this bank, west of the river, had been cast adrift without political organization on the admission of Missouri in 1821. Now the appearance of a vigorous population in an unorganized region compelled Congress to take some action, and thus, for temporary purposes, Michigan was enlarged in 1834. Her new boundary extended west to the Missouri River, between the state of Missouri and Canada. The new Northwest, which may be held to include Iowa, Wisconsin, and Minnesota, started its political history as a remote settlement in a vast territory of Michigan, with its seat of

government at Detroit.   Before it was cut off as the
territory of Wisconsin in 1836 much had been done
in the way of populating it.

The boom of the thirties brought Arkansas and
Michigan into the Union as states, and started the
growth of the new Northwest.   The industrial activity of the period was based on speculation in public
lands and routes of transportation.   America was
transportation mad.   New railways were building
in the East and being projected West.   Canals were
turning the western portage paths into water highways.   The speculative excitement touched the field
of religion as well as economics, producing new sects
by the dozen, and bringing schisms into the old.
And population moving already in its inherent restlessness was made more active in migration by the
hard times of the East in 1833 and 1834.

The immigrants brought to the Black Hawk
purchase and its vicinity, in the boom of the thirties,
came chiefly by the river route.   The lake route
was just beginning to be used; not until the Civil
War did the traffic of the upper Mississippi naturally and generally seek its outlet by Lake Michigan.
The Mississippi now carried more than its share of
the home seekers.

Steamboats had been plying on western waters in
increasing numbers since 1811.   By 1823, one had
gone as far north on the Mississippi as Fort Snelling,
while by 1832 the Missouri had been ascended to
Fort Union.   In the thirties an extensive packet

service gathered its passengers and freight at Pittsburg and other points on the Ohio, carrying them by a devious voyage of 1400 miles to Keokuk, near the southeast corner of the new Black Hawk lands. Wagons and cattle, children and furniture, crowded the decks of the boats. The aristocrats of emigration rode in the cabins provided for them, but the great majority of home seekers lived on deck and braved the elements upon the voyage. Explosions, groundings, and collisions enlivened the reckless river traffic. But in 1836 Governor Dodge found more than 22,000 inhabitants in his new territory of Wisconsin, most of whom had reached the promised land by way of the river.

For those whom the long river journey did not please, or who lived inland in Ohio or Indiana, the national road was a help. In 1825 the continuation of the Cumberland Road through Ohio had been begun. By 1836 enough of it was done to direct the overland course of migration through Indianapolis towards central Illinois. The Conestoga wagon, which had already done its share in crossing the Alleghanies, now carried a second generation to the Mississippi. At Dubuque and Buffalo and Burlington ferries were established before 1836 to take the immigrants across the Mississippi into the new West.

By the terms of its treaty, the Black Hawk purchase was to be vacated by the Indians in the summer of 1833. Before that year closed, its settlement had begun, despite the fact that the government surveys had not yet been made. Here, as elsewhere, the frontier farmer paid little regard to the legal basis of his life. He settled upon unoccupied lands as he needed them, trusting to the public opinion of the future to secure his title.

The legislature of Michigan watched the migration of 1833 and 1834, and in the latter year created the two counties of Dubuque and Demoine, beyond the Mississippi, embracing these settlements. At the old claim a town of miners appeared by magic, able shortly to boast "that the first white man hung in Iowa in a Christian-like manner was Patrick O'Conner, at Dubuque, in June, 1834." Dubuque was a mining camp, differing from the other villages in possessing a larger proportion of the lawless element. Generally, however, this Iowa frontier was peaceful in comparison with other frontiers. Life and property were safe, and except for its dealings with the Indians and the United States government, in which frontiers have rarely recognized a law, the community was law-abiding. It stands in some contrast with another frontier building at the same time up the valley of the Arkansas. "Fent Noland of Batesville," wrote a contemporary of one of the heroes of this frontier, "is in every way one of the most remarkable men of the West; for such is the versatility of his genius that he seems equally adapted to every species of effort, intellectual or physical. With a like unerring aim he shoots a bullet or a *bon mot;* and wields the pen or the Bowie

knife with the same thought, swift rapidity of
motion, and energetic fury of manner. Sunday he
will write an eloquent dissertation on religion;
Monday he rawhides a rogue; Tuesday he com-
poses a sonnet, set in silver stars and breathing the
perfume of roses to some fair maid's eyebrows;
Wednesday he fights a duel; Thursday he does up
brown the personal character of Senators Sevier
and Ashley; Friday he goes to the ball dressed in
the most finical superfluity of fashion and shines
the soul of wit and the sun of merry badinage among
all the gay gentlemen; and to close the triumphs of
the week, on Saturday night he is off thirty miles
to a country dance in the Ozark Mountains, where
they trip it on the light fantastic toe in the famous
jig of the double-shuffle around a roaring log heap
fire in the woods all night long, while between the
dances Fent Noland sings some beautiful wild song,
as 'Lucy Neal' or 'Juliana Johnson.' Thus Fent
is a myriad-minded Proteus of contradictory characters, many-hued as the chameleon fed on the dews
and suckled at the breast of the rainbow.'' Much
of this luxuriant imagery was lacking farther north.

The first phase of this development of the new
Northwest was ended in 1837, when the general panic
brought confusion to speculation throughout the
United States. For four years the sanguine hopes
of the frontier had led to large purchases of public
lands, to banking schemes of wildest extravagance,
and to railroad promotion without reason or de-

mand. The specie circular of 1836 so deranged the currency of the whole United States that the effort to distribute the surplus in 1837 was fatal to the speculative boom. The new communities suffered for their hopeful attempts. When the panic broke, the line of agricultural settlement had been pushed considerably beyond the northern and western limits of Illinois. The new line ran near to the Fox and Wisconsin portage route and the west line of the Black Hawk purchase. Milwaukee and Southport had been founded on the lake shore, hopeful of a great commerce that might rival the possessions of Chicago. Madison and its vicinity had been developed. The lead country in Wisconsin had grown in population. Across the river, Dubuque, Davenport, and Burlington gave evidence of a growing community in the country still farther west. Nearly the whole area intended for white occupation by the Indian policy had been settled, so that any further extension must be at the expense of the Indians' guaranteed lands.

On the eve of the panic, which depopulated many of the villages of the new strip, Michigan had been admitted. Her possessions west of Lake Michigan had been reorganized as a new territory of Wisconsin, with a capital temporarily at Belmont, where Henry Dodge, first governor, took possession in the fall of 1836. A territorial census showed that Wisconsin had a population of 22,214 in 1836, divided nearly equally by the Mississippi. Most of the population

was on the banks of the great river, near the lead
mines and the Black Hawk purchase, while only a
fourth could be found near the new cities along the
lake.   The outlying settlements were already pressing against the Indian neighbors, so that the new
governor soon was obliged to conduct negotiations
for further cessions.   The Chippewa, Menominee,
and Sioux all came into council within two years,
the Sioux agreeing to retire west of the Mississippi,
while the others receded far into the north, leaving
most of the present Wisconsin open to development.
These treaties completed the line of the Indian frontier as it was established in the thirties.

The Mississippi divided the population of Wisconsin nearly equally in 1836, but subsequent years
witnessed greater growth upon her western bank.
Never in the westward movement had more attractive farms been made available than those on the
right bank now reached by the river steamers and
the ferries from northern Illinois.   Two years after
the erection of Wisconsin the western towns received their independent establishment, when in
1838 Iowa Territory was organized by Congress,
including everything between the Mississippi and
Missouri rivers, and north of the state of Missouri.
Burlington, a village of log houses with perhaps five
hundred inhabitants, became the seat of government of the new territory, while Wisconsin retired
east of the river to a new capital at Madison.   At
Burlington a first legislature met in the autumn, to

choose for a capital Iowa City, and to do what it could for a community still suffering from the results of the panic.

The only Iowa lands open to lawful settlement were those of the Black Hawk purchase, many of which were themselves not surveyed and on the market. But the pioneers paid little heed to this. Leaving titles to the future, they cleared their farms, broke the sod, and built their houses.

IOWA SOD PLOW

The heavy sod of the Iowa prairies was beyond the strength of the individual settler. In the years of first development the professional sod breaker was on hand, a most important member of his community, with his great plough, and large teams of from six to twelve oxen, making the ground ready for the first crop. In the frontier mind the land belonged to him who broke it, regardless of mere title. The quarrel between the squatter and the speculator was perennial. Congress in its laws sought to dispose of lands by auction to the highest bidder, — a scheme through which the sturdy impecunious farmer saw his clearing in danger of being bought over his modest bid by an undeserving speculator. Accordingly the history of Iowa and Wisconsin is full of the claims associations by which the squatters endeavored to protect their rights and succeeded well. By voluntary association they agreed upon their claims and bounds. Transfers and sales were recorded on their books. When at last the advertised day came for the formal sale of the township by the federal land officer the population attended the auction in a body, while their chosen delegate bid off the whole area for them at the minimum price, and without competition. At times it happened that the speculator or the casual purchaser tried to bid, but the squatters present with their cudgels and air of anticipation were usually able to prevent what they believed to be unfair interference with their rights. The claims associations were entirely illegal; yet they reveal, as few American institutions do, the orderly tendencies of an American community even when its organization is in defiance of existing law.

The development of the new territories of Iowa and Wisconsin in the decade after their erection carried both far towards statehood. Burlington, the earliest capital of Iowa, was in 1840 "the largest, wealthiest, most business-doing and most fashionable city, on or in the neighborhood of the

Upper Mississippi. . . . We have three or four churches," said one of its papers, "a theatre, and a dancing school in full blast." As early as 1843 the Black Hawk purchase was overrun. The Sauk and Foxes had ceded provisionally all their Iowa lands and the Potawatomi were in danger. "Although it is but ten years to-day," said their agent, speaking of their Chicago treaty of 1833, "the tide of emigration has rolled onwards to the far West, until the whites are now crowded closely along the southern side of these lands, and will soon swarm along the eastern side, to exhibit the very worst traits of the white man's character, and destroy, by fraud and illicit intercourse, the remnant of a powerful people, now exposed to their influence." Iowa was admitted to the Union in 1846, after bickering over her northern boundary; Wisconsin followed in 1848; the remnant of both, now known as Minnesota, was erected as a territory in its own right in the next year.

Fort Snelling was nearly twenty years old before it came to be more than a distant military outpost. Until the treaties of 1837 it was in the midst of the Sioux with no white neighbors save the agents of the fur companies, a few refugees from the Red River country, and a group of more or less disreputable hangers-on. An enlargement of the military reserve in 1837 led to the eviction by the troops of its near-by squatters, with the result that one of these took up his grog shop, left the peninsula between the Mississippi and St. Peter's, and erected the first permanent settlement across the former, where St. Paul now stands. Iowa had desired a northern boundary which should touch the St. Peter's River, but when she was admitted without it and Wisconsin followed with the St. Croix as her western limit, Minnesota was temporarily without a government.

The Minnesota territorial act of 1849 preceded the active colonization of the country around St. Paul. Mendota, Fort Snelling, St. Anthony's, and Stillwater all came into active being, while the most enterprising settlers began to push up the Minnesota River, as the St. Peter's now came to be called. As usual the Indians were in the way. As usual the claims associations were resorted to. And finally, as usual the Indians yielded. At Mendota and Traverse des Sioux, in the autumn of 1851, the magnates of the young territory witnessed great treaties by which the Sioux, surrendering their portion of the permanent Indian frontier, gave up most of their vast hunting grounds to accept valley reserves along the Minnesota. And still more rapidly population came in after the cession.

The new Northwest was settled after the great day of the keelboat on western waters. Iowa and the lead country had been reached by the steamboats of the Mississippi. The Milwaukee district was reached by the steamboats from the lakes. The upper Mississippi frontier was now even more thoroughly dependent on the river navigation than

E

its neighbors had been, while its first period was over before any railroad played an immediate part in its development.

The boom period between the panics of 1837 and 1857 thus added another concentric band along the northwest border, disregarding the Indian frontier and introducing a large population where the prophet of the early thirties had declared that civilization could never go. The Potawatomi of Iowa had yielded in 1846, the Sioux in 1851. The future of the other tribes in their so-called permanent homes was in grave question by the middle of the decade. The new frontier by 1857 touched the tip of Lake Superior, included St. Paul and the lower Minnesota valley, passed around Spirit Lake in northwest Iowa, and reached the Missouri near Sioux City. In a few more years the right wing of the frontier would run due north from the bend of the Missouri.

The hopeful life of the fifties surpassed that of the thirties in its speculative zeal. The home seeker had to struggle against the occasional Indian and the unscrupulous land agent as well as his own too sanguine disposition. Fictitious town sites had to be distinguished from the real. Fraudulent dealers more than once sold imaginary lots and farms from beautifully lithographed maps to eastern investors. Occasionally whole colonies of migrants would appear on the steamboat wharves bound for non-existent towns. And when the settler had escaped fraud, and avoided or survived the racking torments of fever or cholera, the Indian danger was sometimes real.

Iowa had advanced her northwest frontier up the Des Moines River, past the old frontier fort, until in 1856 a couple of trading houses and a few families had reached the vicinity of Spirit Lake. Here, in March, 1857, one of the settlers quarrelled with a wandering Indian over a dog. The Indian belonged to Inkpaduta's band of Sioux, one not included in the treaty of 1851. Forty-seven dead settlers slaughtered by the band were found a few days later by a visitor to the village. A hard winter campaign by regulars from Fort Ridgely resulted in the rescue of some of the captives, but the indignant demand of the frontier for retaliation was never granted.

In spite of fraud and danger the population grew. For the first time the railroad played a material part in its advance. The great eastern trunk lines had crossed the Alleghanies into the Ohio valley. Chicago had received connection with the East in 1852. The Mississippi had been reached by 1854. In the spring of 1856 all Iowa celebrated the opening of a railway bridge at Davenport.

The new Northwest escaped its dangers only to fall a victim to its own ambition. An earlier decade of expansion had produced panic in 1837. Now greater expansion and prosperity stimulated an over-development that chartered railways and even built them between points that scarcely existed and through country rank in its prairie growth,

wild with game, and without inhabitants. Over-
speculation on borrowed money finally brought retribution in the panic of 1857, with Minnesota about
to frame a constitution and enter the Union. The
panic destroyed the railways and bankrupted the
inhabitants. At Duluth, a canny pioneer, who
lived in the present, refused to swap a pair of boots
for a town lot in the future city. At the other end
of the line a floating population was prepared to
hurry west on the first news of Pike's Peak gold.

But a new Northwest had come into life in spite
of the vicissitudes of 1837 and 1857. Wisconsin, Minnesota, and Iowa had in 1860 ten times the population of Illinois at the opening of the Black Hawk
War. More than a million and a half of pioneers had
settled within these three new states, building their
towns and churches and schools, pushing back the
right flank of the Indian frontier, and reiterating
their perennial demand that the Indian must go.
This was the first departure from the policy laid
down by Monroe and carried out by Adams and
Jackson. Before this movement had ended, that
policy had been attacked from another side, and was
once more shown to be impracticable. The Indian
had too little strength to compel adherence to the
contract, and hence suffered from this encroachment
by the new Northwest. His final destruction came
from the overland traffic, which already by 1857 had
destroyed the fiction of the American desert, and
introduced into his domain thousands of pioneers
lured by the call of the West and the lust for gold.

CHAPTER IV

THE SANTA FÉ TRAIL

ENGLAND had had no colonies so remote and inaccessible as the interior provinces of Spain, which stretched up into the country between the Rio Grande and the Pacific for more than fifteen hundred miles above Vera Cruz. Before the English seaboard had received its earliest colonists, the hand of Spain was already strong in the upper waters of the Rio Grande, where her outposts had been planted around the little adobe village of Santa Fé. For more than two hundred years this life had gone on, unchanged by invention or discovery, unenlightened by contact with the world or admixture of foreign blood. Accepting, with a docility characteristic of the colonists of Spain, the hard conditions and restrictions of the law, communication with these villages of Chihuahua and New Mexico had been kept in the narrow rut worn through the hills by the pack-trains of the king.

It was no stately procession that wound up into the hills yearly to supply the Mexican frontier. From Vera Cruz the port of entry, through Mexico City, and thence north along the highlands through San Luis Potosi and Zacatecas to Durango, and thence to Chihuahua, and up the valley of the Rio Grande to Santa Fé climbed the long pack-trains and the clumsy ox-carts that carried into the provinces their whole supply from outside. The civilization of the provincial life might fairly be measured by the length, breadth, and capacity of this transportation route. Nearly two thousand miles, as the road meandered, of river, mountain gorge, and arid desert had to be overcome by the mule-drivers of the caravans. What their pack-animals could not carry, could not go. What had large bulk in proportion to its value must stay behind. The ancient commerce of the Orient, carried on camels across the Arabian desert, could afford to deal in gold and silver, silks, spices, and precious drugs; in like manner, though in less degree, the world's contribution to these remote towns was confined largely to textiles, drugs, and trinkets of adornment. Yet the Creole and Mestizo population of New Mexico bore with these meagre supplies for more than two centuries without an effort to improve upon them. Their resignation gives some credit to the rigors of the Spanish colonial system which restricted their importation to the defined route and the single port. It is due as much, however, to the hard geographic fact which made Vera Cruz and Mexico, distant as they were, their nearest neighbors, until in the nineteenth century another civilization came within hailing distance, at its frontier in the bend of the Missouri.

The Spanish provincials were at once willing to endure the rigors of the commercial system and to smuggle when they had a chance. So long as it was cheaper to buy the product of the annual caravan than to develop other sources of supply the caravans flourished without competition. It was not until after the expulsion of Spain and the independence of Mexico that a rival supply became important, but there are enough isolated events before this time to show what had to occur just so soon as the United States frontier came within range.

The narrative of Pike after his return from Spanish captivity did something to reveal the existence of a possible market in Santa Fé. He had been engaged in exploring the western limits of the Louisiana purchase, and had wandered into the valley of the Rio Grande while searching for the head waters of the Red River. Here he was arrested, in 1807, by Spanish troops, and taken to Chihuahua for examination. After a short detention he was escorted to the limits of the United States, where he was released. He carried home the news of high prices and profitable markets existing among the Mexicans.

In 1811 an organized expedition set out to verify the statements of Pike. Rumor had come to the States of an insurrection in upper Mexico, which might easily abolish the trade restriction. But the revolt had been suppressed before the dozen or so of reckless Americans who crossed the plains had arrived at their destination. The Spanish authorities, restored to power and renewed vigor, received them with open prisons. In jail they were kept at Chihua-hua, some for ten years, while the traffic which they had hoped to inaugurate remained still in the future. Their release came only with the independence of Mexico, which quickly broke down the barrier against importation and the foreigner.

The Santa Fé trade commenced when the news of the Mexican revolution reached the border. Late in the fall of 1821 one William Becknell, chancing a favorable reception from Iturbide's officials, took a small train from the Missouri to New Mexico, in what proved to be a profitable speculation. He returned to the States in time to lead out a large party in the following summer. So long as the United States frontier lay east of the Missouri River there could have been no western traffic, but now that settlement had reached the Indian Country, and river steamers had made easy freighting from Pittsburg to Franklin or Independence, Santa Fé was nearer to the United States seaboard markets than to Vera Cruz. Hence the breach in the American desert and the Indian frontier made by this earliest of the overland trails.

The year 1822 was not only the earliest in the Santa Fé trade, but it saw the first wagons taken across the plains. The freight capacity of the mule-train placed a narrow limit upon the profits and extent of trade. Whether a wagon could be hauled over the rough trails was a matter of considerable doubt when Becknell and Colonel Cooper attempted it in this year. The experiment was so successful that within two years the pack-train was generally abandoned for the wagons by the Santa Fé traders.

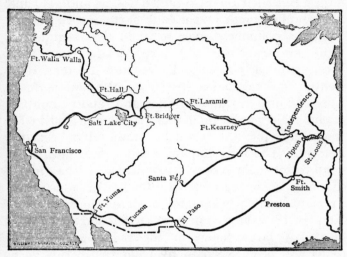

OVERLAND TRAILS

The main trail to Oregon was opened before 1840; that to California appeared about 1845; the Santa Fé trail had been used since 1821. The overland mail of 1858 followed the southern route.

The wagons carried a miscellaneous freight. "Cotton goods, consisting of coarse and fine cambrics, calicoes, domestic, shawls, handkerchiefs, steam-loom shirtings, and cotton hose," were in high demand. There were also "a few woollen goods, consisting of super blues, stroudings, pelisse cloths, and shawls, crapes, bombazettes, some light articles of cutlery, silk shawls, and looking-glasses." Backward bound their freights were lighter. Many of the wagons, indeed, were sold as part of the cargo. The returning merchants brought some beaver skins and mules, but their Spanish-milled dollars and gold and silver bullion made up the bulk of the return freight.

Such a commerce, even in its modest beginnings, could not escape the public eye. The patron of the West came early to its aid. Senator Thomas Hart Benton had taken his seat from the new state of Missouri just in time to notice and report upon the traffic. No public man was more confirmed in his friendship for the frontier trade than Senator Benton. The fur companies found him always on hand to get them favors or to "turn aside the whip of calamity." Because of his influence his son-in-law, Frémont, twenty years later, explored the wilderness. Now, in 1824, he was prompt to demand encouragement. A large policy in the building of public roads had been accepted by Congress in this year. In the following winter Senator Benton's bill provided $30,000 to mark and build a wagon road from Missouri to the United States border on the Arkansas. The earliest travellers over the road reported some annoyance from the Indians, whose hungry, curious, greedy bands would hang around their camps to beg and steal. In the Osage and Kansa treaties of 1825 these tribes agreed to let the traders traverse the country in peace.

Indian treaties were not sufficient to protect the

Santa Fé trade. The long journey from the fringe of settlement to the Spanish towns eight hundred miles southwest traversed both American and Mexican soil, crossing the international boundary on the Arkansas near the hundredth meridian. The Indians of the route knew no national lines, and found a convenient refuge against pursuers from either nation in crossing the border. There was no military protection to the frontier at the American end of the trail until in 1827 the war department erected a new post on the Missouri, above the Kansas, calling it Fort Leavenworth. Here a few regular troops were stationed to guard the border and protect the traders. The post was due as much to the new Indian concentration policy as to the Santa Fé trade. Its significance was double. Yet no one seems to have foreseen that the development of the trade through the Indian Country might prevent the accomplishment of Monroe's ideal of an Indian frontier.

From Fort Leavenworth occasional escorts of regulars convoyed the caravans to the Southwest. In 1829 four companies of the sixth infantry, under Major Riley, were on duty. They joined the caravan at the usual place of organization, Council Grove, a few days west of the Missouri line, and marched with it to the confines of the United States. Along the march there had been some worry from the Indians. After the caravan and escort had separated at the Arkansas the former, going on alone into Mexico, was scarcely out of sight of its guard before it was dangerously attacked. Major Riley rose promptly to the occasion. He immediately crossed the Arkansas into Mexico, risking the consequences of an invasion of friendly territory, and chastised the Indians. As the caravan returned, the Mexican authorities furnished an escort of troops which marched to the crossing. Here Major Riley, who had been waiting for them at Chouteau's Island all summer, met them. He entertained the Mexican officers with drill while they responded with a parade, chocolate, and "other refreshments," as his report declares, and then he brought the traders back to the States by the beginning of November.

There was some criticism in the United States of this costly use of troops to protect a private trade. Hezekiah Niles, who was always pleading for high protection to manufactures and receiving less than he wanted, complained that the use of four companies during a whole season was extravagant protection for a trade whose annual profits were not over $120,000. The special convoy was rarely repeated after 1829. Fort Leavenworth and the troops gave moral rather than direct support. Colonel Dodge, with his dragoons, — for infantry were soon seen to be ridiculous in Indian campaigning, — made long expeditions and demonstrations in the thirties, reaching even to the slopes of the Rockies. And the Santa Fé caravans continued until the forties in relative safety.

Two years after Major Riley's escort occurred an

event of great consequence in the history of the Santa Fé trail. Josiah Gregg, impelled by ill health to seek a change of climate, made his first trip to Santa Fé in 1831. As an individual trader Gregg would call for no more comment than would any one who crossed the plains eight times in a single decade. But Gregg was no mere frontier merchant. He was watching and thinking during his entire career, examining into the details of Mexican life and history and tabulating the figures of the traffic. When he finally retired from the plains life which he had come to love so well, he produced, in two small volumes, the great classic of the trade: "The Commerce of the Prairies, or the Journal of a Santa Fé Trader." It is still possible to check up details and add small bits of fact to supplement the history and description of this commerce given by Gregg, but his book remains, and is likely to remain, the fullest and best source of information. Gregg had power of scientific observation and historical imagination, which, added to unusual literary ability, produced a masterpiece.

The Sante Fé trade, begun in 1822, continued with moderate growth until 1843. This was its period of pioneer development. After the Mexican War the commerce grew to a vastly larger size, reaching its greatest volume in the sixties, just before the construction of the Pacific railways. But in its later years it was a matter of greater routine and less general interest than in those years of commence-

ment during which it was educating the United States
to a more complete knowledge of the southern portion of the American desert. Gregg gives a table
in which he shows the approximate value of the trade
for its first twenty-two years. To-day it seems
strange that so trifling a commerce should have been
national in its character and influence. In only one
year, 1843, does he find that the eastern value of the
goods sent to Santa Fé was above a quarter of a
million dollars; in that year it reached $450,000,
but in only two other years did it rise to the quarter
million mark. In nine years it was under $100,000.
The men involved were a mere handful. At the
start nearly every one of the seventy men in the
caravan was himself a proprietor. The total number increased more rapidly than the number of independent owners. Three hundred and fifty were the
most employed in any one year. The twenty-six
wagons of 1824 became two hundred and thirty
in 1843, but only four times in the interval were
there so many as a hundred.

Yet the Santa Fé trade was national in its importance. Its romance contained a constant appeal
to a public that was reading the Indian tales of James
Fenimore Cooper, and that loved stories of hardship
and adventure. New Mexico was a foreign country
with quaint people and strange habitations. The
American desert, not much more than a chartless
sea, framed and emphasized the traffic. If one must
have confirmation of the truth that frontier causes

have produced results far beyond their normal measure, such confirmation may be found here.

The traders to Santa Fé commonly travelled together in a single caravan for safety. In the earlier years they started overland from some Missouri town — Franklin most often — to a rendezvous at Council Grove. The erection of Fort Leavenworth and an increasing navigation of the Missouri River made possible a starting-point further west than Franklin; hence when this town was washed into the Missouri in 1828 its place was taken by the new settlement of Independence, further up the river and only twelve miles from the Missouri border. Here at Independence was done most of the general outfitting in the thirties. For the greater part of the year the town was dead, but for a few weeks in the spring it throbbed with the rough-and-ready life of the frontier. Landing of traders and cargoes, bartering for mules and oxen, building and repairing wagons and ox-yokes, and in the evening drinking and gambling among the hard men soon to leave port for the Southwest, — all these gave to Independence its name and place. From Independence to Council Grove, some one hundred and fifty miles, across the border, the wagons went singly or in groups. At the Grove they halted, waiting for an escort, or to organize in a general company for self-defence. Here in ordinary years the assembled traders elected a captain whose responsibility was complete, and whose authority was as great as he could make it by his own force.

Under him were lieutenants, and under the command of these the whole company was organized in guards and watches, for once beyond the Grove the company was in dangerous Indian Country in which eternal vigilance was the price of safety.

The unit of the caravan was the wagon, — the same Pittsburg or Conestoga wagon that moved frontiersmen whenever and wherever they had to travel on land.   It was drawn by from eight to twelve mules or oxen, and carried from three to five thousand pounds of cargo.   Over the wagon were large arches covered with Osnaburg sheetings to turn water and protect the contents.   The careful freighter used two thicknesses of sheetings, while the canny one slipped in between them a pair of blankets, which might thus increase his comfort outward bound, and be in an inconspicuous place to elude the vigilance of the customs officials at Santa Fé. Arms, mounts, and general equipment were innumerable in variation, but the prairie schooner, as its white canopy soon named it, survived through its own superiority.

At Council Grove the desert trip began. The journey now became one across a treeless prairie, with water all too rare, and habitations entirely lacking. The first stage of the trail crossed the country, nearly west, to the great bend of the Arkansas River, two hundred and seventy miles from Independence. Up the Arkansas it ran on, past Chouteau's Island, to Bent's Fort, near La Junta, Colorado, where fur traders had established a post. Water was most scarce. Whether the caravan crossed the river at the Cimarron crossing or left it at Bent's Fort to follow up the Purgatoire, the pull was hard on trader and on stock. His oxen often reached Santa Fé with scarcely enough strength left to stand alone. But with reasonable success and skilful guidance the caravan might hope to surmount all these difficulties and at last enter Santa Fé, seven hundred and eighty miles away, in from six to seven weeks from Independence.

When the Mexican War came in 1846, the Missouri frontier was familiar with all of the long trail to Santa Fé. Even in the East there had come to be some real interest in and some accurate knowledge of the desert and its thoroughfares. One of the earliest steps in the strategy of the war was the organization of an Army of the West at Fort Leavenworth, with orders to march overland against Mexico and Upper California. Colonel Stephen W. Kearny was given command of the invading army, which he recruited largely from the frontier and into which he incorporated a battalion of the Mormon emigrants who were, in the summer of 1846, near Council Bluffs, on their way to the Rocky Mountains and the country beyond. Kearny himself knew the frontier, duty having taken him in 1845 all the way to the mountains and back in the interest of policing the trails. By the end of June he was ready to begin the march towards Bent's Fort on the upper Arkansas, where there was

F

to be a common rendezvous. To this point the army marched in separate columns, far enough apart to secure for all the force sufficient water and fodder from the plains. Up to Bent's Fort the march was little more than a pleasure jaunt. The trail was well known, and Indians, never likely to run heedlessly into danger, were well behaved. Beyond Bent's Fort the advance assumed more of a military aspect, for the enemy's country had been entered and resistance by the Mexicans was anticipated in the mountain passes north of Santa Fé. But the resistance came to naught, while the army, footsore and hot, marched easily into Santa Fé on August 18, 1846. In the palace of the governor the conquering officers were entertained as lavishly as the resources of the provinces would permit. "We were too thirsty to judge of its merits," wrote one of them of the native wines and brandy which circulated freely; "anything liquid and cool was palatable." With little more than the formality of taking possession New Mexico thus fell into the hands of the United States, while the war of conquest advanced further to the West. In the end of September Kearny started out from Santa Fé for California, where he arrived early in the following January.

The conquest of the Southwest extended the boundary of the United States to the Gila and the Pacific, broadening the area of the desert within the United States and raising new problems of long-distance government in connection with the populations of

New Mexico and California. The Santa Fé trail, with its continuance west of the Rio Grande, became the attenuated bond between the East and the West. From the Missouri frontier to California the way was through the desert and the Indian Country, with regular settlements in only one region along the route. The reluctance of foreign customs officers to permit trade disappeared with the conquest, so that the traffic with the Southwest and California boomed during the fifties.

The volume of the traffic expanded to proportions which had never been dreamed of before the conquest. Kearny's baggage-trains started a new era in plains freighting. The armies had continuously to be supplied. Regular communication had to be maintained for the new Southwest. But the freighting was no longer the adventurous pioneering of the Santa Fé traders. It became a matter of business, running smoothly along familiar channels. It ceased to have to do with the extension of geographic knowledge and came to have significance chiefly in connection with the organization of overland commerce. Between the Mexican and Civil wars was its new period of life. Finally, in the seventies, it gradually receded into history as the tentacles of the continental railway system advanced into the desert.

The Santa Fé trail was the first beaten path thrust in advance of the western frontier. Even to-day its course may be followed by the wheel ruts for much of the distance from the bend of the Missouri to Santa

Fé. Crossing the desert, it left civilized life behind it at the start, not touching it again until the end was reached. For nearly fifty years after the trade began, this character of the desert remained substantially unchanged. Agricultural settlement, which had rushed west along the Ohio and Missouri, stopped at the bend, and though the trail continued, settlement would not follow it. The Indian country and the American desert remained intact, while the Santa Fé trail, in advance of settlement, pointed the way of manifest destiny, as no one of the eastern trails had ever done. When the new states grew up on the Pacific, the desert became as an ocean traversed only by the prairie schooners in their beaten paths. Islands of settlement served but to accentuate the unpopulated condition of the Rocky Mountain West.

The bend of the Missouri had been foreseen by the statesmen of the twenties as the limit of American advance. It might have continued thus had there really been nothing beyond it. But the profits of the trade to Santa Fé created a new interest and a connecting road. In nearly the same years the call of the fur trade led to the tracing of another path in the wilderness, running to a new goal. Oregon and the fur trade had stirred up so much interest beyond the Rockies that before Kearny marched his army into Santa Fé another trail of importance equal to his had been run to Oregon.

The maintenance of the Indian frontier depended

upon the ability of the United States to keep whites out of the Indian Country. But with Oregon and Santa Fé beyond, this could never be. The trails had already shown the fallacy of the frontier policy before it had become a fact in 1840.

CHAPTER V

THE OREGON TRAIL

THE Santa Fé trade had just been started upon its long career when trappers discovered in the Rocky Mountains, not far from where the forty-second parallel intersects the continental divide, an easy crossing by which access might be had from the waters of the upper Platte to those of the Pacific Slope. South Pass, as this passage through the hills soon came to be called, was the gateway to Oregon. As yet the United States had not an inch of uncontested soil upon the Pacific, but in years to come a whole civilization was to pour over the upper trail to people the valley of the Columbia and claim it for new states. The Santa Fé trail was chiefly the route of commerce. The Oregon trail became the pathway of a people westward bound.

In its earliest years the Oregon trail knew only the fur traders, those nameless pioneers who possessed an accurate rule-of-thumb knowledge of every hill and valley of the mountains nearly a generation before the surveyor and his transit brought them within the circle of recorded facts. The historian of the fur trade, Major Hiram Martin Chittenden, has tracked out many of them with the same laborious

70

industry that carried them after the beaver and the other marketable furs. When they first appeared is lost in tradition. That they were everywhere in the period between the journey of Lewis and Clark, in 1805, and the rise of Independence as an outfitting post, in 1832, is clearly manifest. That they discovered every important geographic fact of the West is quite as certain as it is that their discoveries were often barren, were generally unrecorded in a formal way, and exercised little influence upon subsequent settlement and discovery. Their place in history is similar to that of those equally nameless ship captains of the thirteenth century who knew and charted the shore of the Mediterranean at a time when scientific geographers were yet living on a flat earth and shaping cosmographies from the Old Testament. Although the fur-traders, with their great companies behind them, did less to direct the future than their knowledge of geography might have warranted, they managed to secure a foothold upon the Pacific coast early in the century. Astoria, in 1811, was only a pawn in the game between the British and American organizations, whose control over Oregon was so confusing that Great Britain and the United States, in 1818, gave up the task of drawing a boundary when they reached the Rockies, and allowed the country beyond to remain under joint occupation.

In the thirties, religious enthusiasm was added to the profits of the fur trade as an inducement to visit Oregon. By 1832 the trading prospects had incited

migration outside the regular companies.   Nathaniel
J. Wyeth took out his first party in this year.   He
repeated the journey with a second party in 1834.
The Methodist church sent a body of missionaries
to convert the western Indians in this latter year.
The American Board of Foreign Missions sent out
the redoubtable Marcus Whitman in 1835.   Before
the thirties were over Oregon had become a household word through the combined reports of traders
and missionaries.   Its fertility and climate were
common themes in the lyceums and on the lecture
platform; while the fact that this garden might
through prompt migration be wrested from the
British gave an added inducement.   Joint occupation was yet the rule, but the time was approaching
when the treaty of 1818 might be denounced, a time
when Oregon ought to become the admitted property
of the United States.   The thirties ended with no
large migration begun.   But the financial crisis of
1837, which unsettled the frontier around the Great
Lakes, provided an impoverished and restless population ready to try the chance in the farthest West.

A growing public interest in Oregon roused the
United States government to action in the early
forties.   The Indians of the Northwest were in need
of an agent and sound advice.   The exact location
of the trail, though the trail itself was fairly well
known, had not been ascertained.   Into the hands
of the senators from Missouri fell the task of inspir-
ing the action and directing the result.   Senator

Linn was the father of bills and resolutions looking towards a territory west of the mountains; while Benton, patron of the fur trade, received for his new son-in-law, John C. Frémont, a detail in command of an exploring party to the South Pass.

The career of Frémont, the Pathfinder, covers twenty years of great publicity, beginning with his first command in 1842. On June 10, of this year, with some twenty-one guides and men, he departed from Cyprian Chouteau's place on the Kansas, ten miles above its mouth. He shortly left the Kansas, crossed country to Grand Island in the Platte, and followed the Platte and its south branch to St. Vrain's Fort in northern Colorado, where he arrived in thirty days. From St. Vrain's he skirted the foothills north to Fort Laramie. Thence, ascending the Sweetwater, he reached his destination at South Pass on August 8, just one day previous to the signing of the great English treaty at Washington. At South Pass his journey of observation was substantially over. He continued, however, for a few days along the Wind River Range, climbing a mountain peak and naming it for himself. By October he was back in St. Louis with his party.

In the spring of 1843, Frémont started upon a second and more extended governmental exploration to the Rockies. This time he followed a trail along the Kansas River and its Republican branch to St. Vrain's, whence he made a detour south to Boiling Spring and Bent's trading-post on the Arkansas River.

Mules were scarce, and Colonel Bent was relied upon for a supply. Returning to the Platte, he divided his company, sending part of it over his course of 1842 to Laramie and South Pass, while he led his own detachment directly from St. Vrain's into the Medicine Bow Range, and across North Park, where rises the North Platte. Before reaching Fort Hall, where he was to reunite his party, he made another detour to Great Salt Lake, that he might feel like Balboa as he looked upon the inland sea. From Fort Hall, which he reached on September 18, he followed the emigrant route by the valley of the Snake to the Dalles of the Columbia.

Whether the ocean could be reached by any river between the Columbia and Colorado was a matter of much interest to persons concerned with the control of the Pacific. The facts, well enough known to the trappers, had not yet received scientific record when Frémont started south from the Dalles in November, 1843, to ascertain them. His march across the Nevada desert was made in the dead of winter under difficulties that would have brought a less resolute explorer to a stop. It ended in March, 1844, at Sutter's ranch in the Sacramento Valley, with half his horses left upon the road. His homeward march carried him into southern California and around the sources of the Colorado, proving by recorded observation the difficult character of the country between the mountains and the Pacific.

In following years the Pathfinder revisited the

scenes of these two expeditions upon which his reputation is chiefly based. A man of resolution and moderate ability, the glory attendant upon his work turned his head. His later failures in the face of military problems far beyond his comprehension tended to belittle the significance of his earlier career, but history may well agree with the eminent English traveller, Burton, who admits that: "Every foot of ground passed over by Colonel Frémont was perfectly well known to the old trappers and traders, as the interior of Africa to the Arab and Portuguese pombeiros. But this fact takes nothing away from the honors of the man who first surveyed and scientifically observed the country." Through these two journeys the Pacific West rose in clear definition above the American intellectual horizon. "The American Eagle," quoth the *Platte* (*Missouri*) *Eagle* in 1843, "is flapping his wings, the precurser [*sic*] of the end of the British lion, on the shores of the Pacific. Destiny has willed it."

The year in which Frémont made his first expedition to the mountains was also the year of the first formal, conducted emigration to Oregon. Missionaries beyond the mountains had urged upon Congress the appointment of an American representative and magistrate for the country, with such effect that Dr. Elijah White, who had some acquaintance with Oregon, was sent out as sub-Indian agent in the spring of 1842. With him began the regular migration of homeseekers that peopled Oregon during the next ten years. His emigration was not large, perhaps eighteen Pennsylvania wagons and 130 persons; but it seems to have been larger than he expected, and large enough to raise doubt as to the practicability of taking so many persons across the plains at once. In the decade following, every May, when pasturage was fresh and green, saw pioneers gathering, with or without premeditation, at the bend of the Missouri, bound for Oregon. Independence and its neighbor villages continued to be the posts of outfit. How many in the aggregate crossed the plains can never be determined, in spite of the efforts of the pioneer societies of Oregon to record their names. The distinguishing feature of the emigration was its spontaneous individualistic character. Small parties, too late for the caravan, frequently set forth alone. Single families tried it often enough to have their wanderings recorded in the border papers. In the spring following the crossing of Elijah White emigrants gathered by hundreds at the Missouri ferries, until an estimate of a thousand in all is probably not too high. In 1844 the tide subsided a little, but in 1845 it established a new mark in the vicinity of three thousand, and in 1847 ran between four and five thousand. These were the highest figures, yet throughout the decade the current flowed unceasingly.

The migration of 1843, the earliest of the fat years, may be taken as typical of the Oregon movement. Early in the year faces turned toward the Missouri rendezvous. Men, women, and children, old and young, with wagons and cattle, household equipment, primitive sawmills, and all the impedimenta of civilization were to be found in the hopeful crowd. For some days after departure the unwieldy party, a thousand strong, with twice as many cattle and beasts of burden, held together under Burnett, their chosen captain. But dissension beyond his control soon split the company. In addition to the general fear that the number was dangerously high, the poorer emigrants were jealous of the rich. Some of the latter had in their equipment cattle and horses by the score, and as the poor man guarded these from the Indian thieves during his long night watches he felt the injustice which compelled him to protect the property of another. Hence the party broke early in June. A "cow column" was formed of those who had many cattle and heavy belongings; the lighter body went on ahead, though keeping within supporting distance; and under two captains the procession moved on. The way was tedious rather than difficult, but habit soon developed in the trains a life that was full and complete. Oregon, one of the migrants of 1842 had written, was a "great country for unmarried gals." Courtship and marriage began almost before the States were out of sight. Death and burial, crime and punishment, filled out the round of human experience, while Dr. Whitman was more than once called upon in his professional capacity to aid in the enlargement of the band.

The trail to Oregon was the longest road yet developed in the United States. It started from the Missouri River anywhere between Independence and Council Bluffs. In the beginning, Independence was the common rendezvous, but as the agricultural frontier advanced through Iowa in the forties numerous new crossings and ferries were made further up the stream. From the various ferries the start began, as did the Santa Fé trade, sometime in May. By many roads the wagons moved westward towards the point from which the single trail extended to the mountains. East of Grand Island, where the Platte River reaches its most southerly point, these routes from the border were nearly as numerous as the caravans, but here began the single highway along the river valley, on its southern side. At this point, in the years immediately after the Mexican War, the United States founded a military post to protect the emigrants, naming it for General Stephen W. Kearny, commander of the Army of the West. From Fort Kearney (custom soon changed the spelling of the name) to the fur-trading post at Laramie Creek the trail followed the river and its north fork. Fort Laramie itself was bought from the fur company and converted into a military post which became a second great stopping-place for the emigrants. Shortly west of Laramie, the Sweetwater guided the trail to South Pass, where, through a gap twenty miles in width, the main commerce between the Mississippi Valley and the Pacific was forced to go.

Beyond South Pass, Wyeth's old Fort Hall was the next post of importance on the road. From Fort Hall to Fort Boisé the trail continued down the Snake, cutting across the great bend of the river to meet the Columbia near Walla Walla.

The journey to Oregon took about five months. Its deliberate, domesticated progress was as different as might be from the commercial rush to Santa Fé. Starting too late, the emigrant might easily get caught in the early mountain winter, but with a prompt start and a wise guide, or pilot, winter always found the homeseeker in his promised land. "This is the right manner to settle the Oregon question," wrote Niles, after he had counted over the emigrants of 1844.

Before the great migration of 1843 reached Oregon the pioneers already there had taken the law to themselves and organized a provisional government in the Willamette Valley. The situation here, under the terms of the joint occupation treaty, was one of considerable uncertainty. National interests prompted settlers to hope and work for future control by one country or the other, while advantage seemed to incline to the side of Dr. McLoughlin, the generous factor of the British fur companies. But the aggressive Americans of the early migrations were restive under British leadership. They were fearful also lest future American emigration might carry political control out of their hands into the management of newcomers. Death and inheritance among their number had pointed to a need for civil institutions. In May, 1843, with all the ease invariably shown by men of Anglo-Saxon blood when isolated together in the wilderness, they formed a voluntary association for government and adopted a code of laws.

Self-confidence, the common asset of the West, was not absent in this newest American community. "A few months since," wrote Elijah White, "at our Oregon lyceum, it was unanimously voted that the colony of Wallamette held out the most flattering encouragement to immigrants of any colony on the globe." In his same report to the Commissioner of Indian Affairs, the sub-Indian agent described the course of events. "During my up-country excursion, the whites of the colony convened, and formed a code of laws to regulate intercourse between themselves during the absence of law from our mother country, adopting in almost all respects the Iowa code. In this I was consulted, and encouraged the measure, as it was so manifestly necessary for the collection of debts, securing rights in claims, and the regulation of general intercourse among the whites."

A messenger was immediately sent east to beg Congress for the extension of United States laws and jurisdiction over the territory. His journey was six months later than the winter ride of Marcus Whitman, who went to Boston to save the missions of the American Board from abandonment, and might with better justice than Whitman's be called the ride to save Oregon. But Oregon was in no danger of being lost, however dilatory Congress might be. The little illegitimate government settled down to work, its legislative committee enacted whatever laws were needed for local regulation, and a high degree of law and order prevailed.

Sometimes the action of the Americans must have been meddlesome and annoying to the English and Canadian trappers. In the free manners of the first half of the nineteenth century the use of strong drink was common throughout the country and universal along the frontier. "A family could get along very well without butter, wheat bread, sugar, or tea, but whiskey was as indispensable to housekeeping as corn-meal, bacon, coffee, tobacco, and molasses. It was always present at the house raising, harvesting, road working, shooting matches, corn husking, weddings, and dances. It was never out of order where two or three were gathered together.'" Yet along with this frequent intemperance, a violent abstinence movement was gaining way. Many of the Oregon pioneers came from Iowa and the new Northwest, full of the new crusade and ready to support it. Despite the lack of legal right, though with every moral justification, attempts were made to crush the liquor traffic with the Indians. White tells of a mass meeting authorizing him to take action on his own responsibility; of his enlisting a band of coadjutors; and, finally, of finding "the distillery in a deep, dense thicket, 11 miles from town, at 3 o'clock

G

P.M. The boiler was a large size potash kettle, and all the apparatus well accorded. Two hogsheads and eight barrels of slush or beer were standing ready for distillation, with part of one barrel of molasses. No liquor was to be found, nor as yet had much been distilled. Having resolved on my course, I left no time for reflection, but at once upset the nearest cask, when my noble volunteers immediately seconded my measures, making a river of beer in a moment; nor did we stop till the kettle was raised, and elevated in triumph at the prow of our boat, and every cask, with all the distilling apparatus, was broken to pieces and utterly destroyed. We then returned, in high cheer, to the town, where our presence and report gave general joy."

The provisional government lasted for several years, with a fair degree of respect shown to it by its citizens. Like other provisional governments, it was weakest when revenue was in question, but its courts of justice met and satisfied a real need of the settlers. It was long after regular settlement began before Congress acquired sure title to the country and could pass laws for it.

The Oregon question, muttering in the thirties, thus broke out loudly in the forties. Emigrants then rushed west in the great migrations with deliberate purpose to have and to hold. Once there, they demanded, with absolute confidence, that Congress protect them in their new homes. The stories of the election of 1844, the Oregon treaty of 1846, and the erection of a territorial government in 1848 would all belong to an intimate study of the Oregon trail.

In the election of 1844 Oregon became an important question in practical politics. Well-informed historians no longer believe that the annexation of Texas was the result of nothing but a deep-laid plot of slaveholders to acquire more lands for slave states and more southern senators. All along the frontier, whether in Illinois, Wisconsin, and Iowa, or in Arkansas, Alabama, and Mississippi, population was restive under hard times and its own congenital instinct to move west to cheaper lands. Speculation of the thirties had loaded up the eastern states with debts and taxes, from which the states could not escape with honor, but from under which their individual citizens could emigrate. Wherever farm lands were known, there went the home-seekers, and it needs no conspiracy explanation to account for the presence, in the platform, of a party that appealed to the great plain people, of planks for the reannexation of Texas and the whole of Oregon. With a Democratic party strongest in the South, the former extension was closer to the heart, but the whole West could subscribe to both.

Oregon included the whole domain west of the Rockies, between Spanish Mexico at 42° and Russian America, later known as Alaska, at 54° 40′. Its northern and southern boundaries were clearly established in British and Spanish treaties. Its eastern limit by the old treaty of 1818 was the conti-

nental divide, since the United States and Great
Britain were unable either to allot or apportion it.
Title which should justify a claim to it was so equally
divided between the contesting countries that it would
be difficult to make out a positive claim for either,
while in fact a compromise based upon equal division
was entirely fair.   But the West wanted all of Oregon with an eagerness that saw no flaw in the United
States title.   That the democratic party was sincere
in asking for all of it in its platform is clearer with
respect to the rank and file of the organization than
with the leaders of the party.   Certain it is that just
so soon as the execution of the Texas pledge provoked
a war with Mexico, President Polk, himself both a
westerner and a frontiersman, was ready to eat his
words and agree with his British adversary quickly.

Congress desired, after Polk's election in 1844, to
serve a year's notice on Great Britain and bring joint
occupation to an end.   But more pacific advices
prevailed in the mouth of James Buchanan, Secretary
of State, so that the United States agreed to accept
an equitable division instead of the whole or none.
The Senate, consulted in advance upon the change of
policy, gave its approval both before and after to the
treaty which, signed June 15, 1846, extended the
boundary line of 49° from the Rockies to the Pacific.
The settled half of Oregon and the greater part of
the Columbia River thus became American territory, subject to such legislation as Congress should
prescribe.

A territory of Oregon, by law of 1848, was the result of the establishment of the first clear American title on the Pacific. All that the United States had secured in the division was given the popular name. Missionary activity and the fur trade, and, above all, popular agricultural conquest, had established the first detached American colony, with the desert separating it from the mother country. The trail was already well known to thousands, and so clearly defined by wheel ruts and débris along the sides that even the blind could scarce wander from the beaten path. A temporary government, sufficient for the immediate needs of the inhabitants, had at once paved the way for the legitimate territory and revealed the high degree of law and morality prevailing in the population. Already the older settlers were prosperous, and the first chapter in the history of Oregon was over. A second great trail had still further weakened the hold of the American desert over the American mind, endangering, too, the Indian policy that was dependent upon the desert for its continuance.

CHAPTER VI

OVERLAND WITH THE MORMONS

THE story of the settlement and winning of Oregon is but a small portion of the whole history of the Oregon trail. The trail was not only the road to Oregon, but it was the chief road across the continent. Santa Fé dominated a southern route that was important in commerce and conquest, and that could be extended west to the Pacific. But the deep ravine of the Colorado River splits the United States into sections with little chance of intercourse below the fortieth parallel. To-day, in only two places south of Colorado do railroads bridge it; only one stage route of importance ever crossed it. The southern trail could not be compared in its traffic or significance with the great middle highway by South Pass which led by easy grades from the Missouri River and the Platte, not only to Oregon but to California and Great Salt Lake.

Of the waves of influence that drew population along the trail, the Oregon fever came first; but while it was still raging, there came the Mormon trek that is without any parallel in American history. Throughout the lifetime of the trails the American desert extended almost unbroken from the bend of the

Missouri to California and Oregon. The Mormon settlement in Utah became at once the most considerable colony within this area, and by its own fertility emphasized the barren nature of the rest.

Of the Mormons, Joseph Smith was the prophet, but it would be fair to ascribe the parentage of the sect to that emotional upheaval of the twenties and thirties which broke down barriers of caste and politics, ruptured many of the ordinary Christian churches, and produced new revelations and new prophets by the score. Joseph Smith was merely one of these, more astute perhaps than the others, having much of the wisdom of leadership, as Mohammed had had before him, and able to direct and hold together the enthusiasm that any prophet might have been able to arouse. History teaches that it is easy to provoke religious enthusiasm, however improbable or fraudulent the guides or revelations may be; but that the founding of a church upon it is a task for greatest statesmanship.

The discovery of the golden plates and the magic spectacles, and the building upon them of a militant church has little part in the conquest of the frontier save as a motive force. It is difficult for the gentile mind to treat the Book of Mormon other than as a joke, and its perpetrator as a successful charlatan. Mormon apologists and their enemies have gone over the details of its production without establishing much sure evidence on either side. The theological teaching of the church seems to put less stress upon it than its supposed miraculous origin would dictate. It is, wrote Mark Twain, with his light-hearted penetration, "rather stupid and tiresome to read, but there is nothing vicious in its teachings. Its code of morals is unobjectionable — it is 'smouched' from the New Testament and no credit given." Converts came slowly to the new prophet at the start, for he was but one of many teachers crying in the wilderness, and those who had known him best in his youth were least ready to see in him a custodian of divinity. Yet by the spring of 1830 it was possible to organize, in western New York, the body which Rigdon was later to christen the "Church of Jesus Christ of Latter-day Saints." By the spring of 1831 headquarters had moved to Kirtland, Ohio, where proselyting had proved to be successful in both religion and finance.

Kirtland was but a temporary abode for the new sect. Revelations came in upon the prophet rapidly, pointing out the details of organization and administration, the duty of missionary activity among the Indians and gentiles, and the future home further to the west. Scouts were sent to the Indian Country at an early date, leaving behind at Kirtland the leaders to build their temple and gather in the converts who, by 1833 and 1834, had begun to appear in hopeful numbers. The frontier of this decade was equally willing to speculate in religion, agriculture, banking, or railways, while Smith and his intimates possessed the germ of leadership to take advantage of every chance. Until the panic of 1837 they flourished, apparently not always beyond reproach in financial affairs, but with few neighbors who had the right to throw the stone. Antagonism, already appearing against the church, was due partly to an essential intolerance among their frontier neighbors and partly to the whole-souled union between church and life which distinguished the Mormons from the other sects. Their political complexion was identical with their religion, — a combination which always has aroused resentment in America.

For a western home, the leaders fell upon a tract in Missouri, not far from Independence, close to the Indians whose conversion was a part of the Mormon duty. In the years when Oregon and Santa Fé were by-words along the Missouri, the Mormons were getting a precarious foothold near the commencement of the trails. The population around Independence was distinctly inhospitable, with the result that petty violence appeared, in which it is hard to place the blame. There was a calm assurance among the Saints that they and they alone were to inherit the earth. Their neighbors maintained that poultry and stock were unsafe in their vicinity because of this belief. The Mormons retaliated with charges of well-spoiling, incendiarism, and violence. In all the bickerings the sources of information are partisan and cloudy with prejudice, so that it is easier to see the disgraceful scuffle than to find the culprit. From the south side of the Missouri around Independence the Saints were finally driven across the river by armed mobs; a transaction in which the Missourians spoke of a sheriff's posse and maintaining the peace. North of the river the unsettled frontier was reached in a-few miles, and there at Far West, in Caldwell County, they settled down at last, to build their tabernacle and found their Zion. In the summer of 1838 their corner-stone was laid.

Far West remained their goal in belief longer than in fact. Before 1838 ended they had been forced to agree to leave Missouri; yet they returned in secret to relay the corner-stone of the tabernacle and continued to dream of this as their future home. Up to the time of their expulsion from Missouri in 1838 they are not proved to have been guilty of any crime that could extenuate the gross intolerance which turned them out. As individuals they could live among Gentiles in peace. It seems to have been the collective soul of the church that was unbearable to the frontiersmen. The same intolerance which had facilitated their departure from Ohio and compelled it from Missouri, in a few more years drove them again on their migrations. The cohesion of the church in politics, economics, and religion explains the opposition which it cannot well excuse.

In Hancock County, Illinois, not far from the old Fort Madison ferry which led into the half-breed country of Iowa, the Mormons discovered a village of Commerce, once founded by a communistic settlement from which the business genius of Smith now purchased it on easy terms. It was occupied in 1839, renamed Nauvoo in 1840, and in it a new tabernacle was begun in 1841. From the poverty-stricken young clairvoyant of fifteen years before, the prophet had now developed into a successful man of affairs, with ambitions that reached even to the presidency at Washington. With a strong sect behind him, money at his disposal, and supernatural powers in which all faithful saints believed, Joseph could go far. Nauvoo had a population of about fifteen thousand by the end of 1840.

Coming into Illinois upon the eve of a closely contested presidential election, at a time when the state feared to lose its population in an emigration to avoid taxation, and with a vote that was certain to be cast for one candidate or another as a unit, the Mormons insured for themselves a hearty welcome from both Democrats and Whigs. A complaisant legislature gave to the new Zion a charter full of privilege in the making and enforcing of laws, so that the ideal of the Mormons of a state within the state was fully realized. The town council was emancipated from state control, its courts were independent, and its militia was substantially at the beck of Smith. Proselyting and good management built up the town rapidly. To an importunate creditor Smith described it as a "deathly sickly hole," but to the possible convert it was advertised as a land of milk and honey. Here it began to be noticed that desertions from the church were not uncommon; that conversion alone kept full and swelled its ranks. It was noised about that the wealthy convert had the warmest reception, but was led on to let his religious passion work his impoverishment for the good of the cause.

Here in Nauvoo it was that the leaders of the church took the decisive step that carried Mormonism beyond the pale of the ordinary, tolerable, religious sects. Rumors of immorality circulated among the Gentile neighbors. It was bad enough, they thought, to have the Mormons chronic petty thieves, but the license that was believed to prevail among the leaders was more than could be endured by a community that did not count this form of iniquity among its own excesses. The Mormons were in general of the same stamp as their fellow frontiersmen until they took to this. At the time, all immorality was denounced and denied by the prophet and his friends, but in later years the church made public a revelation concerning celestial or plural marriage, with the admission that Joseph Smith had received it in the summer of 1843. Never does Mormon polygamy seem to have been as prevalent as its enemies have charged. But no church countenancing the practice could hope to be endured by an American community. The odium of practising it was increased by the hypocrisy which denied it. It was only a matter of time until the Mormons should resume their march.

The end of Mormon rule at Nauvoo was precipi-

tated by the murder of Joseph Smith, and Hyrum
his brother, by a mob at Carthage jail in the summer
of 1844. Growing intolerance had provoked an
attack upon the Saints similar to that in Missouri.
Under promise of protection the Smiths had surrendered themselves. Their martyrdom at once
disgraced the state in which it could be possible, and
gave to Mormonism in a murdered prophet a mighty
bond of union. The reins of government fell into
hands not unworthy of them when Brigham Young
succeeded Joseph Smith.

Not until December, 1847, did Brigham become in a
formal way president of the church, but his authority
was complete in fact after the death of Joseph.
A hard-headed Missouri River steamboat captain
knew him, and has left an estimate of him which
must be close to truth. He was "a man of great
ability. Apparently deficient in education and
refinement, he was fair and honest in his dealings,
and seemed extremely liberal in conversation upon
religious subjects. He impressed La Barge," so
Chittenden, the biographer of the latter relates,
"as anything but a religious fanatic or even enthusiast; but he knew how to make use of the fanati-
cism of others and direct it to great ends." Shortly
after the murder of Joseph it became clear that
Nauvoo must be abandoned, and Brigham began to
consider an exodus across the plains so familiar
by hearsay to every one by 1845, to the Rocky
Mountains beyond the limits of the United States.

Persecution, for the persecuted can never see two sides, had soured the Mormons. The threatened eviction came in the autumn of 1845. In 1846 the last great trek began.

The van of the army crossed the Mississippi at Nauvoo as early as February, 1846. By the hundred, in the spring of the year, the wagons of the persecuted sect were ferried across the river. Five hundred and thirty-nine teams within a single week in May is the report of one observer. Property which could be commuted into the outfit for the march was carefully preserved and used. The rest, the tidy houses, the simple furniture, the careful farms (for the backbone of the church was its well-to-do middle class), were abandoned or sold at forced sale to the speculative purchaser. Nauvoo was full of real estate vultures hoping to thrive upon the Mormon wreckage. Sixteen thousand or more abandoned the city and its nearly finished temple within the year.

Across southern Iowa the "Camp of Israel," as Brigham Young liked to call his headquarters, advanced by easy stages, as spring and summer allowed. To-day, the Chicago, Burlington, and Quincy railway follows the Mormon road for many miles, but in 1846 the western half of Iowa territory was Indian Country, the land of the Chippewa, Ottowa, and Potawatomi, who sold out before the year was over, but who were in possession at this time. Along the line of march camps were built by advance parties to be used in succession by the following thousands. The extreme advance hurried on to the Missouri River, near Council Bluffs, where as yet no city stood, to plant a crop of grain, since manna could not be relied upon in this migration. By autumn much of the population of Nauvoo had settled down in winter quarters not far above the present site of Omaha, preserving the orderly life of the society, and enduring hardships which the leaders sought to mitigate by gaiety and social gatherings. In the Potawatomi country of Iowa, opposite their winter quarters, Kanesville sprang into existence; while all the way from Kanesville to Grand Island in the Platte Mormon detachments were scattered along the roads. The destination was yet in doubt. Westward it surely was, but it is improbable that even Brigham knew just where.

The Indians received the Mormons, persecuted and driven westward like themselves, kindly at first, but discontent came as the winter residence was prolonged. From the country of the Omaha, west of the Missouri, it was necessary soon to prohibit Mormon settlement, but east, in the abandoned Potawatomi lands, they were allowed to maintain Kanesville and other outfitting stations for several years. A permanent residence here was not desired even by the Mormons themselves. Spring in 1847 found them preparing to resume the march.

In April, 1847, an advance party under the guidance of no less a person than Brigham Young started out the Platte trail in search of Zion. One hundred and forty-three men, seventy-two wagons, one hundred and seventy-five horses, and six months' rations, they took along, if the figures of one of their historians may be accepted. Under strict military order, the detachment proceeded to the mountains. It is one of the ironies of fate that the Mormons had no sooner selected their abode beyond the line of the United States in their flight from persecution than conquest from Mexico extended the United States beyond them to the Pacific. They themselves aided in this defeat of their plan, since from among them Kearny had recruited in 1846 a battalion for his army of invasion.

Up the Platte, by Fort Laramie, to South Pass and beyond, the prospectors followed the well-beaten trail. Oregon homeseekers had been cutting it deep in the prairie sod for five years. West of South Pass they bore southwest to Fort Bridger, and on the 24th of July, 1847, Brigham gazed upon the waters of the Great Salt Lake. Without serious premeditation, so far as is known, and against the advice of one of the most experienced of mountain guides, this valley by a later-day Dead Sea was chosen for the future capital. Fields were staked out, ground was broken by initial furrows, irrigation ditches were commenced at once, and within a month the town site was baptized the City of the Great Salt Lake.

Behind the advance guard the main body remained in winter quarters, making ready for their difficult search for the promised land; moving at last in the late spring in full confidence that a Zion somewhere would be prepared for them. The successor of Joseph relied but little upon supernatural aid in keeping his flock under control. Commonly he depended upon human wisdom and executive direction. But upon the eve of his own departure from winter quarters he had made public, for the direction of the main body, a written revelation: "The Word and Will of the Lord concerning the Camp of Israel in their Journeyings to the West." Such revelations as this, had they been repeated, might well have created or renewed popular confidence in the real inspiration of the leader. The order given was such as a wise source of inspiration might have formed after constant intercourse with emigrants and traders upon the difficulties of overland migration and the dangers of the way.

"Let all the people of the Church of Jesus Christ of Latter-day Saints, and those who journey with them," read the revelation, "be organized into companies, with a covenant and a promise to keep all the commandments and statutes of the Lord our God. Let the companies be organized with captains of hundreds, and captains of fifties, and captains of tens, with a president and counsellor at their head, under direction of the Twelve Apostles: and this shall be our covenant, that we will walk in all the ordinances of the Lord.

"Let each company provide itself with all the

H

teams, wagons, provisions, and all other necessaries for the journey that they can. When the companies are organized, let them go with all their might, to prepare for those who are to tarry. Let each company, with their captains and presidents, decide how many can go next spring; then choose out a sufficient number of able-bodied and expert men to take teams, seed, and farming utensils to go as pioneers to prepare for putting in the spring crops. Let each company bear an equal proportion, according to the dividend of their property, in taking the poor, the widows, and the fatherless, and the families of those who have gone with the army, that the cries of the widow and the fatherless come not up into the ears of the Lord against his people.

"Let each company prepare houses and fields for raising grain for those who are to remain behind this season; and this is the will of the Lord concerning this people.

"Let every man use all his influence and property to remove this people to the place where the Lord shall locate a stake of Zion: and if ye do this with a pure heart, with all faithfulness, ye shall be blessed in your flocks, and in your herds, and in your fields, and in your houses, and in your families. . . ."

The rendezvous for the main party was the Elk Horn River, whence the head of the procession moved late in June and early in July. In careful organization, with camps under guard and wagons always in corral at night, detachments moved on in quick succession. Kanesville and a large body remained behind for another year or longer, but before Brigham had laid out his city and started east the emigration of 1847 was well upon its way. The foremost began to come into the city by September. By October the new city in the desert had nearly four thousand inhabitants. The march had been made with little suffering and slight mortality. No better pioneer leadership had been seen upon the trail.

The valley of the Great Salt Lake, destined to become an oasis in the American desert, supporting the only agricultural community existing therein during nearly twenty years, discouraged many of the Mormons at the start. In Illinois and Missouri they were used to wood and water; here they found neither. In a treeless valley they were forced to carry their water to their crops in a way in which their leader had more confidence than themselves. The urgency of Brigham in setting his first detachment to work on fields and crops was not unwise, since for two years there was a real question of food to keep the colony alive. Inexperience in irrigating agriculture and plagues of crickets kept down the early crops. By 1850 the colony was safe, but its maintenance does still more credit to its skilful leadership. Its people, apart from foreign converts who came in later years, were of the stuff that had colonized the middle West and won a foothold in Oregon; but nowhere did an emigration so nearly create a land which it enjoyed as here. A paternal government dictated every effort, outlined the streets and farms, detailed parties to explore the vicinity and start new centres of life. Little was left to chance or unguided enthusiasm. Practical success and a high state of general welfare rewarded the Saints for their implicit obedience to authority.

Mormon emigration along the Platte trail became as common as that to Oregon in the years following 1847, but, except in the disastrous hand-cart episode of 1856, contains less of novelty than of substantial increase to the colony. Even to-day men are living in the West, who, walking all the way, with their own hands pushed and pulled two-wheeled carts from the Missouri to the mountains in the fifties. To bad management in handling proselytes the hand-cart catastrophe was chiefly due. From the beginning missionary activity had been pressed throughout the United States and even in Europe. In England and Scandinavia the lower classes took kindly to the promises, too often impracticable, it must be believed, of enthusiasts whose standing at home depended upon success abroad. The convert with property could pay his way to the Missouri border and join the ordinary annual procession. But the poor, whose wealth was not equal to the moderately costly emigration, were a problem until the emigration society determined to cut expenses by reducing equipment and substituting pushcarts and human power for the prairie schooner with its long train of oxen.

In 1856 well over one thousand poor emigrants left Liverpool, at contract rates, for Iowa City, where the parties were to be organized and ample equipment in handcarts and provisions were promised to be ready. On arrival in Iowa City it was found that slovenly management had not built enough of the carts. Delayed by the necessary construction of these carts, some of the bands could not get on the trail until late in the summer, — too late for a successful trip, as a few of their more cautious advisers had said. The earliest company got through to Salt Lake City in September with considerable success. It was hard and toilsome to push the carts; women and children suffered badly, but the task was possible. Snow and starvation in the mountains broke down the last company. A friendly historian speaks of a loss of sixty-seven out of a party of four hundred and twenty. Throughout the United States the picture of these poor deluded immigrants, toiling against their carts through mountain pass and river-bottom, with clothing going and food quite gone, increased the conviction that the Mormon hierarchy was misleading and abusing the confidence of thousands.

That the hierarchy was endangering the peace of the whole United States came to be believed as well. In 1850, with the Salt Lake settlement three years old, Congress had organized a territory of Utah, extending from the Rockies to California, between 37° and 42°, and the President had made Brigham Young its governor. The close association of the Mormon church and politics had prevented peaceful relations from existing between its people and the federal officers of the territory, while Washington prejudiced a situation already difficult by sending to Utah officers and judges, some of whom could not have commanded respect even where the sway of United States authority was complete. The vicious influence of politics in territorial appointments, which the territories always resented, was specially dangerous in the case of a territory already feeling itself persecuted for conscience' sake. Yet it was not impossible for a tactful and respectable federal officer to do business in Utah. For several years relations increased in bad temper, both sides appealing constantly to President and Congress, until it appeared, as was the fact, that the United States authority had become as nothing in Utah and with the church. Among the earliest of President Buchanan's acts was the preparation of an army which should reëstablish United States prestige among the Mormons. Large wagon trains were sent out from Fort Leavenworth in the summer of 1857, with an army under Albert Sidney Johnston following close behind, and again the old Platte trail came before the public eye.

The Utah war was inglorious. Far from its base, and operating in a desert against plainsmen of remarkable skill, the army was helpless. At will, the Mormon cavalry cut out and burned the supply trains, confining their attacks to property rather than to armed forces. When the army reached Fort Bridger, it found Brigham still defiant, his people bitter against conquest, and the fort burned. With difficulty could the army of invasion have lived through the winter without aid. In the spring of 1858 a truce was patched up, and the Mormons, being invulnerable, were forgiven. The army marched down the trail again.

The Mormon hegira planted the first of the island settlements in the heart of the desert. The very isolation of Utah gave it prominence. What religious enthusiasm lacked in aiding organization, shrewd leadership and resulting prosperity supplied. The first impulse moving population across the plains had been chiefly conquest, with Oregon as the result. Religion was the next, producing Utah. The lust for gold followed close upon the second, calling into life California, and then in a later decade sprinkling little camps over all the mountain West. The Mormons would have fared much worse had their leader not located his stake of Zion near the point where the trail to the Southwest deviated from the Oregon road, and where the forty-niners might pay tribute to his commercial skill as they passed through his oasis on their way to California.

CHAPTER VII

CALIFORNIA AND THE FORTY-NINERS

On his second exploring trip, John C. Frémont had worked his way south over the Nevada desert until at last he crossed the mountains and found himself in the valley of the Sacramento. Here in 1844 a small group of Americans had already been established for several years. Mexican California was scantily inhabited and was so far from the inefficient central government that the province had almost fallen away of its own weight. John A. Sutter, a Swiss of American proclivities, was the magnate of the Sacramento region, whence he dispensed a liberal hospitality to the Pathfinder's party.

In 1845, Frémont started on his third trip, this time entering California by a southern route and finding himself at Sutter's early in 1846. In some respects his detachment of engineers had the appearance of a filibustering party from the start. When it crossed the Rockies, it began to trespass upon the territory belonging to Mexico, with whom the United States was yet at peace. Whether the explorer was actually instructed to detach California from Mexico, or whether he only imagined that such action would be approved at home, is likely never to be explained. Naval officers on the Pacific were already under orders in the event of war to seize California at once; and Polk was from the start ambitious to round out the American territory on the Southwest. The Americans in the Sacramento were at variance with their Mexican neighbors, who resented the steady influx of foreign blood. Between 1842 and 1846 their numbers had rapidly increased. And in June, 1846, certain of them, professing to believe that they were to be attacked, seized the Mexican village of Sonoma and broke out the colors of what they called their Bear Flag Republic. Frémont, near at hand, countenanced and supported their act, if he did not suggest it.

The news of actual war reached the Pacific shortly after the American population in California had begun its little revolution. Frémont was in his glory for a time as the responsible head of American power in the province. Naval commanders under their own orders coöperated along the coast so effectively that Kearny, with his army of the West, learned that the conquest was substantially complete, soon after he left Santa Fé, and was able to send most of his own force back. California fell into American hands almost without a struggle, leaving the invaders in possession early in 1847. In January of that year the little village of Yerba Buena was rebaptized San Francisco, while the

American occupants began the sale of lots along the water front and the construction of a great seaport.

The relations of Oregon and California to the occupation of the West were much the same in 1847. Both had been coveted by the United States. Both had now been acquired in fact. Oregon had come first because it was most easily reached by the great trail, and because it had no considerable body of foreign inhabitants to resist invasion. It was, under the old agreement for joint occupation, a free field for colonization. But California had been the territory of Mexico and was occupied by a strange population. In the early forties there were from 4000 to 6000 Mexicans and Spaniards in the province, living the easy agricultural life of the Spanish colonist. The missions and the Indians had decayed during the past generation. The population was light hearted and generous. It quarrelled loudly, but had the Latin-American knack for bloodless revolutions. It was partly Americanized by long association with those trappers who had visited it since the twenties, and the settlers who had begun in the late thirties. But as an occupied foreign territory it had not invited American colonization as Oregon had done. Hence the Oregon movement had been going on three or four years before any considerable bodies of emigrants broke away from the trail, near Salt Lake, and sought out homes in California. If war had not come, American immigration into California would have progressed after 1846 quite as rapidly as the Mexican authorities would have allowed. As it was, the actual conquest removed the barrier, so that California migration in 1846 and 1847 rivalléd that to Oregon under the ordinary stimulus of the westward movement. The settlement of the Mormons at Salt Lake developed a much-needed outfitting post at the head of the most perilous section of the California trail. Both Mormons and Californians profited by its traffic.

With respect to California, the treaty which closed the Mexican War merely recognized an accomplished fact. By right of conquest California had changed hands. None can doubt that Mexico here paid the penalty under that organic law of politics which forbids a nation to sit still when others are moving. In no conceivable way could the occupation of California have been prevented, and if the war over Texas had not come in 1846, a war over California must shortly have occurred. By the treaty of Guadalupe-Hidalgo Mexico relinquished the territory which she had never been able to develop, and made way for the erection of the new America on the Pacific.

Most notable among the ante-bellum pioneers in California was John A. Sutter, whose establishment on the Sacramento had been a centre of the new life. Upon a large grant from the Mexican government he had erected his adobe buildings in the usual semi-fortified style that distinguished the isolated ranch. He was ready for trade, or agriculture, or war if need be, possessing within his own domain equipment for the ordinary simple manufactures and supplies. As his ranch prospered, and as Americans increased in San Francisco and on the Sacramento, the prospects of Sutter steadily improved. In 1847 he made ready to reap an additional share of profit from the boom by building a sawmill on his estate. Among his men there had been for some months a shiftless jack-of-all-trades, James W. Marshall, who had been chiefly carpenter while in Sutter's employ. In the summer of 1847 Marshall was sent out to find a place where timber and water-power should be near enough together to make a profitable mill site. He found his spot on the south bank of the American, which is a tributary of the Sacramento, some forty-five miles northeast of Sacramento.

In the autumn of the year Sutter and Marshall came to their agreement by which the former was to furnish all supplies and the latter was to build the mill and operate it on shares. Construction was begun before the year ended, and was substantially completed in January, 1848. Experience showed the amateur constructor that his mill-race was too shallow. To remedy this he started the practice of turning the river into it by night to wash out earth and deepen the channel. Here it was that after one of these flushings, toward the end of January, he picked up glittering flakes which looked to him like gold.

With his first find, Marshall hurried off to Sutter, at the ranch. Together they tested the flakes in the apothecary's shop, proving the reality of the discovery before returning to the mill to prospect more fully.

For Sutter the discovery was a calamity. None could tell how large the field might be, but he saw clearly that once the news of the find got abroad, the whole population would rush madly to the diggings. His ranch, the mill, and a new mill which was under way, all needed labor. But none would work for hire with free gold to be had for the taking. The discoverers agreed to keep their secret for six weeks, but the news leaked out, carried off all Sutter's hands in a few days, and reached even to San Francisco in the form of rumor before February was over. A new force had appeared to change the balance of the West and to excite the whole United States.

The rush to the gold fields falls naturally into two parts: the earlier including the population of California, near enough to hear of the find and get to the diggings in 1848. The later came from all the world, but could not start until the news had percolated by devious and tedious courses to centres of population thousands of miles away. The movement within California started in March and April.

Further prospecting showed that over large areas around the American and Sacramento rivers free gold could be obtained by the simple processes of placer mining. A wooden cradle operated by six or eight men was the most profitable tool, but a tin dishpan would do in an emergency. San Francisco was sceptical when the rumor reached it, and was not excited even by the first of April, but as nuggets and bags of dust appeared in quantity, the doubters turned to enthusiasts. Farms were abandoned, town houses were deserted, stores were closed, while every able-bodied man tramped off to the north to try his luck. The city which had flourished and expanded since the beginning of 1847 became an empty shell before May was over. Its newspaper is mute witness of the desertion, lapsing into silence for a month after May 29th because its hands had disappeared. Farther south in California the news spread as spring advanced, turning by June nearly every face toward Sacramento.

The public authorities took cognizance of the find during the summer. It was forced upon them by the wholesale desertions of troops who could not stand the strain. Both Consul Larkin and Governor Mason, who represented the sovereignty of the United States, visited the scenes in person and described the situation in their official letters home. The former got his news off to the Secretary of State by the 1st of June; the latter wrote on August 17; together they became the authoritative messengers that confirmed the rumors to the world, when Polk published some of their documents in his message to Congress in December, 1848. The rumors had reached the East as early as September, but now, writes Bancroft, "delirium seized upon the community."

How to get to California became a great popular question in the winter of 1848–1849. The public mind was well prepared for long migrations through the news of Pacific pioneers which had filled the journals for at least six years. Route, time, method, and cost were all to be considered. Migration, of a sort, began at once.

Land and water offered a choice of ways to California. The former route was now closed for the winter and could not be used until spring should produce her crop of necessary pasturage. But the impetuous and the well-to-do could start immediately by sea. All along the seaboard enterprising ship-owners announced sailings for California, by the Horn or by the shorter Isthmian route. Retired hulks were called again into commission for the purpose. Fares were extortionate, but many were willing to pay for speed. Before the discovery, Congress had arranged for a postal service, *via* Panama, and the Pacific Mail Steamship Company had been organized to work the contracts. The *California* had left New York in the fall of 1848 to run on the western end of the route. It had sailed without passengers, but, meeting the news of gold on the South American coast, had begun to load up at Latin ports. When it reached Panama, a crowd of clamorous emigrants, many times beyond its capacity, awaited its coming and quarrelled over its accommodations. On February 28, 1849, it reached San Francisco at last, starting the influx from the world at large.

The water route was too costly for most of the gold-seekers, who were forced to wait for spring, when the trails would be open. Various routes then guided them, through Mexico and Texas, but most of all they crowded once more the great Platte trail. Oregon migration and the Mormon flight had familiarized this route to all the world. For its first stages it was "already broad and well beaten as any turnpike in our country."

The usual crowd, which every May for several years had brought to the Missouri River crossings around Fort Leavenworth, was reënforced in 1849 and swollen almost beyond recognition. A rifle regiment of regulars was there, bound for Forts Laramie and Hall to erect new frontier posts. Lieutenant Stansbury was there, gathering his surveying party which was to prospect for a railway route to Salt Lake. By thousands and tens of thousands others came, tempted by the call of gold. This was the cheap and popular route. Every western farmer was ready to start, with his own wagons and his own stock. The townsman could easily buy the simple equipment of the plains. The poor could work their way, driving cattle for the better-off. Through inexperience and congestion the journey was likely to be hard, but any one might undertake it. Niles reported in June that up to May 18, 2850 wagons had crossed the river at St. Joseph, and 1500 more at the other ferries.

Familiarity had done much to divest the overland journey of its terrors. We hear in this, and even in earlier years, of a sort of plains travel de luxe, of wagons "fitted up so as to be secure from the weather and . . . the women knitting and sewing, for all the world as if in their ordinary farm-houses." Stansbury, hurrying out in June and overtaking the trains, was impressed with the picturesque character of the emigrants and their equipment. "We have been in company with multitudes of emigrants the whole day," he wrote on June 12. "The road has been lined to a long extent with their wagons, whose white covers, glittering in the sunlight, resembled, at a distance, ships upon the ocean. . . . We passed also an old Dutchman, with an immense wagon, drawn by six yoke of cattle, and loaded with household furniture. Behind followed a covered cart containing the wife, driving herself, and a host of babies — the whole bound to the land of promise, of the distance to which, however, they seemed to have not the most remote idea. To the tail of the cart was attached a large chicken-coop, full of fowls; two milch-cows followed, and next came an old mare, upon the back of which was perched a little, brown-faced, barefooted girl, not more than seven years old, while a small sucking colt brought up the rear." Travellers eastward bound, meeting the procession, reported the hundreds and thousands whom they met.

I

The organization of the trains was not unlike that of the Oregonians and the Mormons, though generally less formal than either of these. The wagons were commonly grouped in companies for protection, little needed, since the Indians were at peace during most of 1849. At nightfall the long columns came to rest and worked their wagons into the corral which was the typical plains encampment. To form this the wagons were ranged in a large circle, each with its tongue overlapping the vehicle ahead, and each fastened to the next with the brake or yoke chains. An opening at one end allowed for driving in the stock, which could here be protected from stampede or Indian theft. In emergency the circle of wagons formed a fortress strong enough to turn aside ordinary Indian attacks. When the companies had been on the road for a few weeks the forming of the corral became an easy military manœuvre. The itinerant circus is to-day the thing most like the fleet of prairie schooners.

The emigration of the forty-niners was attended by worse sufferings than the trail had yet known. Cholera broke out among the trains at the start. It stayed by them, lining the road with nearly five thousand graves, until they reached the hills beyond Fort Laramie. The price of inexperience, too, had to be paid. Wagons broke down and stock died. The wreckage along the trail bore witness to this. On July 27, Stansbury observed: "To-day we find additional and melancholy evidence of the difficulties encountered by those who are ahead of us. Before halting at noon, we passed eleven wagons that had been broken up, the spokes of the wheels taken to make pack-saddles, and the rest burned or otherwise destroyed. The road has been literally strewn with articles that have been thrown away. Bar-iron and steel, large blacksmiths' anvils and bellows, crowbars, drills, augers, gold-washers, chisels, axes, lead, trunks, spades, ploughs, large grindstones, baking-ovens, cooking-stoves without number, kegs, barrels, harness, clothing, bacon, and beans, were found along the road in pretty much the order in which they have been here enumerated. The carcasses of eight oxen, lying in one heap by the roadside, this morning, explained a part of the trouble." In twenty-four miles he passed seventeen abandoned wagons and twenty-seven dead oxen.

Beyond Fort Hall, with the journey half done, came the worst perils. In the dust and heat of the Humboldt Valley, stock literally faded away, so that thousands had to turn back to refuge at Salt Lake, or were forced on foot to struggle with thirst and starvation.

The number of the overland emigrants can never be told with accuracy. Perhaps the truest estimate is that of the great California historian who counts it that, in 1849, 42,000 crossed the continent and reached the gold fields.

It was a mixed multitude that found itself in California after July, 1849, when the overland folk began to arrive. All countries and all stations in society had contributed to fill the ranks of the 100,000 or more whites who were there in the end of the year. The farmer, the amateur prospector, and the professional gambler mingled in the crowd. Loose women plied their trade without rebuke. Those who had come by sea contained an over-share of the undesirable element that proposed to live upon the recklessness and vices of the miners. The overland emigrants were largely of farmer stock; whether they had possessed frontier experience or not before the start, the 3000-mile journey toughened and seasoned all who reached California. Nearly all possessed the essential virtues of strength, boldness, and initiative.

The experience of Oregon might point to the future of California when its strenuous population arrived upon the unprepared community. The Mexican government had been ejected by war. A military government erected by the United States still held its temporary sway, but felt out of place as the controlling power over a civilian American population. The new inhabitants were much in need of law, and had the American dislike for military authority. Immediately Congress was petitioned to form a territorial government for the new El Dorado. But Congress was preoccupied with the relations of slavery and freedom in the Southwest during its session of 1848–1849. It adjourned with nothing done for California. The mining population was irritated but not deeply troubled by this neglect. It had already organized its miners' courts and begun to execute summary justice in emergencies. It was quite able and willing to act upon the suggestion of its administrative officers and erect its state government without the consent of Congress. The military governor called the popular convention; the constitution framed during September, 1849, was ratified by popular vote on November 13; a few days later Governor Riley surrendered his authority into the hands of the elected governor, Burnett, and the officials of the new state. All this was done spontaneously and easily. There was no sanction in law for California until Congress admitted it in September, 1850, receiving as one of its first senators, John C. Frémont.

The year 1850 saw the great compromise upon slavery in the Southwest, a compromise made necessary by the appearance on the Pacific of a new America. The "call of the West and the lust for gold" had done their work in creating a new centre of life beyond the quondam desert.

The census of 1850 revealed something of the nature of this population. Probably 125,000 whites, though it was difficult to count them and impossible to secure absolute accuracy, were found in Oregon and California. Nine-tenths of these were in the latter colony. More than 11,000 were found in the settlements around Great Salt Lake. Not many more than 3000 Americans were scattered among the Mexican population along the Rio Grande. The great trails had seen most of these home-seekers marching westward over the desert and across the Indian frontier which in the blindness of statecraft had been completed for all time in 1840.

CHAPTER VIII

KANSAS AND THE INDIAN FRONTIER

THE long line separating the Indian and agricultural frontiers was in 1850 but little farther west than the point which it had reached by 1820. Then it had arrived at the bend of the Missouri, where it remained for thirty years. Its flanks had swung out during this generation, including Arkansas on the south and Iowa, Minnesota, and Wisconsin on the north, so that now at the close of the Mexican War the line was nearly a true meridian crossing the Missouri at its bend. West of this spot it had been kept from going by the tradition of the desert and the pressure of the Indian tribes. The country behind had filled up with population, Oregon and California had appeared across the desert, but the barrier had not been pushed away.

Through the great trails which penetrated the desert accurate knowledge of the Far West had begun to come. By 1850 the tradition which Pike and Long had helped to found had well-nigh disappeared, and covetous eyes had been cast upon the Indian lands across the border, — lands from which the tribes were never to be removed without their con-

sent, and which were never to be included in any
organized territory or state. Most of the traffic
over the trails and through this country had been in
defiance of treaty obligations. Some of the tribes
had granted rights of transit, but such privileges as
were needed and used by the Oregon, and California,
and Utah hordes were far in excess of these. Most
of the emigrants were technically trespassers upon
Indian lands as well as violators of treaty provisions.
Trouble with the Indians had begun early in the migrations.

At the very beginning of the Oregon movement the
Indian office had foreseen trouble: "Frequent diffi-

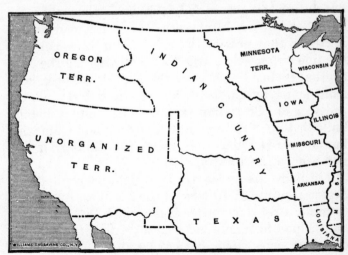

THE WEST IN 1849

Texas still claimed the Rio Grande as her western boundary. The Southwest
acquired in 1848 was yet unorganized.

culties have occurred during the spring of the last and present year [1845] from the passing of emigrants for Oregon at various points into the Indian Country. Large companies have frequently rendezvoused on the Indian lands for months previous to the period of their starting. The emigrants have two advantages in crossing into the Indian Country at an early period of the spring; one, the facility of grazing their stock on the rushes with which the lands abound; and the other, that they cross the Missouri River at their leisure. In one instance a large party had to be forced by the military to put back. This passing of the emigrants through the Indian Country without their permission must, I fear, result in an unpleasant collision, if not bloodshed. The Indians say that the whites have no right to be in their country without their consent; and the upper tribes, who subsist on game, complain that the buffalo are wantonly killed and scared off, which renders their only means of subsistence every year more precarious." Frémont had seen, in 1842, that this invasion of the Indian Country could not be kept up safely without a show of military force, and had recommended a post at the point where Fort Laramie was finally placed.

The years of the great migrations steadily aggravated the relations with the tribes, while the Indian agents continually called upon Congress to redress or stop the wrongs being done as often by panic-stricken emigrants as by vicious ones. "By alternate persuasion and force," wrote the Commissioner in

1854, "some of these tribes have been removed, step by step, from mountain to valley, and from river to plain, until they have been pushed halfway across the continent. They can go no further; on the ground they now occupy the crisis must be met, and their future determined. . . . [There] they are, and as they are, with outstanding obligations in their behalf of the most solemn and imperative character, voluntarily assumed by the government." But a relentless westward movement that had no regard for rights of Mexico in either Texas or California could not be expected to notice the rights of savages even less powerful. It demanded for its own citizens rights not inferior to those conceded by the government "to wandering nations of savages." A shrewd and experienced Indian agent, Fitzpatrick, who had the confidence of both races, voiced this demand in 1853. "But one course remains," he wrote, "which promises any permanent relief to them, or any lasting benefit to the country in which they dwell. That is simply to make such modifications in the 'intercourse laws' as will invite the residence of traders amongst them, and *open the whole Indian territory to settlement*. In this manner will be introduced amongst them those who will set the example of developing the resources of the soil, of which the Indians have not now the most distant idea; who will afford to them employment in pursuits congenial to their nature; and who will accustom them, imperceptibly, to those modes of life which can alone

secure them from the miseries of penury.   Trade is
the only civilizer of the Indian.   It has been the pre-
cursor of all civilization heretofore, and it will be of
all hereafter. . . .   The present 'intercourse laws'
too, so far as they are calculated to protect the
Indians from the evils of civilized life — from the
sale of ardent spirits and the prostitution of morals —
are nothing more than a dead letter; while, so far
as they contribute to exclude the benefits of civilization from amongst them, they can be, and are, strictly
enforced."

In 1849 the Indian Office was transferred by Congress from the War Department to the Interior, with
the idea that the Indians would be better off under
civilian than military control, and shortly after this
negotiations were begun looking towards new settlements with the tribes.   The Sioux were persuaded
in the summer of 1851 to make way for increasing
population in Minnesota, while in the autumn of the
same year the tribes of the western plains were induced to make concessions.

The great treaties signed at the Upper Platte
agency at Fort Laramie in 1851 were in the interest
of the migrating thousands.   Fitzpatrick had spent
the summer of 1850 in summoning the bands of Cheyenne and Arapaho to the conference.   Shoshoni
were brought in from the West.   From the north of
the Platte came Sioux and Assiniboin, Arickara,
Grosventres, and Crows.   The treaties here concluded were never ratified in full, but for fifteen years

Congress paid various annuities provided by them, and in general the tribes adhered to them.   The right of the United States to make roads across the plains and to fortify them with military posts was fully agreed to, while the Indians pledged themselves to commit no depredations upon emigrants.   Two years later, at Fort Atkinson, Fitzpatrick had a conference with the plains Indians of the south, Comanche and Apache, making "a renewal of faith, which the Indians did not have in the Government, nor the Government in them."

Overland traffic was made more safe for several years by these treaties.   Such friction and fighting as occurred in the fifties were due chiefly to the excesses and the fears of the emigrants themselves. But in these treaties there was nothing for the eastern tribes along the Iowa and Missouri border, who were in constant danger of dispossession by the advance of the frontier itself.

The settlement of Kansas, becoming probable in the early fifties, was the impending danger threatening the peace of the border.   There was not as yet any special need to extend colonization across the Missouri, since Arkansas, Missouri, Iowa, and Minnesota were but sparsely inhabited.   Settlers for years might be accommodated farther to the east. But the slavery debate of 1850 had revealed and aroused passions in both North and South.   Motives were so thoroughly mixed that participants were rarely able to give satisfactory accounts of themselves. Love of struggle, desire for revenge, political ambition, all mingled with pure philanthropy and a reasonable fear of outside interference with domestic institutions. The compromise had settled the future of the new lands, but between Missouri and the mountains lay the residue of the Louisiana purchase, divided truly by the Missouri compromise line of 36° 30', but not yet settled. Ambition to possess it, to convert it to slavery, or to retain it for freedom was stimulated by the debate and the fears of outside interference. The nearest part of the unorganized West was adjacent to Missouri. Hence it was that Kansas came within the public vision first.

It is possible to trace a movement for territorial organization in the Indian Country back to 1850 or even earlier. Certain of the more intelligent of the Indian colonists had been able to read the signs of the times, with the result that organized effort for a territory of Nebraska had emanated from the Wyandot country and had besieged Congress between 1851 and 1853. The obstacles in the road of fulfilment were the Indians and the laws. Experience had long demonstrated the unwisdom of permitting Indians and emigrants to live in the same districts. The removal and intercourse acts, and the treaties based upon them, had guaranteed in particular that no territory or state should ever be organized in this country. Good faith and the physical presence of the tribes had to be overcome before a new territory could appear.

The guarantee of permanency was based upon treaty, and in the eye of Congress was not so sacred that it could not be modified by treaty. As it became clear that the demand for the opening of these lands would soon have to be granted, Congress prepared for the inevitable by ordering, in March, 1853, a series of negotiations with the tribes west of Missouri with a view to the cession of more country. The Commissioner of Indian Affairs, George W. Manypenny, who later wrote a book on "Our Indian Wards," spent the next summer in breaking to the Indians the hard news that they were expected once more to vacate. He found the tribes uneasy and sullen. Occasional prospectors, wandering over their lands, had set them thinking. There had been no actual white settlement up to October, 1853, so Manypenny declared, but the chiefs feared that he was contemplating a seizure of their lands. The Indian mind had some difficulty in comprehending the difference between ceding their land by treaty and losing it by force.

At a long series of council fires the Commissioner soothed away some of the apprehensions, but found a stubborn resistance when he came to talk of ceding all the reserves and moving to new homes. The tribes, under pressure, were ready to part with some of their lands, but wanted to retain enough to live on. When he talked to them of the Great Father in Washington, Manypenny himself felt the irony of the situation; the guarantee of permanency had been simple and explicit. Yet he arranged for a series of treaties in the following year.

In the spring of 1854 treaties were concluded with most of the tribes fronting on Missouri between 37° and 42° 40'. Some of these had been persuaded to move into the Missouri Valley in the negotiations of the thirties. Others, always resident there, had accepted curtailed reserves. The Omaha faced the Missouri, north of the Platte. South of the Platte were the Oto and Missouri, the Sauk and Foxes of Missouri, the Iowa, and the Kickapoo. The Delaware reserve, north of the Kansas, and around Fort Leavenworth, was the seat of Indian civilization of a high order. The Shawnee, immediately south of the Kansas, were also well advanced in agriculture in the permanent home they had accepted. The confederated Kaskaskia and Peoria, and Wea and Piankashaw, and the Miami were further south. From those tribes more than thirteen million acres of land were bought in the treaties of 1854. In scattered and reduced reserves the Indians retained for themselves about one-tenth of what they ceded. Generally, when the final signing came, under the persuasion of the Indian Office, and often amid the strange surroundings of Washington, the chiefs surrendered the lands outright and with no condition.

Certain of the tribes resisted all importunities to give title at once and held out for conditions of sale. The Iowa, the confederated minor tribes, and notably the Delawares, ceded their lands in trust to the United States, with the treaty pledge that the lands so yielded should be sold at public auction to the highest bidder, the remainders should then be offered privately for three years at $1.25 per acre, and the final remnants should be disposed of by the United States, the accruing funds being held in trust by the United States for the Indians.   By the end of May the treaties were nearly all concluded.   In July, 1854, Congress provided a land office for the territory of Kansas.

While the Indian negotiations were in progress, Senator Douglas was forcing his Kansas-Nebraska bill at Washington.   The bill had failed in 1853, partly because the Senate had felt the sanctity of the Indian agreement; but in 1854 the leader of the Democratic party carried it along relentlessly.   With words of highest patriotism upon his lips, as Rhodes has told it, he secured the passage of a bill not needed by the westward movement, subversive of the national pledge, and, blind as he was, destructive as well of his party and his own political future.   The support of President Pierce and the coöperation of Jefferson Davis were his in the struggle.   It was not his intent, he declared, to legislate slavery into or out of the territories; he proposed to leave that to the people themselves.   To this principle he gave the name of "popular sovereignty," "and the name was a far greater invention than the doctrine."   With rising opposition all about him, he repealed the Mis-

souri compromise which in 1820 had divided the
Indian Country by the line of 36° 30′ into free and
slave areas, and created within these limits the new
territories of Kansas and Nebraska. His bill was
signed by the President on May 30, 1854. In later
years this day has been observed as a memorial to
those who lost their lives in fighting the battle which
he provoked.

With public sentiment excited, and the Missouri
compromise repealed, eager partisans prepared in
the spring of 1854 to colonize the new territories
in the interests of slavery and freedom. On the
slavery side, Senator Atchison, of Missouri, was
to be reckoned as one of the leaders. Young men
of the South were urged to move, with their slaves
and their possessions, into the new territories,
and thus secure these for their cherished institution. If votes should fail them in the future, the
Missouri border was not far removed, and colonization of voters might be counted upon. Missouri,
directly adjacent to Kansas, and a slave state,
naturally took the lead in this matter of preventing
the erection of a free state on her western boundary.
The northern states had been stirred by the act as
deeply as the South. In New England the bill was
not yet passed when leaders of the abolition movement prepared to act under it. One Eli Thayer,
of Worcester, urged during the spring that friends of
freedom could do no better work than aid in the
colonization of Kansas. He secured from his own

K

state, in April, a charter for a Massachusetts Emigrant Aid Society, through which he proposed to aid suitable men to move into the debatable land. Churches and schools were to be provided for them. A stern New England abolition spirit was to be fostered by them. And they were not to be left without the usual border means of defence. Amos A. Lawrence, of Boston, a wealthy philanthropist, made Thayer's scheme financially possible. Dr. Charles Robinson was their choice for leader of emigration and local representative in Kansas.

The resulting settlement of Kansas was stimulated little by the ordinary westward impulse but greatly by political ambition and sectional rivalry. As late as October, 1853, there had been almost no whites in the Indian Country. Early in 1854 they began to come in, in increasing numbers. The Emigrant Aid Society sent its parties at once, before the ink was dry on the treaties of cession and before land offices had been opened. The approach was by the Missouri River steamers to Kansas City and Westport, near the bend of the river, where was the gateway into Kansas. The Delaware cession, north of the Kansas River, was not yet open to legal occupation, but the Shawnee lands had been ceded completely and would soon be ready. So the New England companies worked their way on foot, or in hired wagons, up the right bank of the Kansas, hunting for eligible sites. About thirty miles west of the Missouri line and the old Shawnee mission they picked their spot late in July. The town of Lawrence grew out of their cluster of tents and cabins.

It was more than two months after the arrival of the squatters at Lawrence before the first governor of the new territory, Andrew H. Reeder, made his appearance at Fort Leavenworth and established civil government in Kansas. One of his first experiences was with the attempt of United States officers at the post to secure for themselves pieces of the Delaware lands which surrounded it. "While lying at the fort," wrote a surveyor who left early in September to run the Nebraska boundary line, "we heard a great deal about those d—d squatters who were trying to steal the Leavenworth site." None of the Delaware lands were open to settlement, since the United States had pledged itself to sell them all at public auction for the Indians' benefit. But certain speculators, including officers of the regular army, organized a town company to preëmpt a site near the fort, where they thought they foresaw the great city of the West. They relied on the immunity which usually saved pilferers on the Indian lands, and seem even to have used United States soldiers to build their shanties. They had begun to dispose of their building lots "in this discreditable business" four weeks before the first of the Delaware trust lands were put on sale.

However bitter toward each other, the settlers were agreed in their attitude toward the Indians, and squatted regardless of Indian rights or United States

laws. Governor Reeder himself convened his legislature, first at Pawnee, whence troops from Fort
Riley ejected it; then at the Shawnee mission, close
to Kansas City, where his presence and its were
equally without authority of law. He established
election precincts in unceded lands, and voting places
at spots where no white man could go without vio-
lating the law. The legal snarl into which the
settlers plunged reveals the inconsistencies in the
Indian policy. It is even intimated that Governor
Reeder was interested in a land scheme at Pawnee
similar to that at Fort Leavenworth.

The fight for Kansas began immediately after the
arrival of Governor Reeder and the earliest immigrants. The settlers actually in residence at the
commencement of 1855 seem to have been about
8500. Propinquity gave Missouri an advantage at
the start, when the North was not yet fully aroused.
At an election for territorial legislature held on
March 30, 1855, the threat of Senator Atchison was
revealed in all its fulness when more than 6000
votes were counted among a population which
had under 3000 qualified voters. Missouri men
had ridden over in organized bands to colonize
the precincts and carry the election. The whole
area of settlement was within an easy two days' ride
of the Missouri border. The fraud was so crude that
Governor Reeder disavowed certain of the results,
yet the resulting legislature, meeting in July, 1855,
was able to expel some of its anti-slavery members,

while the rest resigned. It adopted the Missouri code of law, thus laying the foundations for a slave state.

The political struggle over Kansas became more intense on the border and more absorbing in the nation in the next four years. The free-state men, as the settlers around Lawrence came to be known, disavowed the first legislature on the ground of its fraudulent election, while President Pierce steadily supported it from Washington. Governor Reeder was removed during its session, seemingly because he had thrown doubts upon its validity. Protesting against it, the northerners held a series of meetings in the autumn, around Lawrence, and Topeka, some twenty-five miles further up the Kansas River, and crystallized their opposition under Dr. Robinson. Their efforts culminated at Topeka in October in a spontaneous, but in this instance revolutionary, convention which framed a free-state constitution for Kansas and provided for erecting a rival administration. Dr. Robinson became its governor.

Before the first legislature under the Topeka constitution assembled, Kansas had still further trouble. Private violence and mob attacks began during the fall of 1855. What is known as the Wakarusa War occurred in November, when Sheriff Jones of Douglas County tried to arrest some free-state men at Lecompton, and met with strong resistance reënforced with Sharpe rifles from New England. Governor Wilson Shannon, who had succeeded Reeder, patched up peace, but hostility continued through the winter. Lawrence was increasingly the centre of northern settlement and the object of pro-slave aggression. A Missouri mob visited it on May 21, 1856, and in the approving presence, it is said, of Sheriff Jones, sacked its hotel and printing shop, and burned the residence of Dr. Robinson.

In the fall a free-state crowd marched up the river and attacked Lecompton, but within a week of the sacking of Lawrence retribution was visited upon the pro-slave settlers. In cold blood, five men were murdered at a settlement on Potawatomi Creek, by a group of fanatical free-state men. Just what provocation John Brown and his family had received which may excuse his revenge is not certain. In many instances individual anti-slavery men retaliated lawlessly upon their enemies. But the leaders of the Lawrence party have led also in censuring Brown and in disclaiming responsibility for his acts. It is certain that in this struggle the free-state party, in general, wanted peaceful settlement of the country, and were staking their fortunes and families upon it. They were ready for defence, but criminal aggression was no part of their platform.

The course of Governor Shannon reached its end in the summer of 1856. He was disliked by the free-state faction, while his personal habits gave no respectability to the pro-slave cause. At the end of his régime the extra-legal legislature under the Topeka constitution was prevented by federal troops from convening in session at Topeka. A few weeks later Governor John W. Geary superseded him and established his seat of government in Lecompton, by this time a village of some twenty houses. It took Geary, an honest, well-meaning man, only six weeks to fall out with the pro-slave element and the federal land officers. He resigned in March, 1857.

Under Governor Robert J. Walker, who followed Geary, the first official attempt at a constitution was entered upon. The legislature had already summoned a convention which sat at Lecompton during September and October. Its constitution, which was essentially pro-slavery, however it was read, was ratified before the end of the year and submitted to Congress. But meanwhile the legislature which called the convention had fallen into free-state hands, disavowed the constitution, and summoned another convention. At Leavenworth this convention framed a free-state constitution in March, which was ratified by popular vote in May, 1858. Governor Walker had already resigned in December, 1857. Through holding an honest election and purging the returns of slave-state frauds he had enabled the free-state party to secure the legislature. Southerner though he was, he choked at the political dishonesty of the administration in Kansas. He had yielded to the evidence of his eyes, that the population of Kansas possessed a large free-state majority. But so yielding he had lost the confidence of Washington.

Even Senator Douglas, the patron of the popular
sovereignty doctrine, had now broken with President
Buchanan, recognizing the right of the people to
form their own institutions. No attention was ever
paid by Congress to this Leavenworth constitution,
but when the Lecompton constitution was finally
submitted to the people by Congress, in August,
1858, it was defeated by more than 11,000 votes in a
total of 13,000.   Kansas was henceforth in the hands
of the actual settlers. A year later, at Wyandotte,
it made a fourth constitution, under which it at last
entered the union on January 29, 1861. "In the
Wyandotte Convention," says one of the local historians, "there were a few Democrats and one or
two cranks, and probably both were of some use in
their way."

There had been no white population in Kansas in
1853, and no special desire to create one. But the
political struggle had advertised the territory on a
large scale, while the whole West was under the influence of the agricultural boom that was extending
settlement into Wisconsin, Minnesota, and Iowa.
Governor Reeder's census in 1855 found that about
8500 had come in since the erection of the territory.
The rioting and fighting, the rumors of Sharpe rifles
and the stories of Lawrence and Potawatomi,
instead of frightening settlers away, drew them there
in increasing thousands. Some few came from the
South, but the northern majority was overwhelming before the panic of 1857 laid its heavy hand

upon expansion.   There was a white population of
106,390 in 1860.

The westward movement, under its normal influences, had extended the range of prosperous agricultural settlement into the Northwest in this past
decade.   It had coöperated in the extension into that
part of the old desert now known as Kansas.   But
chiefly politics, and secondly the call of the West,
is the order of causes which must explain the first
westward advance of the agricultural frontier since
1820.   Even in 1860 the population of Kansas was
almost exclusively within a three days' journey of
the Missouri bend.

CHAPTER IX

"PIKE'S PEAK OR BUST"[1]

THE territory of Kansas completed the political organization of the prairies. Before 1854 there had been a great stretch of land beyond Missouri and the Indian frontier without any semblance of organization or law. Indeed within the area whites had been forbidden to enter, since here was the final abode of the Indians. But with the Kansas-Nebraska act all this was changed. In five years a series of amorphous territories had been provided for by law.

Along the line of the frontier were now three distinct divisions. From the Canadian border to the fortieth parallel, Nebraska extended. Kansas lay between 40° and 37°. Lying west of Arkansas, the old Indian Country, now much reduced by partition, embraced the rest. The whole plains country, east of the mountains, was covered by these territorial projects. Indian Territory was without the government which its name implied, but popular parlance regarded it as the others and refused to see any difference among them.

[1] This chapter is in part based upon my article on "The Territory of Colorado" which was published in *The American Historical Review* in October, 1906.

Beyond the mountain wall which formed the western boundary of Kansas and Nebraska lay four other territories equally without particular reason for their shape and bounds. Oregon, acquired in 1846, had been divided in 1853 by a line starting at the mouth of the Columbia and running east to the Rockies, cutting off Washington territory on its northern side. The Utah territory which figured in the compromise of 1850, and which Mormon migration had made necessary, extended between California and the Rockies, from Oregon at 42° to New Mexico at 37°. New Mexico, also of the compromise year, reached from Texas to California, south of 37°, and possessed at its northeast corner a panhandle which carried it north to 38° in order to leave in it certain old Mexican settlements.

These divisions of the West embraced in 1854 the whole of the country between California and the states. As yet their boundaries were arbitrary and temporary, but they presaged movements of population which during the next quarter century should break them up still further and provide real colonies in place of the desert and the Indian Country. Congress had no formative part in the work. Population broke down barriers and showed the way, while laws followed and legalized what had been done. The map of 1854 reveals an intent to let the mountain summit remain a boundary, and contains no prophecy of the four states which were shortly to appear.

For several decades the area of Kansas territory, and the southern part of Nebraska, had been well known as the range of the plains Indians, — Pawnee and Sioux, Arapaho and Cheyenne, Kiowa, Comanche and Apache.   Through this range the cara-

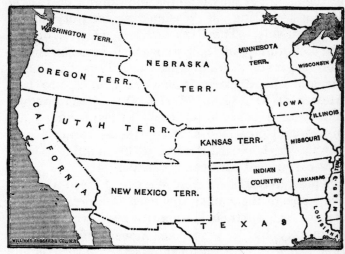

THE WEST IN 1854

Great amorphous territories now covered all the plains, and the Rocky Mountains were recognized only as a dividing line.

vans had gone.   Here had been constant military expeditions as well.   It was a common summer's campaign for a dragoon regiment to go out from Fort Leavenworth to the mountains by either the Arkansas or Platte route, to skirt the eastern slopes along the southern fork of the Platte, and return home by the other trail.   Those military demonstrations,

which were believed to be needed to impress the
tribes, had made this march a regular performance.
Colonel Dodge had done it in the thirties, Sumner
and Sedgwick did it in 1857, and there had been numerous others in between.   A well-known trail had
been worn in this wise from Fort Laramie, on the
north, through St. Vrain's, crossing the South Platte
at Cherry Creek, past the Fontaine qui Bouille, and
on to Bent's Fort and the New Mexican towns.
Yet Kansas had slight interest in its western end.
Along the Missouri the sections were quarrelling
over slavery, but they had scarcely scratched the
soil for one-fourth of the length of the territory.

The crest of the continent, lying at the extreme
west of Kansas, lay between the great trails, so that
it was off the course of the chief migrations, and
none visited it for its own sake.   The deviating
trails, which commenced at the Missouri bend, were
some 250 miles apart at the one hundred and third
meridian.   Here was the land which Kansas baptized
in 1855 as the county of Arapahoe, and whence arose
the hills around Pike's Peak, which rumor came in
three years more to tip with gold.

The discovery of gold in California prepared the
public for similar finds in other parts of the West.
With many of the emigrants prospecting had become
a habit that sent small bands into the mountain
valleys from Washington to New Mexico.   Stories
of success in various regions arose repeatedly during
the fifties and are so reasonable that it is not possible

to determine with certainty the first finds in many
localities. Any mountain stream in the whole
system might be expected to contain some gold, but
deposits large enough to justify a boom were slow
in coming.

In January, 1859, six quills of gold, brought in to
Omaha from the mountains, confirmed the rumors
of a new discovery that had been persistent for several months. The previous summer had seen organized attempts to locate in the Pike's Peak region
the deposits whose existence had been believed in,
more or less, since 1850. Parties from the gold
fields of Georgia, from Lawrence, and from Lecompton are known to have been in the field and to have
started various mushroom settlements. El Paso,
near the present site of Colorado Springs, appeared,
as well as a group of villages at the confluence of the
South Platte and the half-dry bottom of Cherry
Creek, — Montana, Auraria, Highland, and St.
Charles. Most of the gold-seekers returned to the
States before winter set in, but a few, encouraged by
trifling finds, remained to occupy their flimsy cabins
or to jump the claims of the absentees. In the
sands of Cherry Creek enough gold was found to hold
the finders and to start a small migration thither
in the autumn. In the early winter the groups on
Cherry Creek coalesced and assumed the name of
Denver City.

The news of Pike's Peak gold reached the Missouri
Valley at the strategic moment when the newness of

Kansas had worn off, and the depression of 1857 had brought bankruptcy to much of the frontier. The adventurous pioneers, who were always ready to move, had been reënforced by individuals down on their luck and reduced to any sort of extremity. The way had been prepared for a heavy emigration to the new diggings which started in the fall of 1858 and assumed great volume in the spring of 1859.

The edge of the border for these emigrants was not much farther west than it had been for emigrants of the preceding decade. A few miles from the Missouri River all traces of Kansas or Nebraska disappeared, whether one advanced by the Platte or the Arkansas, or by the intermediate routes of the Smoky Hill and Republican. The destination was less than half as far away as California had been. No mountains and no terrible deserts were to be crossed. The costs and hardships of the journey were less than any that had heretofore separated the frontier from a western goal. There is a glimpse of the bustling life around the head of the trails in a letter which General W. T. Sherman wrote to his brother John from Leavenworth City, on April 30, 1859: "At this moment we are in the midst of a rush to Pike's Peak. Steamboats arrive in twos and threes each day, loaded with people for the new gold region. The streets are full of people buying flour, bacon, and groceries, with wagons and outfits, and all around the town are little camps preparing to go west. A daily stage goes west to Fort Riley, 135 miles, and every morning two spring wagons, drawn by four mules and capable of carrying six passengers, start for the Peak, distance six hundred miles, the journey to be made in twelve days. As yet the stages all go out and don't return, according to the plan for distributing the carriages; but as soon as they are distributed, there will be two going and two returning, making a good line of stages to Pike's Peak. Strange to say, even yet, although probably 25,000 people have actually gone, we are without authentic advices of gold. Accounts are generally favorable as to words and descriptions, but no positive physical evidence comes in the shape of gold, and I will be incredulous until I know some considerable quantity comes in in way of trade."

Throughout the United States newspapers gave full notice to the new boom, while a "Pike's Peak Guide," based on a journal kept by one of the early parties, found a ready sale. No single movement had ever carried so heavy a migration upon the plains as this, which in one year must have taken nearly 100,000 pioneers to the mountains. "Pike's Peak or Bust!" was a common motto blazoned on their wagon covers. The sawmill, the press, and the stage-coach were all early on the field. Byers, long a great editor in Denver, arrived in April to distribute an edition of his *Rocky Mountain News*, which he had printed on one side before leaving Omaha. Thenceforth the diggings were consistently advertised by a resident enthusiast. Early in May the first coach of the Leavenworth and Pike's Peak Express Company brought Henry Villard into Denver. In June came no less a personage than Horace Greeley to see for himself the new wonder. "Mine eyes have never yet been blessed with the sight of any floor whatever in either Denver or Auraria," he could write of the village of huts which he inspected. The seal of approval which his letters set upon the enterprise did much to encourage it.

With the rush of prospectors to the hills, numerous new camps quickly appeared. Thirty miles north along the foothills and mesas Boulder marked the exit of a mountain creek upon the plains. Behind Denver, in Clear Creek Valley, were Golden, at the mouth, and Black Hawk and Central City upon the north fork of the stream. Idaho Springs and Georgetown were on its south fork. Here in the Gregory district was the active life of the diggings. The great extent of the gold belt to the southwest was not yet fully known. Farther south was Pueblo, on the Arkansas, and a line of little settlements working up the valley, by Canyon City to Oro, where Leadville now stands.

Reaction followed close upon the heels of the boom, beginning its work before the last of the outward bound had reached the diggings. Gold was to be found in trifling quantities in many places, but the mob of inexperienced miners had little chance for fortune. The great deposits, which were some months in being discovered, were in refractory

L

quartz lodes, calling for heavy stamp mills, chemical processes, and, above all, great capital for their working. Even for laborers there was no demand commensurate with the number of the fifty-niners. Hence, more than half of these found their way back to the border before the year was over, bitter, disgusted, and poor, scrawling on deserted wagons, in answer to the outward motto, "Busted! By Gosh!"

The problem of government was born when the first squatters ran the lines of Denver City. Here was a new settlement far away from the seat of territorial government, while the government itself was impotent. Kansas had no legislature competent to administer law at home — far less in outlying colonies. But spontaneous self-government came easily to the new town. "Just to think," wrote one of the pioneers in his diary, "that within two weeks of the arrival of a few dozen Americans in a wilderness, they set to work to elect a Delegate to the United States Congress, and ask to be set apart as a new Territory! But we are of a fast race and in a fast age and must prod along." An early snow in November, 1858, had confined the miners to their cabins and started politics. The result had been the election of two delegates, one to Congress and one to Kansas legislature, both to ask for governmental direction. Kansas responded in a few weeks, creating five new counties west of 104°, and chartering a city of St. Charles, long after St. Charles had been merged into Denver. Congress did nothing.

The prospective immigration of 1859 inspired further and more comprehensive attempts at local government. It was well understood that the news of gold would send in upon Denver a wave of population and perhaps a reign of lawlessness. The adjournment of Congress without action in their behalf made it certain that there could be no aid from this quarter for at least a year, and became the occasion for a caucus in Denver over which William Larimer presided on April 11, 1859. As a result of this caucus, a call was issued for a convention of representatives of the neighboring mining camps to meet in the same place four days later. On April 15, six camps met through their delegates, "being fully impressed with the belief, from early and recent precedents, of the power and benefits and duty of self-government," and feeling an imperative necessity "for an immediate and adequate government, for the large population now here and soon to be among us . . . and also believing that a territorial government is not such as our large and peculiarly situated population demands."

The deliberations thus informally started ended in a formal call for a constitutional convention to meet in Denver on the first Monday in June, for the purpose, as an address to the people stated, of framing a constitution for a new "state of Jefferson." "Shall it be," the address demanded, "the government of the knife and the revolver, or shall we unite in forming here in our golden country, among the ravines and gulches of the Rocky Mountains, and the fertile valleys of the Arkansas and the Platte, a new and independent State?" The boundaries of the prospective state were named in the call as the one hundred and second and one hundred and tenth meridians of longitude, and the thirty-seventh and forty-third parallels of north latitude — including with true frontier amplitude large portions of Utah and Nebraska and nearly half of Wyoming, in addition to the present state of Colorado.

When the statehood convention met in Denver on June 6, the time was inopportune for concluding the movement, since the reaction had set in. The height of the gold boom was over, and the return migration left it somewhat doubtful whether any permanent population would remain in the country to need a state. So the convention met on the 6th, appointed some eight drafting committees, and adjourned, to await developments, until August 1. By this later date, the line had been drawn between the confident and the discouraged elements in the population, and for six days the convention worked upon the question of statehood. As to permanency there was now no doubt; but the body divided into two nearly equal groups, one advocating immediate statehood, the other shrinking from the heavy taxation incident to a state establishment and so preferring a territorial government with a federal treasury behind it. The body, too badly split to reach a conclusion itself, compromised by preparing the way for either development and leaving the choice to a public vote. A state constitution was drawn up on one hand; on the other, was prepared a memorial to Congress praying for a territorial government, and both documents were submitted to a vote on September 5. Pursuant to the memorial, which was adopted, another election was held on October 3, at which the local agent of the new Leavenworth and Pike's Peak Express Company, Beverly D. Williams, was chosen as delegate to Congress.

The adoption of the territorial memorial failed to meet the need for immediate government or to prevent the advocates of such government from working out a provisional arrangement pending the action of Congress. On the day that Williams was elected, these advocates chose delegates for a preliminary territorial constitutional convention which met a week later. "Here we go," commented Byers, "a regular triple-headed government machine; south of 40 deg. we hang on to the skirts of Kansas; north of 40 deg. to those of Nebraska; straddling the line, we have just elected a Delegate to the United States Congress from the 'Territory of Jefferson,' and ere long we will have in full blast a provisional government of Rocky Mountain growth and manufacture." In this convention of October 10, 1859, the name of Jefferson was retained for the new territory; the boundaries of April 15 were retained, and a government similar to the highest type of territorial establishment was provided for. If the

convention had met on the authority of an enabling
act, its career could not have been more dignified.
Its constitution was readily adopted, while officers
under it were chosen in an orderly election on October
24.   Robert W. Steele, of Ohio, became its governor.
On November 7 he met his legislature and delivered
his first inaugural address.

The territory of Jefferson which thus came into
existence in the Pike's Peak region illustrates well
the spirit of the American frontier. The fundamental
principle of American government which Byers expressed in connection with it is applicable at all
times in similar situations.   "We claim," he wrote
in his *Rocky Mountain News*, "that any body, or
community of American citizens, which from any
cause or under any circumstance is cut off from, or
from isolation is so situated as not to be under, any
active and protecting branch of the central government, have a right, if on American soil, to frame a
government, and enact such laws and regulations as
may be necessary for their own safety, protection,
and happiness, always with the condition precedent,
that they shall, at the earliest moment when the central government shall extend an *effective* organization
and laws over them, give it their unqualified support
and obedience."   The life of the spontaneous commonwealth thus called into existence is a creditable
witness to the American instinct for orderly government.

When Congress met in December, 1859, the pro-

visional territory of Jefferson was in operation, while
its delegates in Washington were urging the need for
governmental action. To their influence, President
Buchanan added, on February 20, 1860, a message
transmitting the petition from the Pike's Peak country. The Senate, upon April 3, received a report
from the Committee on Territories introducing Senate Bill No. 366, for the erection of Colorado territory, while Grow of Pennsylvania reported to the
House on May 10 a bill to erect in the same region a
territory of Idaho. The name of Jefferson disappeared from the project in the spring of 1860, its
place being taken by sundry other names for the same
mountain area. Several weeks were given, in part,
to debate over this Colorado-Idaho scheme, though
as usual the debate turned less upon the need for
this territorial government than upon the attitude
which the bill should take toward the slavery issue.
The slavery controversy prevented territorial legislation in this session, but the reasonableness of the
Colorado demand was well established.

The territory of Jefferson, as organized in November, 1859, had been from the first recognized as
merely a temporary expedient. The movement
for it had gained weight in the summer of that year
from the probability that it need not be maintained
for many months. When Congress, however, failed
in the ensuing session of 1859–1860 to grant the
relief for which the pioneers had prayed, the wisdom
of continuing for a second year the life of a govern-

ment admitted to be illegal came into question.
The first session of its legislature had lasted from
November 7, 1859, to January 25, 1860. It
had passed comprehensive laws for the regulation of
titles in lands, water, and mines, and had adopted
civil and criminal codes. Its courts had been established and had operated with some show of
authority. But the service and obedience to the
government had been voluntary, no funds being on
hand for the payment of salaries and expenses. One
of the pioneers from Vermont wrote home, "There is
no hopes [sic] of perfect quiet in our governmental
matters until we are securely under the wing of our
National Eagle." In his proclamation calling the
second election Governor Steele announced that
"all persons who expect to be elected to any of the
above offices should bear in mind that there will be
no salaries or per diem allowed from this territory,
but that the General Government will be memorial-
ized to aid us in our adversity."

Upon this question of revenue the territory of
Jefferson was wrecked. Taxes could not be collected, since citizens had only to plead grave doubts
as to the legality in order to evade payment. "We
have tried a Provisional Government, and how has
it worked," asked William Larimer in announcing
his candidacy for the office of territorial delegate.
"It did well enough until an attempt was made to
tax the people to support it." More than this, the
real need for the government became less apparent

as 1860 advanced, for the scattered communities learned how to obtain a reasonable peace without it. American mining camps are peculiarly free from the need for superimposed government. The new camp at once organizes itself on a democratic basis, and in mass meeting registers claims, hears and decides suits, and administers summary justice. Since the Pike's Peak country was only a group of mining camps, there proved to be little immediate need for a central government, for in the local mining-district organizations all of the most pressing needs of the communities could be satisfied. So loyalty to the territory of Jefferson, in the districts outside of Denver, waned during 1860, and in the summer of that year had virtually disappeared. Its administration, however, held together. Governor Steele made efforts to rehabilitate its authority, was himself reëlected, and met another legislature in November.

When the thirty-sixth Congress met for its second session in December, 1860, the Jefferson organization was in the second year of its life, yet in Congress there was no better prospect of quick action than there had been since 1857. Indeed the election of Lincoln brought out the eloquence of the slavery question with a renewed vigor that monopolized the time and strength of Congress until the end of January. Had not the departure of the southern members to their states cleared the way for action, it is highly improbable that even this session would have produced results of importance.

Grow had announced in the beginning of the session a territorial platform similar to that which had been under debate for three years. Until the close of January the southern valedictories held the floor, but at last the admission of Kansas, on January 29, 1861, revealed the fact that pro-slavery opposition had departed and that the long-deferred territorial scheme could have a fair chance. On the very day that Kansas was admitted, with its western boundary at the twenty-fifth meridian from Washington, the Senate revived its bill No. 366 of the last session and took up its deliberation upon a territory for Pike's Peak. Only by chance did the name Colorado remain attached to the bill. Idaho was at one time adopted, but was amended out in favor of the original name when the bill at last passed the Senate. The boundaries were cut down from those which the territory had provided for itself. Two degrees were taken from the north of the territory, and three from the west. In this shape, between 37° and 41° north latitude, and 25° and 32° of longitude west of Washington, the bill received the signature of President Buchanan on February 28. The absence of serious debate in the passage of this Colorado act is excellent evidence of the merit of the scheme and the reasons for its being so long deferred.

President Buchanan, content with approving the bill, left the appointment of the first officials for Colorado to his successor. In the multitude of greater problems facing President Lincoln, this was neglected for several weeks, but he finally commissioned General William Gilpin as the first governor of the territory. Gilpin had long known the mountain frontier; he had commanded a detachment on the Santa Fé trail in the forties, and he had written prophetic books upon the future of the country to which he was now sent. His loyalty was unquestioned and his readiness to assume responsibility went so far as perhaps to cease to be a virtue. He arrived in Denver on May 29, 1861, and within a few days was ready to take charge of the government and to receive from the hands of Governor Steele such authority as remained in the provisional territory of Jefferson.

CHAPTER X

THE Pike's Peak boom was only one in a series of mining episodes which, within fifteen years of the discoveries in California, let in the light of exploration and settlement upon hundreds of valleys scattered over the whole of the Rocky Mountain West. The men who exploited California had generally been amateur miners, acquiring skill by bitter experience; but the next decade developed a professional class, mobile as quicksilver, restless and adventurous as all the West, which permeated into the most remote recesses of the mountains and produced before the Civil War was over, as the direct result of their search for gold, not only Colorado, but Nevada and Arizona, Idaho and Montana. Activity was constant during these years all along the continental divide. New camps were being born overnight, old ones were abandoned by magic. Here and there cities rose and remained to mark success in the search. Abandoned huts and half-worked diggings were scars covering a fourth of the continent.

Colorado, in the summer of 1859, attracted the largest of migrations, but while Denver was being settled there began, farther west, a boom which for the present outdid it in significance. The old California trail from Salt Lake crossed the Nevada desert and entered California by various passes through the Sierra Nevadas. Several trading posts had been planted along this trail by Mormons and others during the fifties, until in 1854 the legislature of Utah had created a Carson County in the west end of the territory for the benefit of the settlements along the river of the same name. Small discoveries of gold were enough to draw to this district a floating population which founded a Carson City as early as 1858. But there were no indications of a great excitement until after the finding of a marvellously rich vein of silver near Gold Hill in the spring of 1859. Here, not far from Mt. Davidson and but a few miles east of Lake Tahoe and the Sierras, was the famous Comstock lode, upon which it was possible within five years to build a state.

The California population, already rushing about from one boom to another in perpetual prospecting, seized eagerly upon this new district in western Utah. The stage route by way of Sacramento and Placerville was crowded beyond capacity, while hundreds marched over the mountains on foot. "There was no difficulty in reaching the newly discovered region of boundless wealth," asserted a journalistic visitor. "It lay on the public highway to California, on the borders of the state. From Missouri, from Kansas and Nebraska, from Pike's

Peak and Salt Lake, the tide of emigration poured in. Transportation from San Francisco was easy. I made the trip myself on foot almost in the dead of winter, when the mountains were covered with snow." Carson City had existed before the great discovery. Virginia City, named for a renegade southerner, nicknamed "Virginia," soon followed it, while the typical population of the mining camps piled in around the two.

In 1860 miners came in from a larger area. The new pony express ran through the heart of the fields and aided in advertising them east and west. Colorado was only one year ahead in the public eye. Both camps obtained their territorial acts within the same week, that of Nevada receiving Buchanan's signature on March 2, 1861. All of Utah west of the thirty-ninth meridian from Washington became the new territory which, through the need of the union for loyal votes, gained its admission as a state in three more years.

The rush to Carson valley drew attention away from another mining enterprise further south. In the western half of New Mexico, between the Rio Grande and the Colorado, there had been successful mining ever since the acquisition of the territory. The southwest boundary of the United States after the Mexican War was defined in words that could not possibly be applied to the face of the earth. This fact, together with knowledge that an easy railway grade ran south of the Gila River, had led in 1853 to the purchase of additional land from Mexico and the definition of a better boundary in the Gadsden treaty. In these lands of the Gadsden purchase old mines came to light in the years immediately following. Sylvester Mowry and Charles D. Poston were most active in promoting the mining companies which revived abandoned claims and developed new ones near the old Spanish towns of Tubac and Tucson. The region was too remote and life too hard for the individual miner to have much chance. Organized mining companies here took the place of the detached prospector of Colorado and Nevada. Disappointed miners from California came in, and perhaps "the Vigilance Committee of San Francisco did more to populate the new Territory than the silver mines. Tucson became the headquarters of vice, dissipation, and crime. . . . It was literally a paradise of devils." Excessive dryness, long distances, and Apache depredation discouraged rapid growth, yet the surveys of the early fifties and the passage of the overland mail through the camps in 1858 advertised the Arizona settlement and enabled it to live.

The outbreak of the Civil War extinguished for the time the Mowry mines and others in the Santa Cruz Valley, holding them in check till a second mineral area in western New Mexico should be found. United States army posts were abandoned, confederate agents moved in, and Indians became bold. The federal authority was not reëstablished until

Colonel J. H. Carleton led his California column across the Colorado and through New Mexico to Tucson early in 1862. During the next two years he maintained his headquarters at Santa Fé, carried on punitive campaigns against the Navaho and the Apache, and encouraged mining.

The Indian campaigns of Carleton and his aides in New Mexico have aroused much controversy. There were no treaty rights by which the United States had privileges of colonization and development. It was forcible entry and retention, maintained in the face of bitter opposition. Carleton, with Kit Carson's assistance, waged a war of scarcely concealed extermination. They understood, he reported to Washington, "the direct application of force as a law. If its application be removed, that moment they become lawless. This has been tried over and over and over again, and at great expense. The purpose now is never to relax the application of force with a people that can no more be trusted than you can trust the wolves that run through their mountains; to gather them together little by little, on to a reservation, away from the haunts, and hills, and hiding-places of their country, and then to be kind to them; there teach their children how to read and write, teach them the arts of peace; teach them the truths of Christianity. Soon they will acquire new habits, new ideas, new modes of life; the old Indians will die off, and carry with them all the latent longings for murdering and robbing;

the young ones will take their places without these
longings; and thus, little by little, they will become
a happy and contented people."

Mowry's mines had been seized by Carleton at
the start, as tainted with treason. The whole
Tucson district was believed to be so thoroughly in
sympathy with the confederacy that the commanding
officer was much relieved when rumors came of a
new placer gold field along the left bank of the Colorado River, around Bill Williams Creek. Thither
the population of the territory moved as fast as it
could. Teamsters and other army employees deserted freely. Carleton deliberately encouraged
surveying and prospecting, and wrote personally
to General Halleck and Postmaster-general Blair,
congratulating them because his California column
had found the gold with which to suppress the confederacy. "One of the richest gold countries in
the world," he described it to be, destined to be the
centre of a new territorial life, and to throw into the
shade "the insignificant village of Tucson."

The population of the silver camp had begun
to urge Congress to provide a territory independent
of New Mexico, immediately after the development
of the Mowry mines. Delegates and petitions had
been sent to Washington in the usual style. But
congressional indifference to new territories had
blocked progress. The new discoveries reopened
the case in 1862 and 1863. Forgetful of his Indian
wards and their rights, the Superintendent of Indian

M

Affairs had told of the sad peril of the "unprotected miners" who had invaded Indian territory of clear title. They would offer to the "numerous and warlike tribes" an irresistible opportunity. The territorial act was finally passed on February 24, 1863, while the new capital was fixed in the heart of the new gold field, at Fort Whipple, near which the city of Prescott soon appeared.

The Indian danger in Arizona was not ended by the erection of a territorial government. There never came in a population large enough to intimidate the tribes, while bad management from the start provoked needless wars. Most serious were the Apache troubles which began in 1861 and ceased only after Crook's campaigns in the early seventies. In this struggle occurred the massacre at Camp Grant in 1871, when citizens of Tucson, with careful premeditation, murdered in cold blood more than eighty Apache, men, women, and children. The degree of provocation is uncertain, but the disposition of Tucson, as Mowry has phrased it, was not such as to strengthen belief in the justice of the attack: "There is only one way to wage war against the Apache. A steady, persistent campaign must be made, following them to their haunts — hunting them to the 'fastnesses of the mountains.' They must be surrounded, starved into coming in, surprised or inveigled — by white flags, or any other method, human or divine — and then put to death. If these ideas shock any weak-minded individual who thinks himself a philanthropist, I can only say that I pity without respecting his mistaken sympathy. A man might as well have sympathy for a rattlesnake or a tiger."

The mines of Arizona, though handicapped by climate and inaccessibility, brought life into the extreme Southwest. Those of Nevada worked the partition of Utah. Farther to the north the old Oregon country gave out its gold in these same years as miners opened up the valleys of the Snake and the head waters of the Missouri River. Right on the crest of the continental divide appeared the northern group of mining camps.

The territory of Washington had been cut away from Oregon at its own request and with Oregon's consent in 1853. It had no great population and was the subject of no agricultural boom as Oregon had been, but the small settlements on Puget Sound and around Olympia were too far from the Willamette country for convenient government. When Oregon was admitted in 1859, Washington was made to include all the Oregon country outside the state, embracing the present Washington and Idaho, portions of Montana and Wyoming, and extending to the continental divide. Through it ran the overland trail from Fort Hall almost to Walla Walla. Because of its urging Congress built a new wagon road that was passable by 1860 from Fort Benton, on the upper Missouri, to the junction of the Columbia and Snake. Farther east the active business of the American Fur Company had by 1859 established steamboat communication from St. Louis to Fort Benton, so that an overland route to rival the old Platte trail was now available.

In eastern Washington the most important of the Indians were the Nez Percés, whose peaceful habits and friendly disposition had been noted since the days of Lewis and Clark, and who had permitted their valley of the Snake to become a main route to Oregon. Treaties with these had been made in 1855 by Governor Stevens, in accordance with which most of the tribe were in 1860 living on their reserve at the junction of the Clearwater and Snake, and were fairly prosperous. Here as elsewhere was the specific agreement that no whites save government employees should be allowed in the Indian Country; but in the summer of 1861 the news that gold had been found along the Clearwater brought the agreement to naught. Gold had actually been discovered the summer before. In the spring of 1861 pack trains from Walla Walla brought a horde of miners east over the range, while steamboats soon found their way up the Snake. In the fork between the Clearwater and Snake was a good landing where, in the autumn of 1861, sprang up the new Lewiston, named in honor of the great explorer, acting as centre of life for five thousand miners in the district, and showing by its very existence on the Indian reserve the futility of treaty restrictions in the face of the gold fever. The troubles of the Indian department were great. "To attempt to restrain miners would be, to my mind, like attempting to restrain the whirlwind," reported Superintendent Kendall. "The history of California, Australia, Frazer river, and even of the country of which I am now writing, furnishes abundant evidence of the attractive power of even only reported gold discoveries.

"The mines on Salmon river have become a fixed fact, and are equalled in richness by few recorded discoveries. Seeing the utter impossibility of preventing miners from going to the mines, I have refrained from taking any steps which, by certain want of success, would tend to weaken the force of the law. At the same time I as carefully avoided giving any consent to unauthorized statements, and verbally instructed the agent in charge that, while he might not be able to enforce the laws for want of means, he must give no consent to any attempt to lay out a town at the juncture of the Snake and Clearwater rivers, as he had expressed a desire of doing."

Continued developments proved that Lewiston was in the centre of a region of unusual mineral wealth. The Clearwater finds were followed closely by discoveries on the Salmon River, another tributary of the Snake, a little farther south. The Boisé mines came on the heels of this boom, being followed by a rush to the Owyhee district, south of the great bend of the Snake. Into these various camps poured the usual flood of miners from the whole West. Before 1862 was over eastern Washington had outgrown the bounds of the territorial government on Puget Sound. Like the Pike's Peak diggings, and the placers of the Colorado Valley, and the Carson and Virginia City camps, these called for and received a new territorial establishment.

In 1860 the territories of Washington and Nebraska had met along a common boundary at the top of the Rocky Mountains. Before Washington was divided in 1863, Nebraska had changed its shape under the pressure of a small but active population north of its seat of government. The centres of population in Nebraska north of the Platte River represented chiefly overflows from Iowa and Minnesota. Emigrating from these states farmers had by 1860 opened the country on the left bank of the Missouri, in the region of the Yankton Sioux. The Missouri traffic had developed both shores of the river past Fort Pierre and Fort Union to Fort Benton, by 1859. To meet the needs of the scattered people here Nebraska had been partitioned in 1861 along the line of the Missouri and the forty-third parallel. Dakota had been created out of the country thus cut loose and in two years more shared in the fate of eastern Washington. Idaho was established in 1863 to provide home rule for the miners of the new mineral region. It included a great rectangle, on both sides of the Rockies, reaching south to Utah and Nebraska, west to its present western boundary at Oregon and 117°, east to 104°, the present eastern line of Montana and Wyoming. Dakota and Washington were cut down for its sake.

It seemed, in 1862 and 1863, as though every little rivulet in the whole mountain country possessed its treasures to be given up to the first prospector with the hardihood to tickle its soil. Four important districts along the upper course of the Snake, not to mention hundreds of minor ones, lent substance to this appearance, Almost before Idaho could be organized its area of settlement had broadened enough to make its own division in the near future a certainty. East of the Bitter Root Mountains, in the head waters of the Missouri tributaries, came a long series of new booms.

When the American Fur Company pushed its little steamer *Chippewa* up to the vicinity of Fort Benton in 1859, none realized that a new era for the upper Missouri had nearly arrived. For half a century the fur trade had been followed in this region and had dotted the country with tiny forts and palisades, but there had been no immigration, and no reason for any. The Mullan road, which Congress had authorized in 1855, was in course of construction from Fort Benton to Walla Walla, but as yet there were few immigrants to follow the new route. Considerably before the territory of Idaho was created, however, the active prospectors of the Snake Valley had crossed the range and inspected most of the Blackfoot country in the direction of

Fort Benton. They had organized for themselves a Missoula County, Washington territory, in July, 1862, an act which may be taken as the beginning of an entirely new movement.

Two brothers, James and Granville Stuart, were the leaders in developing new mineral areas east of the main range. After experience in California and several years of life along the trails, they settled down in the Deer Lodge Valley, and began to open up their mines in 1861. They accomplished little this year since the steamboat to Fort Benton, carrying supplies, was burned, and their trip to Walla Walla for shovels and picks took up the rest of the season. But early in 1862 they were hard and successfully at work. Reënforcements, destined for the Salmon River mines farther west, came to them in June; one party from Fort Benton, the other from the Colorado diggings, and both were easily persuaded to stay and join in organizing Missoula County. Bannack City became the centre of their operations.

Alder Gulch and Virginia City were, in 1863, a second focus for the mines of eastern Idaho. Their deposits had been found by accident by a prospecting party which was returning to Bannack City after an unsuccessful trip. The party, which had been investigating the Big Horn Mountains, discovered Alder Gulch between the Beaver Head and Madison rivers, early in June. With an accurate knowledge of the mining population, the discoverers organized the mining district and registered their own claims before revealing the location of the new diggings. Then came a stampede from Bannack City which gave to Virginia City a population of 10,000 by 1864.

Another mining district, in Last Chance Gulch, gave rise in 1864 to Helena, the last of the great boom towns of this period. Its situation as well as its resources aided in the growth of Helena, which lay a little west of the Madison fork of the Missouri, and in the direct line from Bannack and Virginia City to Fort Benton. Only 142 miles of easy staging above the head of Missouri River navigation, it was a natural post on the main line of travel to the northwest fields.

The excitement over Bannack and Virginia and Helena overlapped in years the period of similar boom in Idaho. It had begun even before Idaho had been created. When this was once organized, the same inconveniences which had justified it, justified as well its division to provide home rule for the miners east of the Bitter Root range. An act of 1864 created Montana territory with the boundaries which the state possesses to-day, while that part of Idaho south of Montana, now Wyoming, was temporarily reattached to Dakota. Idaho assumed its present form. The simultaneous development in all portions of the great West of rich mining camps did much to attract public attention as well as population. In 1863 nearly all of the camps were flourishing.

The mountains were occupied for the whole distance from Mexico to Canada, while the trails were crowded with emigrants hunting for fortune. The old trails bore much of the burden of migration as usual, but new spurs were opened to meet new needs. In the north, the Mullan road had made easy travel from Fort Benton to Walla Walla, and had been completed since 1862. Congress authorized in 1864 a new road from eastern Nebraska, which should run north of the Platte trail, and the war department had sent out personally conducted parties of emigrants from the vicinity of St. Paul. The Idaho and Montana mines were accessible from Fort Hall, the former by the old emigrant road, the latter by a new northeast road to Virginia City. The Carson mines were on the main line of the California road. The Arizona fields were commonly reached from California, by way of Fort Yuma.

The shifting population which inhabited the new territories invites and at the same time defies description. It was made up chiefly of young men. Respectable women were not unknown, but were so few in number as to have little measurable influence upon social life. In many towns they were in the minority, even among their sex, since the easily won wealth of the camps attracted dissolute women who cannot be numbered but who must be imagined. The social tone of the various camps was determined by the preponderance of men, the absence of regular labor, and the speculative fever which was the justification of their existence. The political tone was determined by the nature of the population, the character of the industry, and the remoteness from a seat of government. Combined, these factors produced a type of life the like of which America had never known, and whose picturesque qualities have blinded the thoughtless into believing that it was romantic. It was at best a hard bitter struggle with the dark places only accentuated by the tinsel of gambling and adventure.

A single street meandering along a valley, with one-story huts flanking it in irregular rows, was the typical mining camp. The saloon and the general store, sometimes combined, were its representative institutions. Deep ruts along the street bore witness to the heavy wheels of the freighters, while horses loosely tied to all available posts at once revealed the regular means of locomotion, and by the careless way they were left about showed that this sort of property was not likely to be stolen. The mining population centring here lived a life of contrasts. The desolation and loneliness of prospecting and working claims alternated with the excitement of coming to town. Few decent beings habitually lived in the towns. The resident population expected to live off the miners, either in way of trade, or worse. The bar, the gambling-house, the dance-hall have been made too common in description to need further account. In the reaction against loneliness, the extremes of drunkenness, debauchery, and murder were only too frequent in these places of amusement.

That the camps did not destroy themselves in their own frenzy is a tribute to the solid qualities which underlay the recklessness and shiftlessness of much of the population. In most of the camps there came a time when decency finally asserted itself in the only possible way to repress lawlessness. The rapidity with which these camps had drawn their hundreds and their thousands into the fastnesses of the territories carried them beyond the limits of ordinary law and regular institutions. Law and the politician followed fast enough, but there was generally an interval after the discovery during which such peace prevailed as the community itself demanded. In absence of sheriff and constable, and jail in which to incarcerate offenders, the vigilance committee was the only protection of the new camp. Such summary justice as these committees commonly executed is evidence of innate tendency toward law and order, not of their defiance. The typical camp passed through a period of peaceful exploitation at the start, then came an era of invasion by hordes of miners and disreputable hangers-on, with accompanying violence and crime. Following this, the vigilance committee, in its stern repression of a few of the crudest sins, marks the beginning of a reign of law.

The mining camps of the early sixties familiarized the United States with the whole area of the nation, and dispelled most of the remaining tradition of desert which hung over the mountain West. They attracted a large floating population, they secured the completion of the political map through the erection of new territories, and they emphasized loudly the need for national transportation on a larger scale than the trail and the stage coach could permit. But they did not directly secure the presence of permanent population in the new territories. Arizona and Nevada lost most of their inhabitants as soon as the first flush of discovery was over. Montana, Idaho, and Colorado declined rapidly to a fraction of their largest size. None of them was successful in securing a large permanent population until agriculture had gained firm foothold. Many indeed who came to mine remained to plough, but the permanent populating of the Far West was the work of railways and irrigation two decades later. Yet the mining camps had served their purpose in revealing the nature of the whole of the national domain.

CHAPTER XI

CLOSE upon the heels of the overland migrations came an organized traffic to supply their needs. Oregon, Salt Lake, California, and all the later gold fields, drew population away from the old Missouri border, scattered it in little groups over the face of the desert, and left it there crying for sustenance. Many of the new colonies were not self-supporting for a decade or more; few of them were independent within a year or two. In all there was a strong demand for necessities and luxuries which must be hauled from the states to the new market by the routes which the pioneers themselves had travelled. Greater than their need for material supplies was that for intellectual stimulus. Letters, newspapers, and the regular carriage of the mails were constantly demanded of the express companies and the post-office department. To meet this pressure there was organized in the fifties a great system of wagon traffic. In the years from 1858 to 1869 it reached its mighty culmination; while its possibilities of speed, order, and convenience had only just come to be realized when the continental railways brought this agency of transportation to an end.

174

The individual emigrant who had gathered together his family, his flocks, and his household goods, who had cut away from the life at home and staked everything on his new venture, was the unit in the great migrations. There was no regular provision for going unless one could form his own self-contained and self-supporting party. Various bands grouped easily into larger bodies for common defence, but the characteristic feature of the emigration was private initiative. The home-seekers had no power in themselves to maintain communication with the old country, yet they had no disposition to be forgotten or to forget. Professional freighting companies and carriers of mails appeared just as soon as the traffic promised a profit.

A water mail to California had been arranged even before the gold discovery lent a new interest to the Pacific Coast. From New York to the Isthmus, and thence to San Francisco, the mails were to be carried by boats of the Pacific Mail Steamship Company, which sent the nucleus of its fleet around Cape Horn to Pacific waters in 1848. The arrival of the first mail in San Francisco in February, 1849, commenced the regular public communication between the United States and the new colonies. For the places lying away from the coast, mails were hauled under contract as early as 1849. Oregon, Utah, New Mexico, and California were given a measure of irregular and unsatisfactory service.

There is little interest in the earlier phases of the

overland mail service save in that they foreshadowed greater things. A stage line was started from Independence to Santa Fé in the summer of 1849; another contract was let to a man named Woodson for a monthly carriage to Salt Lake City. Neither of the carriers made a serious attempt to stock his route or open stations. Their stages advanced under the same conditions, and with little more rapidity than the ordinary emigrant or freighter. Mormon interests organized a Great Salt Lake Valley Carrying Company at about this time. For four or five years both government and private industry were experimenting with the problems of long-distance wagon traffic, — the roads, the vehicles, the stock, the stations, the supplies. Most picturesque was the effort made in 1856, by the War Department, to acclimate the Saharan camel on the American desert as a beast of burden. Congress had appropriated $30,000 for the experiment, in execution of which Secretary Davis sent Lieutenant H. C. Wayne to the Levant to purchase the animals. Some seventy-five camels were imported into Texas and tested near San Antonio. There is a long congressional document filled with the correspondence of this attempt and embellished with cuts of types of camels and equipment.

While the camels were yet browsing on the Texas plains, Congress made a more definite movement towards supplying the Pacific Slope with adequate service. It authorized the Postmaster-general in

1857 to call for bids for an overland mail which, in a single organization, should join the Missouri to Sacramento, and which should be subsidized to run at a high scheduled speed. The service which the Postmaster-general invited in his advertisement was to be semi-weekly, weekly, or semi-monthly at his discretion; it was to be for a term of six years; it was to carry through the mails in four-horse wagons in not more than twenty-five days. A long list of bidders, including most of the firms engaged in plains freighting, responded with their bids and itineraries; from them the department selected the offer of a company headed by one John Butterfield, and explained to the public in 1857 the reasons for its choice. The route to which the Butterfield contract was assigned began at St. Louis and Memphis, made a junction near the western border of Arkansas, and proceeded thence through Preston, Texas, El Paso, and Fort Yuma. For semi-weekly mails the company was to receive $600,000 a year. The choice of the most southern of routes required considerable explanation, since the best-known road ran by the Platte and South Pass. In criticising this latter route the Postmaster-general pointed out the cold and snow of winter, and claimed that the experience of the department during seven years proved the impossibility of maintaining a regular service here. A second available road had been revealed by the thirty-fifth parallel survey, across northern Texas and through Albuquerque, New Mexico; but

N

this was likewise too long and too severe. The best route, in his mind — the one open all the year, through a temperate climate, suitable for migration as well as traffic — was this southern route, *via* El Paso. It is well to remember that the administration which made this choice was democratic and of strong southern sympathies, and that the Pacific railway was expected to follow the course of the overland mail.

The first overland coaches left the opposite ends of the line on September 15, 1858. The east-bound stage carried an agent of the Post-office Department, whose report states that the through trip to Tipton, Missouri, and thence by rail to St. Louis, was made in 20 days, 18 hours, 26 minutes, actual time. "I cordially congratulate you upon the result," wired President Buchanan to Butterfield. "It is a glorious triumph for civilization and the Union. Settlements will soon follow the course of the road, and the East and West will be bound together by a chain of living Americans which can never be broken." The route was 2795 miles long. For nearly all the way there was no settlement upon which the stages could rely. The company built such stations as it needed.

The vehicle of the overland mail, the most interesting vehicle of the plains, was the coach manufactured by the Abbott-Downing Company of Concord, New Hampshire. No better wagon for the purpose has been devised. Its heavy wheels, with wide, thick

tires, were set far apart to prevent capsizing. Its
body, braced with iron bands, and built of stout white
oak, was slung on leather thoroughbraces which took
the strain better and were more nearly unbreakable
than any other springs.   Inside were generally three
seats, for three passengers each, though at times
as many as fourteen besides the driver and messenger were carried.   Adjustable curtains kept out
part of the rain and cold.   High up in front sat the
driver, with a passenger or two on the box and a large
assortment of packages tucked away beneath his
seat.   Behind the body was the triangular "boot"
in which were stowed the passengers' boxes and the
mail sacks.   The overflow of mail went inside under
the seats.   Mr. Clemens tells of filling the whole
body three feet deep with mail, and of the passengers
being forced to sprawl out on the irregular bed thus
made for them.   Complaining letter-writers tell of
sacks carried between the axles and the body, under
the coach, and of the disasters to letters and contents
resulting from fording streams.   Drawn by four gal-
loping mules and painted a gaudy red or green, the
coach was a visible emblem of spectacular western
advance.   Horace Greeley's coach, bright red, was
once charged by a herd of enraged buffaloes and
overturned, to the discomfort and injury of the ven-
erable editor.

It was no comfortable or luxurious trip that the
overland passenger had, with all the sumptuous
equipment of the new route.   The time limit was

twenty-five days, reduced in practice to twenty-two or twenty-three, at the price of constant travel day and night, regardless of weather or convenience. One passenger who declined to follow this route has left his reason why. The "Southern, known as the Butterfield or American Express, offered to start me in an ambulance from St. Louis, and to pass me through Arkansas, El Paso, Fort Yuma on the Gila River, in fact through the vilest and most desolate portion of the West. Twenty-four mortal days and nights — twenty-five being schedule time — must be spent in that ambulance; passengers becoming crazy by whiskey, mixed with want of sleep, are often obliged to be strapped to their seats; their meals, despatched during the ten-minute halts, are simply abominable, the heats are excessive, the climate malarious; lamps may not be used at night for fear of non-existent Indians: briefly there is no end to this Via Mala's miseries." But the alternative which confronted this traveller in 1860 was scarcely more pleasant. "You may start by stage to the gold regions about Denver City or Pike's Peak, and thence, if not accidentally or purposely shot, you may proceed by an uncertain ox train to Great Salt Lake City, which latter part cannot take less than thirty-five days."

Once upon the road, the passenger might nearly as well have been at sea. There was no turning back. His discomforts and dangers became inevitable. The stations erected along the trail were chiefly for the benefit of the live stock. Horses and mules must be kept in good shape, whatever happened to passengers. Some of the depots, "home stations," had a family in residence, a dwelling of logs, adobe, or sod, and offered bacon, potatoes, bread, and coffee of a sort, to those who were not too squeamish. The others, or "swing" stations, had little but a corral and a haystack, with a few stock tenders. The drivers were often drunk and commonly profane. The overseers and division superintendents differed from them only in being a little more resolute and dangerous. Freighting and coaching were not child's play for either passengers or employees.

The Butterfield Overland Express began to work its six year contract in September, 1858. Other coach and mail services increased the number of continental routes to three by 1860. From New Orleans, by way of San Antonio and El Paso, a weekly service had been organized, but its importance was far less than that of the great route, and not equal to that by way of the Great Salt Lake.

Staging over the Platte trail began on a large scale with the discovery of gold near Pike's Peak in 1858. The Mormon mails, interrupted by the Mormon War, had been revived; but a new concern had sprung up under the name of the Leavenworth and Pike's Peak Express Company. The firm of Jones and Russell, soon to give way to Russell, Majors, and Waddell, had seen the possibilities of the new boom camps, and had inaugurated regular stage service in

May, 1859. Henry Villard rode out in the first coach. Horace Greeley followed in June. After some experimenting in routes, the line accepted a considerable part of the Platte trail, leaving the road at the forks of the river. Here Julesburg came into existence as the most picturesque home station on the plains. It was at this station that Jack Slade, whom Mark Twain found to be a mild, hospitable, coffee-sharing man, cut off the ears of old Jules, after the latter had emptied two barrels of bird-shot into him. It was "celebrated for its desperadoes," wrote General Dodge. "No twenty-four hours passed without its contribution to Boots Hill (the cemetery whose every occupant was buried in his boots), and homicide was performed in the most genial and whole-souled way."

Before the Denver coach had been running for a year another enterprise had brought the central route into greater prominence. Butterfield had given California news in less than twenty-five days from the Missouri, but California wanted more even than this, until the electric telegraph should come. Senator Gwin urged upon the great freight concern the starting of a faster service for light mails only. It was William H. Russell who, to meet this supposed demand, organized a pony express, which he announced to a startled public in the end of March. Across the continent from Placerville to St. Joseph he built his stations from nine to fifteen miles apart, nearly two hundred in all. He supplied these with tenders and riders, stocked them with fodder and fleet American horses, and started his first riders at both ends on the 3d of April, 1860.

Only letters of great commercial importance could be carried by the new express. They were written on tissue paper, packed into a small, light saddle-bag, and passed from rider to rider along the route. The time announced in the schedule was ten days, — two weeks better than Butterfield's best. To make it called for constant motion at top speed, with horses trained to the work and changed every few miles. The carriers were slight men of 135 pounds or under, whose nerve and endurance could stand the strain. Often mere boys were employed in the dangerous service. Rain or snow or death made no difference to the express. Dangers of falling at night, of missing precipitous mountain roads where advance at a walk was perilous, had to be faced. When Indians were hostile, this new risk had to be run. But for eighteen months the service was continued as announced. It ceased only when the overland telegraph, in October, 1861, declared its readiness to handle through business.

In the pony express was the spectacular perfection of overland service. Its best record was some hours under eight days. It was conducted along the well-known trail from St. Joseph to Forts Kearney, Laramie, and Bridger; thence to Great Salt Lake City, and by way of Carson City to Placerville and Sacramento. It carried the news in a time when every day brought new rumors of war and disunion, in the pregnant campaign of 1860 and through the opening of the Civil War. The records of its riders at times approached the marvellous. One lad, William F. Cody, who has since lived to become the personal embodiment of the Far West as Buffalo Bill, rode more than 320 consecutive miles on a single tour. The literature of the plains is full of instances of courage and endurance shown in carrying through the despatches.

The Butterfield mail was transferred to the central route of the pony express in the summer of 1861. For two and a half years it had run steadily along its southern route, proving the entire practicability of carrying on such a service. But its expense had been out of all proportion to its revenue. In 1859 the Postmaster-general reported that its total receipts from mails had been $27,229.94, as against a cost of $600,000. It is not unlikely that the fast service would have been dropped had not the new military necessity of 1861 forbidden any act which might loosen the bonds between the Pacific and the Atlantic states. Congress contemplated the approach of war and authorized early in 1861 the abandonment of the southern route through the confederate territory, and the transfer of the service to the line of the pony express. To secure additional safety the mails were sent by way of Davenport, Iowa, and Omaha, to Fort Kearney a few times, but Atchison became the starting-point at last, while military force was used to keep the route free from interference. The transfer worked a shortening of from five to seven days over the southern route.

In the autumn of 1861, when the overland mail and the pony express were both running at top speed along the Platte trail, the overland service reached its highest point. In October the telegraph brought an end to the express. "The Pacific to the Atlantic sends greeting," ran the first message over the new wire, " and may both oceans be dry before a foot of all the land that lies between them shall belong to any other than one united country." Probably the pony express had done its share in keeping touch between California and the Union. Certainly only its national purpose justified its existence, since it was run at a loss that brought ruin to Russell, its backer, and to Majors and Waddell, his partners.

Russell, Majors, and Waddell, with the biggest freighting business of the plains, had gone heavily into passenger and express service in 1859–1860. Russell had forced through the pony express against the wishes of his partners, carried away from practical considerations by the magnitude of the idea. The transfer of the southern overland to their route increased their business and responsibility. The future of the route steadily looked larger. "Every day," wrote the Postmaster-general, "brings intelligence of the discovery of new mines of gold and silver in the region traversed by this mail route, which gives assurance that it will not be many years before it will be protected and supported throughout the greater part of the route by a civilized population." Under the name of the Central Overland, California, and Pike's Peak Express the firm tried to keep up a struggle too great for them. "Clean out of Cash and Poor Pay" is said to have been an irreverent nickname coined by one of their drivers. As their embarrassments steadily increased, their notes were given to a rival contractor who was already beginning local routes to reach the mining camps of eastern Washington. Ben Holladay had been the power behind the company for several months before the courts gave him control of their overland stage line in 1862. The greatest names in this overland business are first Butterfield, then Russell, Majors, and Waddell, and then Ben Holladay, whose power lasted until he sold out to Wells, Fargo, and Company in 1866. Ben Holladay was the magnate of the plains during the early sixties. A hostile critic, Henry Villard, has written that he was "a genuine specimen of the successful Western pioneer of former days, illiterate, coarse, pretentious, boastful, false, and cunning." In later days he carried his speculation into railways and navigation, but already his was the name most often heard in the West. Mark Twain, who has left in "Roughing It" the best picture of life in the Far West in this decade, speaks lightly of him when he tells of a youth travelling in the Holy Land with a reverend preceptor who was impressing upon him the greatness of Moses, "'the great guide, soldier, poet, lawgiver of ancient Israel! Jack, from this spot where we stand, to Egypt, stretches a fearful desert three hundred miles in extent — and across that desert that wonderful man brought the children of Israel! — guiding them with unfailing sagacity for forty years over the sandy desolation and among the obstructing rocks and hills, and landed them at last, safe and sound, within sight of this very spot. It was a wonderful, wonderful thing to do, Jack. Think of it!'

"'Forty years? Only three hundred miles?'" replied Jack. "'Humph! Ben Holladay would have fetched them through in thirty-six hours!'"

Under Holladay's control the passenger and express service were developed into what was probably the greatest one-man institution in America. He directed not only the central overland, but spur lines with government contracts to upper California, Oregon, Idaho, and Montana. He travelled up and down the line constantly himself, attending in person to business in Washington and on the Pacific. The greatest difficulties in his service were the Indians and progress as stated in the railway. Man and nature could be fought off and overcome, but the life of the stage-coach was limited before it was begun.

The Indian danger along the trails had steadily increased since the commencement of the migrations. For many years it had not been large, since there was room for all and the emigrants held well to the beaten track. But the gold camps had introduced settlers into new sections, and had sent prospectors into all the Indian Country. The opening of new roads to the Pacific increased the pressure, until the Indians began to believe that the end was at hand unless they should bestir themselves. The last years of the overland service, between 1862 and 1868, were hence filled with Indian attacks. Often for weeks no coach could go through. Once, by premeditation, every station for nearly two hundred miles was destroyed overnight, Julesburg, the greatest of them all, being in the list. The presence of troops to defend seemed only to increase the zeal of the red men to destroy.

Besides these losses, which lessened his profits and threatened ruin, Holladay had to meet competition in his own trade, and detraction as well. Captain James L. Fiske, who had broken a new road through from Minnesota to Montana, came east in 1863, "by the 'overland stage,' travelling over the saline plains of Laramie and Colorado Territory and the sand deserts of Nebraska and Kansas. The country was strewed with the skeletons and carcases of cattle, and the graves of the early Mormon and California pilgrims lined the roadside. This is the worst emigrant route that I have ever travelled; much of the road is through deep sand, feed is very scanty, a great deal of the water is alkaline, and the snows in winter render it impassable for trains. The stage line is wretchedly managed. The company undertake to furnish travellers with meals, (at a dollar a meal,) but very frequently on arriving at a station there was nothing to eat, the supplies had not been sent on. On one occasion we fasted for thirty-six hours. The stages were sometimes in a miserable condition. We were put into a coach one night with only two boards left in the bottom. On remonstrating with the driver, we were told to hold on by the sides."

At the close of the Civil War, however, Holladay controlled a monopoly in stage service between the Missouri River and Great Salt Lake. The express companies and railways met him at the ends of his link, but had to accept his terms for intermediate traffic. In the summer of 1865 a competing firm started a Butterfield's Overland Despatch to run on the Smoky Hill route to Denver. It soon found that Indian dangers here were greater than along the Platte, and it learned how near it was to bankruptcy when Holladay offered to buy it out in 1866. He had sent his agents over the rival line, and had in his hand a more detailed statement of resources and conditions than the Overland Despatch itself possessed. He purchased easily at his own price and so ended this danger of competition.

Such was the character of the overland traffic that any day might bring a successful rival, or loss by accident. Holladay seems to have realized that the advantages secured by priority were over, and that the trade had seen its best day. In the end of 1866 he sold out his lines to the greatest of his competitors,

Wells, Fargo, and Company. He sold out wisely. The new concern lost on its purchase through the rapid shortening of the route. During 1866 the Pacific railway had advanced so far that the end of the mail route was moved to Fort Kearney in November. By May, 1869, some years earlier than Wells, Fargo had estimated, the road was done. And on the completion of the Union and Central Pacific railways the great period of the overland mail was ended.

Parallel to the overland mail rolled an overland freight that lacked the seeming romance of the former, but possessed quite as much of real significance. No one has numbered the trains of wagons that supplied the Far West. Santa Fé wagons they were now; Pennsylvania or Pittsburg wagons they had been called in the early days of the Santa Fé trade; Conestoga wagons they had been in the remoter time of the trans-Alleghany migrations. But whatever their name, they retained the characteristics of the wagons and caravans of the earlier period. Holladay bought over 150 such wagons, organized in trains of twenty-six, from the Butterfield Overland Despatch in 1866. Six thousand were counted passing Fort Kearney in six weeks in 1865. One of the drivers on the overland mail, Frank Root, relates that Russell, Majors, and Waddell owned 6250 wagons and 75,000 oxen at the height of their business. The long trains, crawling along half hidden in their clouds of dust, with the noises of the animals and the profanity of the drivers, were the physical bond between the sections. The mail and express served politics and intellect; the freighters provided the comforts and decencies of life.

The overland traffic had begun on the heels of the first migrations. Its growth during the fifties and its triumphant period in the sixties were great arguments in favor of the construction of railways to take its place. It came to an end when the first continental railroad was completed in 1869. For decades after this time the stages still found useful service on branch lines and to new camps, and occasional exhibition in the "Wild West Shows," but the railways were following them closely, for a new period of American history had begun.

CHAPTER XII

THE ENGINEERS' FRONTIER

In a national way, the South struggling against the North prevented the early location of a Pacific railway. Locally, every village on the Mississippi from the Lakes to the Gulf hoped to become the terminus and had advocates throughout its section of the country. The list of claimants is a catalogue of Mississippi Valley towns. New Orleans, Vicksburg, Memphis, Cairo, St. Louis, Chicago, and Duluth were all entered in the competition. By 1860 the idea had received general acceptance; no one in the future need urge its adoption, but the greatest part of the work remained to be done.

Born during the thirties, the idea of a Pacific railway was of uncertain origin and parentage. Just so soon as there was a railroad anywhere, it was inevitable that some enterprising visionary should project one in imagination to the extremity of the continent. The railway speculation, with which the East was seething during the administrations of Andrew Jackson, was boiling over in the young West, so that the group of men advocating a railway to connect the oceans were but the product of their time.

Greatest among these enthusiasts was Asa Whitney, a New York merchant interested in the China trade and eager to win the commerce of the Orient for the United States. Others had declared such a road to be possible before he presented his memorial to Congress in 1845, but none had staked so much upon the idea. He abandoned the business, conducted a private survey in Wisconsin and Iowa, and was at last convinced that "the time is not far distant when Oregon will become . . . a separate nation" unless communication should "unite them to us." He petitioned Congress in January, 1845, for a franchise and a grant of land, that the national road might be accomplished; and for many years he agitated persistently for his project.

The annexation of Oregon and the Southwest, coming in the years immediately after the commencement of Whitney's advocacy, gave new point to arguments for the railway and introduced the sectional element. So long as Oregon constituted the whole American frontage on the Pacific it was idle to debate railway routes south of South Pass. This was the only known, practicable route, and it was the course recommended by all the projectors, down to Whitney. But with California won, the other trails by El Paso and Santa Fé came into consideration and at once tempted the South to make the railway tributary to its own interests.

Chief among the politicians who fell in with the growing railway movement was Senator Benton, who

o

tried to place himself at its head. "The man is alive, full grown, and is listening to what I say (without believing it perhaps)," he declared in October, 1844, "who will yet see the Asiatic commerce traversing the North Pacific Ocean — entering the Oregon River — climbing the western slopes of the Rocky Mountains — issuing from its gorges — and spreading its fertilizing streams over our wide-extended Union!" After this date there was no subject closer to his interest than the railway, and his advocacy was constant. His last word in the Senate was concerning it. In 1849 he carried off its feet the St. Louis railroad convention with his eloquent appeal for a central route: "Let us make the iron road, and make it from sea to sea — States and individuals making it east of the Mississippi, the nation making it west. Let us . . . rise above everything sectional, personal, local. Let us . . . build the great road . . . which shall be adorned with . . . the colossal statue of the great Columbus — whose design it accomplishes, hewn from a granite mass of a peak of the Rocky Mountains, overlooking the road . . . pointing with outstretched arm to the western horizon and saying to the flying passengers, 'There is the East, there is India.'"

By 1850 it was common knowledge that a railroad could be built along the Platte route, and it was believed that the mountains could be penetrated in several other places, but the process of surveying with reference to a particular railway had not yet been

begun. It is possible and perhaps instructive to make a rough grouping, in two classes divided by the year 1842, of the explorations before 1853. So late as Frémont's day it was not generally known whether a great river entered the Pacific between the Columbia and the Colorado. Prior to 1842 the explorations are to be regarded as "incidents" and "adventures" in more or less unknown countries. The narratives were popular rather than scientific, representing the experiences of parties surveying boundary lines or locating wagon roads, of troops marching to remote posts or chastising Indians, of missionaries and casual explorers. In the aggregate they had contributed a large mass of detailed but unorganized information concerning the country where the continental railway must run. But Lieutenant Frémont, in 1842, commenced the effort by the United States to acquire accurate and comprehensive knowledge of the West. In 1842, 1843, and 1845 Frémont conducted the three Rocky Mountain expeditions which established him for life as a popular hero. The map, drawn by Charles Preuss for his second expedition, confined itself in strict scientific fashion to the facts actually observed, and in skill of execution was perhaps the best map made before 1853. The individual expeditions which in the later forties filled in the details of portions of the Frémont map are too numerous for mention. At least twenty-five occurred before 1853, all serving to extend both general and particular knowledge of the West. To these was added a great mass of popular books, prepared by emigrants and travellers. By 1853 there was good, unscientific knowledge of nearly all the West, and accurate information concerning some portions of it. The railroad enthusiasts could tell the general direction in which the roads must run, but no road could well be located without a more comprehensive survey than had yet been made.

The agitation of the Pacific railway idea was founded almost exclusively upon general and inaccurate knowledge of the West. The exact location of the line was naturally left for the professional civil engineer, its popular advocate contented himself with general principles. Frequently these were sufficient, yet, as in the case of Benton, misinformation led to the waste of strength upon routes unquestionably bad. But there was slight danger of the United States being led into an unwise route, since in the diversity of routes suggested there was deadlock. Until after 1850, in proportion as the idea was received with unanimity, the routes were fought with increasing bitterness. Whitney was shelved in 1852 when the choice of routes had become more important than the method of construction.

In 1852–1853 Congress worked upon one of the many bills to construct the much-desired railway to the Pacific. It was discovered that an absolute majority in favor of the work existed, but the enemies of the measure, virulent in proportion as they were in the minority, were able to sow well-fertilized dissent. They admitted and gloried in the intrigue which enabled them to command through the time-honored method of division. They defeated the road in this Congress. But when the army appropriation bill came along in February, 1853, Senator Gwin asked for an amendment for a survey. He doubted the wisdom of a survey, since, "if any route is reported to this body as the best, those that may be rejected will always go against the one selected." But he admitted himself to be as a drowning man who "will catch at straws," and begged that $150,000 be allowed to the President for a survey of the best routes from the Mississippi to the Pacific, the survey to be conducted by the Corps of Topographical Engineers of the regular army. To a non-committal measure like this the opposition could make slight resistance. The Senate, by a vote of 31 to 16, added this amendment to the army appropriation bill, while the House concurred in nearly the same proportion. The first positive official act towards the construction of the road was here taken.

Under the orders of Jefferson Davis, Secretary of War, well-organized exploring parties took to the field in the spring of 1853. Farthest north, Isaac I. Stevens, bound for his post as first governor of Washington territory, conducted a line of survey to the Pacific between the parallels of 47° and 49°, north latitude. South of the Stevens survey, four other lines were worked out. Near the parallels of 41° and 42°, the old South Pass route was again

examined. Frémont's favorite line, between 38°
and 39°, received consideration. A thirty-fifth parallel route was examined in great detail, while on this
and another along the thirty-second parallel the
most friendly attentions of the War Department
were lavished. The second and third routes had
few important friends. Governor Stevens, because
he was a first-rate fighter, secured full space for the
survey in his charge. But the thirty-second and
thirty-fifth parallel routes were those which were
expected to make good.

Governor Stevens left Washington on May 9,
1853, for St. Louis, where he made arrangements with
the American Fur Company to transport a large part
of his supplies by river to Fort Union. From St.
Louis he ascended the Mississippi by steamer to
St. Paul, near which city Camp Pierce, his first
organized camp, had been established. Here he
issued his instructions and worked into shape his
party, — to say nothing of his 172 half-broken mules.
"Not a single full team of broken animals could be
selected, and well broken riding animals were essential, for most of the gentlemen of the scientific corps
were unaccustomed to riding." One of the engineers
dislocated a shoulder before he conquered his steed.

The party assigned to Governor Stevens's command
was recruited with reference to the varied demands
of a general exploring and scientific reconnaissance.
Besides enlisted men and laborers, it included engineers, a topographer, an artist, a surgeon and natu-

ralist, an astronomer, a meteorologist, and a geologist. Its two large volumes of report include elaborate illustrations and appendices on botany and seven different varieties of zoölogy in addition to the geographical details required for the railway.

The expedition, in its various branches, attacked the northernmost route simultaneously in several places. Governor Stevens led the eastern division from St. Paul. A small body of his men, with much of the supplies, were sent up the Missouri in the American Fur Company's boat to Fort Union, there to make local observations and await the arrival of the governor. United there the party continued overland to Fort Benton and the mountains. Six years later than this it would have been possible to ascend by boat all the way to Fort Benton, but as yet no steamer had gone much above Fort Union. From the Pacific end the second main division operated. Governor Stevens secured the recall of Captain George B. McClellan from duty in Texas, and his detail in command of a corps which was to proceed to the mouth of the Columbia River and start an eastward survey. In advance of McClellan, Lieutenant Saxton was to hurry on to erect a supply depot in the Bitter Root Valley, and then to cross the divide and make a junction with the main party.

From Governor Stevens's reports it would seem that his survey was a triumphal progress. To his threefold capacities as commander, governor, and

Indian superintendent, nature had added a magnifying eye and an unrestrained enthusiasm. No formal expedition had traversed his route since the day of Lewis and Clark. The Indians could still be impressed by the physical appearance of the whites. His vanity led him at each success or escape from accident to congratulate himself on the antecedent wisdom which had warded off the danger. But withal, his report was thorough and his party was loyal. The *voyageurs* whom he had engaged received his special praise. "They are thorough woodsmen and just the men for prairie life also, going into the water as pleasantly as a spaniel, and remaining there as long as needed."

Across the undulating fertile plains the party advanced from St. Paul with little difficulty. Its draught animals steadily improved in health and strength. The Indians were friendly and honest. "My father," said Old Crane of the Assiniboin, "our hearts are good; we are poor and have not much. . . . Our good father has told us about this road. I do not see how it will benefit us, and I fear my people will be driven from these plains before the white men." In fifty-five days Fort Union was reached. Here the American Fur Company maintained an extensive post in a stockade 250 feet square, and carried on a large trade with "the Assiniboines, the Gros Ventres, the Crows, and other migratory bands of Indians." At Fort Union, Alexander Culbertson, the agent, became the guide of the party, which proceeded west on August 10. From Fort Union it was nearly 400 miles to Fort Benton, which then stood on the left bank of the Missouri, some eighteen miles below the falls. The country, though less friendly than that east of the Missouri, offered little difficulty to the party, which covered the distance in three weeks. A week later, September 8, a party sent on from Fort Benton met Lieutenant Saxton coming east.

The chief problems of the Stevens survey lay west of Fort Benton, in the passes of the continental divide. Lieutenant Saxton had left Vancouver early in July, crossed the Cascades with difficulty, and started up the Columbia from the Dalles on July 18. He reached Fort Walla Walla on the 27th, and proceeded thence with a half-breed guide through the country of the Spokan and the Cœur d'Alene. Crossing the Snake, he broke his only mercurial barometer and was forced thereafter to rely on his aneroid. Deviating to the north, he crossed Lake Pend d'Oreille on August 10, and reached St. Mary's village, in the Bitter Root Valley, on August 28. St. Mary's village, among the Flatheads, had been established by the Jesuit fathers, and had advanced considerably, as Indian civilization went. Here Saxton erected his supply depot, from which he advanced with a smaller escort to join the main party. Always, even in the heart of the mountains, the country exceeded his expectations. "Nature seemed to have intended it for the great highway across the continent, and it appeared to offer but little obstruction to the passage of a railroad."

Acting on Saxton's advice, Governor Stevens reduced his party at Fort Benton, stored much of his government property there, and started west with a pack train, for the sake of greater speed. He moved on September 22, anxious lest snow should catch him in the mountains. At Fort Benton he left a detachment to make meteorological observations during the winter. Among the Flatheads he left another under Lieutenant Mullan. On October 7 he hurried on again from the Bitter Root Valley for Walla Walla. On the 19th he met McClellan's party, which had been spending a difficult season in the passes of the Cascade range. Because of over-cautious advice which McClellan here gave him, and since his animals were tired out with the summer's hardships, he practically ended his survey for 1853 at this point. He pushed on down the Columbia to Olympia and his new territory.

The energy of Governor Stevens enabled him to make one of the first of the Pacific railway reports. His was the only survey from the Mississippi to the ocean under a single commander. Dated June 30, 1854, it occupies 651 pages of Volume I of the compiled reports. In 1859 he submitted his "narrative and final report" which the Senate ordered Secretary of War, John B. Floyd, to communicate to it in February of that year. This document is printed as supplement to Volume I, but really consists of two large

volumes which are commonly bound together as
Volume XII of the series. Like the other volumes
of the reports, his are filled with lithographs and en-
gravings of fauna, flora, and topography.

The forty-second parallel route was surveyed by
Lieutenant E. G. Beckwith, of the third artillery, in
the summer of 1854. East of Fort Bridger, the War
Department felt it unnecessary to make a special
survey, since Frémont had traversed and described
the country several times and Stansbury had surveyed it carefully as recently as 1849–1850. At
the beginning of his campaign Beckwith was at Salt
Lake. During April he visited the Green River
Valley and Fort Bridger, proving by his surveys the
entire practicability of railway construction here.
In May he skirted the south end of Great Salt Lake
and passed along the Humboldt to the Sacramento
Valley. He had no important adventures and was
impressed most by the squalor of the digger Indians,
whose grass-covered, beehive-shaped "wick-ey-ups"
were frequently seen. As his band approached the
Indians would fearfully cache their belongings in
the undergrowth. In the morning "it was indeed
a novel and ludicrous sight of wretchedness to see
them approach their bush and attempt, slyly (for
they still tried to conceal from me what they were
about), to repossess themselves of their treasures,
one bringing out a piece of old buckskin, a couple of
feet square, smoked, greasy, and torn; another a
half dozen rabbit-skins in an equally filthy condi-

tion, sewed together, which he would swing over his shoulders by a string — his only blanket or clothing; while a third brought out a blue string, which he girded about him and walked away in full dress — one of the lords of the soil." It needed no special emphasis in Beckwith's report to prove that a railway could follow this middle route, since thousands of emigrants had a personal knowledge of its conditions.

Beckwith, who started his forty-second parallel survey from Salt Lake City, had reached that point as one of the officers in Gunnison's unfortunate party. Captain J. W. Gunnison had followed Governor Stevens into St. Louis in 1853. His field of exploration, the route of 38°–39°, was by no means new to him since he had been to Utah with Stansbury in 1849 and 1850, and had already written one of the best books upon the Mormon settlement. He carried his party up the Missouri to a fitting-out camp just below the mouth of the Kansas River, five miles from Westport. Like other commanders he spent much time at the start in "breaking in wild mules," with which he advanced in rain and mud on June 23. For more than two weeks his party moved in parallel columns along the Santa Fé road and the Smoky Hill fork of the Kansas. Near Walnut creek on the Santa Fé road they united, and soon were following the Arkansas River towards the mountains. At Fort Atkinson they found a horde of the plains Indians waiting for Major Fitzpatrick to make a treaty with them.   Always their observations were taken with regularity.   One day Captain Gunnison spent in vain efforts to secure specimens of the elusive prairie dog.   On August 1, when they were ready to leave the Arkansas and plunge southwest into the Sangre de Cristo range, they were gratified "by a clear and beautiful view of the Spanish Peaks."

This thirty-ninth parallel route, which had been a favorite with Frémont, crossed the divide near the head of the Rio Grande.   Its grades, which were difficult and steep at best, followed the Huerfano Valley and Cochetopa Pass.   Across the pass, Gunnison began his descent of the arid alkali valley of the Uncompahgre, — a valley to-day about to blossom as the rose because of the irrigation canal and tunnel bringing to it the waters of the neighboring Gunnison River.   With heavy labor, intense heat, and weakening teams, Gunnison struggled on through September and October towards Salt Lake in Utah territory.   Near Sevier Lake he lost his life.   Before daybreak, on October 26, he and a small detachment of men were surprised by a band of young Paiute. When the rest of his party hurried up to the rescue, they found his body "pierced with fifteen arrows," and seven of his men lying dead around him.   Beckwith, who succeeded to the command, led the remainder of the party to Salt Lake City, where public opinion was ready to charge the Mormons with the murder.   Beckwith believed this to be entirely false, and made use of the friendly assistance of Brigham Young, who persuaded the chiefs of the tribe to return the instruments and records which had been stolen from the party.

The route surveyed by Captain Gunnison passed around the northern end of the ravine of the Colorado River, which almost completely separates the Southwest from the United States. Farther south, within the United States, were only two available points at which railways could cross the cañon, at Fort Yuma and near the Mojave River. Towards these crossings the thirty-fifth and thirty-second parallel surveys were directed.

Second only to Governor Stevens's in its extent was the exploration conducted by Lieutenant A. W. Whipple from Fort Smith on the Arkansas to Los Angeles along the thirty-fifth parallel. Like that of Governor Stevens this route was not the channel of any regular traffic, although later it was to have some share in the organized overland commerce. Here also was found a line that contained only two or three serious obstacles to be overcome. Whipple's instructions planned for him to begin his observations at the Mississippi, but he believed that the navigable Arkansas River and the railways already projected in that state made it needless to commence farther east than Fort Smith, on the edge of the Indian Country. He began his survey on July 14, 1853. His westward march was for two months up the right bank of the Canadian River, as it traversed the Choctaw and Chickasaw reserves, to the hundredth meridian, where it emerged from the panhandle of Texas, and across the panhandle into New Mexico. After crossing the upper waters of the Rio Pecos he reached the Rio Grande at Albuquerque, where his party tarried for a month or more, working over their observations, making local explorations, and sending back to Washington an account of their proceedings thus far. Towards the middle of November they started on toward the Colorado Chiquita and the Bill Williams Fork, through "a region over which no white man is supposed to have passed." The severest difficulties of the trip were found near the valley of the Colorado River, which was entered at the junction of the Bill Williams Fork and followed north for several days. A crossing here was made near the supposed mouth of the Mojave River at a place where porphyritic and trap dykes, outcropping, gave rise to the name of the Needles. The river was crossed February 27, 1854, three weeks before the party reached Los Angeles.

South of the route of Lieutenant Whipple, the thirty-second parallel survey was run to the Fort Yuma crossing of the Colorado River. No attempt was made in this case at a comprehensive survey under a single leader. Instead, the section from the Rio Grande at El Paso to the Red River at Preston, Texas, was run by John Pope, brevet captain in the topographical engineers, in the spring of 1854. Lieutenant J. G. Parke carried the line at the same

time from the Pimas villages on the Gila to the Rio
Grande.   West of the Pimas villages to the Colorado,
a reconnoissance made by Lieutenant-colonel Emory
in 1847 was drawn upon.   The lines in California
were surveyed by yet a different party.   Here again
an easy route was discovered to exist.   Within the
states of California and Oregon various connecting
lines were surveyed by parties under Lieutenant
R. S. Williamson in 1855.

The evidence accumulated by the Pacific railway
surveys began to pour in upon the War Department
in the spring of 1854.   Partial reports at first, elaborate and minute scientific articles following later, made
up a series which by the close of the decade filled the
twelve enormous volumes of the published papers.
Rarely have efforts so great accomplished so little
in the way of actual contribution to knowledge.   The
chief importance of the surveys was in proving by
scientific observation what was already a common-
place among laymen — that the continent was
traversable in many places, and that the incidental
problems of railway construction were in finance
rather than in engineering.   The engineers stood
ready to build the road any time and almost anywhere.

The Secretary of War submitted to Congress the
first instalment of his report under the resolution
of March 3, 1853, on February 27, 1855.   As yet the
labors of compilation and examination of the field
manuscripts were by no means completed, but he

was able to make general statements about the probability of success. At five points the continental divide had been crossed; over four of these railways were entirely practicable, although the shortest of the routes to San Francisco ran by the one pass, Cochetopa, where it would be unreasonable to construct a road.

From the routes surveyed, Secretary Davis recommended one as "the most practicable and economical route for a railroad from the Mississippi River to the Pacific Ocean." In all cases cost, speed of construction, and ease in operation needed to be ascertained and compared. The estimates guessed at by the parties in the field, and revised by the War Department, pointed to the southernmost as the most desirable route. To reach this conclusion it was necessary to accuse Governor Stevens of underestimating the cost of labor along his northern line; but the figures as taken were conclusive. On this thirty-second parallel route, declared the Secretary of War, "the progress of the work will be regulated chiefly by the speed with which cross-ties and rails can be delivered and laid. . . . The few difficult points . . . would delay the work but an inconsiderable period. . . . The climate on this route is such as to cause less interruption to the work than on any other route. Not only is this the shortest and least costly route to the Pacific, but it is the shortest and cheapest route to San Francisco, the greatest commercial city on our western coast; while the aggregate length of railroad lines connecting it at its eastern terminus with the Atlantic and Gulf seaports is less than the aggregate connection with any other route.''

The Pacific railway surveys had been ordered as the only step which Congress in its situation of deadlock could take. Senator Gwin had long ago told his fears that the advocates of the disappointed routes would unite to hinder the fortunate one. To the South, as to Jefferson Davis, Secretary of War, the thirty-second parallel route was satisfactory; but there was as little chance of building a railway as there had been in 1850. In days to come, discussion of railways might be founded upon facts rather than hopes and fears, but either unanimity or compromise was in a fairly remote future. The overland traffic, which was assuming great volume as the surveys progressed, had yet nearly fifteen years before the railway should drive it out of existence. And no railway could even be started before war had removed one of the contesting sections from the floor of Congress.

Yet in the years since Asa Whitney had begun his agitation the railways of the East had constantly expanded. The first bridge to cross the Mississippi was under construction when Davis reported in 1855. The Illinois Central was opened in 1856. When the Civil War began, the railway frontier had become coterminous with the agricultural frontier, and both were ready to span the gap which separated them from the Pacific.

CHAPTER XIII

THE UNION PACIFIC RAILROAD

IT has been pointed out by Davis in his history of the Union Pacific Railroad that the period of agitation was approaching probable success when the latter was deferred because of the rivalry of sections and localities into which the scheme was thrown. From about 1850 until 1853 it indeed seemed likely that the road would be built just so soon as the terminus could be agreed upon. To be sure, there was keen rivalry over this; yet the rivalry did not go beyond local jealousies and might readily be compromised. After the reports of the surveys were completed and presented to Congress the problem took on a new aspect which promised postponement until a far greater question could be solved. Slavery and the Pacific railroad are concrete illustrations of the two horns of the national dilemma.

As a national project, the railway raised the problem of its construction under national auspices. Was the United States, or should it become, a nation competent to undertake the work? With no hesitation, many of the advocates of the measure answered yes. Yet even among the friends of the road the query frequently evoked the other answer.

Slavery had already taken its place as an institution peculiar to a single section. Its defence and perpetuation depended largely upon proving the contrary of the proposition that the Pacific railroad demanded. For the purposes of slavery defence the United States must remain a mere federation, limited in powers and lacking in the attributes of sovereignty and nationality. Looking back upon this struggle, with half a century gone by, it becomes clear that the final answer upon both questions, slavery and railway, had to be postponed until the more fundamental question of federal character had been worked out. The antitheses were clear, even as Lincoln saw them in 1858. Slavery and localism on the one hand, railway and nationalism on the other, were engaged in a vital struggle for recognition. Together they were incompatible. One or the other must survive alone. Lincoln saw a portion of the problem, and he sketched the answer: "I do not expect the Union to be dissolved, — I do not expect the house to fall, but I do expect it will cease to be divided."

The stages of the Pacific railroad movement are clearly marked through all these squabbles. Agitation came first, until conviction and acceptance were general. This was the era of Asa Whitney. Reconnoissance and survey followed, in a decade covering approximately 1847–1857. Organization came last, beginning in tentative schemes which counted for little, passing through a long series of intricate debates in Congress, and being merged in the larger question of nationality, but culminating finally in the first Pacific railroad bills of 1862 and 1864.

When Congress began its session of 1853–1854, most of the surveying parties contemplated by the act of the previous March were still in the field. The reports ordered were not yet available, and Congress recognized the inexpediency of proceeding farther without the facts. It is notable, however, that both houses at this time created select committees to consider propositions for a railway. Both of these committees reported bills, but neither received sanction even in the house of its friends. The next session, 1854–1855, saw the great struggle between Douglas and Benton.

Stephen A. Douglas, who had triumphantly carried through his Kansas-Nebraska bill in the preceding May, started a railway bill in the Senate in 1855. As finally considered and passed by the Senate, his bill provided for three railroads: a Northern Pacific, from the western border of Wisconsin to Puget Sound; a Southern Pacific, from the western border of Texas to the Pacific; and a Central Pacific, from Missouri or Iowa to San Francisco. They were to be constructed by private parties under contracts to be let jointly by the Secretaries of War and Interior and the Postmaster-general. Ultimately they were to become the property of the United States and the states through which they passed. The House of Representatives, led by Benton in the interests of a central road, declined to pass the Douglas measure. Before its final rejection, it was amended to please Benton and his allies by the restriction to a single trunk line from San Francisco, with eastern branches diverging to Lake Superior, Missouri or Iowa, and Memphis.

During the two years following the rejection of the Douglas scheme by the allied malcontents, the select committees on the Pacific railways had few propositions to consider, while Congress paid little attention to the general matter. Absorbing interest in politics, the new Republican party, and the campaign of 1856 were responsible for part of the neglect. The conviction of the dominant Democrats that the nation had no power to perform the task was responsible for more. The transition from a question of selfish localism to one of national policy which should require the whole strength of the nation for its solution was under way. The northern friends of the railway were disheartened by the southern tendencies of the Democratic administration which lasted till 1861. Jefferson Davis, as Secretary of War, was followed by Floyd, of Virginia, who believed with his predecessor that the southern was the most eligible route. At the same time, Aaron V. Brown, of Tennessee, Postmaster-general, was awarding the postal contract for an overland mail to Butterfield's southern route in spite of the fact that Congress had probably intended the central route to be employed.

Between 1857 and 1861 the debates of Congress show the difficulties under which the railroad labored. Many bills were started, but few could get through the committees. In 1859 the Senate passed a bill. In 1860 the House passed one which the Senate amended to death. In the session of 1860–1861 its serious consideration was crowded out by the incipiency of war.

Through the long years of debate over the organization of the road, the nature of its management and the nature of its governmental aid were much in evidence. Save only the Cumberland road the United States had undertaken no such scheme, while the Cumberland road, vastly less in magnitude than this, had raised enough constitutional difficulties to last a generation. That there must be some connection between the road and the public lands had been seen even before Whitney commenced his advocacy. The nature of that connection was worked out incidentally to other movements while the Whitney scheme was under fire.

The policy of granting lands in aid of improvements in transportation had been hinted at as far back as the admission of Ohio, but it had not received its full development until the railroad period began. To some extent, in the thirties and forties, public lands had been allotted to the states to aid in canal building, but when the railroad promoters started their campaign in the latter decade, a new era in the history of the public domain was commenced. The definitive fight over the issue of land grants for railways took place in connection with the Illinois Central and Mobile and Ohio scheme in the years from 1847 to 1850.

The demand for a central railroad in Illinois made its appearance before the panic of 1837. The northwest states were now building their own railroads, and this enterprise was designed to connect the Galena lead country with the junction of the Ohio and Mississippi by a road running parallel to the Mississippi through the whole length of the state of Illinois. Private railways in the Northwest ran naturally from east to west, seeking termini on the Mississippi and at the Alleghany crossings. This one was to intersect all the horizontal roads, making useful connections everywhere. But it traversed a country where yet the prairie hen held uncontested sway. There was little population or freight to justify it, and hence the project, though it guised itself in at least three different corporate garments before 1845, failed of success. No one of the multitude of transverse railways, on whose junctions it had counted, crossed its right-of-way before 1850. La Salle, Galena, and Jonesboro were the only villages on its line worth marking on a large-scale map, while Chicago was yet under forty thousand in population.

Men who in the following decade led the Pacific railway agitation promoted the Illinois Central idea in the years immediately preceding 1850. Both Breese and Douglas of Illinois claimed the parentage of the bill which eventually passed Congress in 1850, and by opening the way to public aid for railway transportation commenced the period of the land-grant railroads.   Already in some of the canal grants the method of aid had been outlined, alternate sections of land along the line of the canal being conveyed to the company to aid it in its work.   The theory underlying the granting of alternate sections in the familiar checker-board fashion was that the public lands, while inaccessible, had slight value, but once reached by communication the alternate sections reserved by the United States would bring a higher price than the whole would have done without the canal, while the construction company would be aided without expense to any one.   The application of this principle to railroads came rather slowly in a Congress somewhat disturbed by a doubt as to its power to devote the public resources to internal improvements.   The sectional character of the Illinois Central railway was against it until its promoters enlarged the scheme into a Lake-to-Gulf railway by including plans for a continuation to Mobile from the Ohio.   With southern aid thus enticed to its support, the bill became a law in 1850.   By its terms, the alternate sections of land in a strip ten miles wide were given to the interested states to be used for the construction of the Illinois Central and the Mobile and Ohio.   The grants were made directly to the states because of constitutional objections to construction within a state without its consent and approval. It was twelve years before Congress was ready to give the lands directly to the railroad company.

The decade following the Illinois Central grant was crowded with applications from other states for grants upon the same terms. In this period of speculative construction before the panic of 1857, every western state wanted all the aid it could get. In a single session seven states asked for nearly fourteen million acres of land, while before 1857 some five thousand miles of railway had been aided by land grants.

When Asa Whitney began his agitation for the Pacific railway, he asked for a huge land grant, but the machinery and methods of the grants had not yet become familiar to Congress. During the subsequent fifteen years of agitation and survey the method was worked out, so that when political conditions made it possible to build the road, there had ceased to be great difficulty in connection with its subsidy.

The sectional problem, which had reached its full development in Congress by 1857, prevented any action in the interest of a Pacific railway so long as it should remain unchanged. As the bickerings widened into war, the railway still remained a practical impossibility. But after war had removed from Congress the representatives of the southern states the way was cleared for action. When Congress met in its war session of July, 1861, all agitation in favor of southern routes was silenced by disunion. It remained only to choose among the routes lying north of the thirty-fifth parallel, and to authorize the construction along one of them of the railway which all admitted to be possible of construction, and to which military need in preservation of the union had now added an imperative quality.

The summer session of 1861 revived the bills for a Pacific railway, and handed them over to the regular session of 1861–1862 as unfinished business. In the lobby at this later session was Theodore D. Judah, a young graduate of the Troy Polytechnic, who gave powerful aid to the final settlement of route and means. Judah had come east in the autumn in company with one of the newly elected California representatives. During the long sea voyage he had drilled into his companion, who happily was later appointed to the Pacific Railroad Committee, all of the elaborate knowledge of the railway problem which he had acquired in his advocacy of the railway on the Pacific Coast. California had begun the construction of local railways several years before the war broke out; a Pacific railway was her constant need and prayer. Her own corporations were planned with reference to the time when tracks from the East should cross her border and find her local creations waiting for connections with them.

When the advent of war promised an early maturity for the scheme, a few Californians organized the most significant of the California railways, the

Central Pacific. On June 28, 1861, this company
was incorporated, having for its leading spirits Judah,
its chief engineer, and Collis Potter Huntington,
Mark Hopkins, Charles Crocker, and Leland Stanford, soon to be governor of the state. Its founders
were all men of moderate means, but they had the best
of that foresight and initiative in which the frontier
was rich. Diligently through the summer of 1861
Judah prospected for routes across the mountains
into Utah territory, where the new silver fields
around Carson indicated the probable course of a
route. With his plans and profiles, he hurried on
to Washington in the fall to aid in the quick settlement of the long-debated question.

Judah's interest in a special California road coin-
cided well with the needs and desires of Congress.
Already various bills were in the hands of the select
committees of both houses. The southern interest
was gone. The only remaining rivalries were
among St. Louis, Chicago, and the new Minnesota;
while the first of these was tainted by the doubtful
loyalty of Missouri, and the last was embarrassed
by the newness of its territory and its lack of population. The Sioux were yet in control of much
of the country beyond St. Paul. Out of this rivalry
Chicago and a central route could emerge triumphant.

The spring of 1862 witnessed a long debate over a
Union Pacific railroad to meet the new military needs
of the United States as well as to satisfy the old eco-

nomic necessities. Why it was called "Union" is somewhat in doubt. Bancroft thinks its name was descriptive of the various local roads which were bound together in the single continental scheme. Davis, on the contrary, is inclined to believe that the name was in contrast to the "Disunion" route of the thirty-second parallel, since the route chosen was to run entirely through loyal territory. Whatever the reason, however, the Union Pacific Railroad Company was incorporated on the 1st of July, 1862.

Under the act of incorporation a continental railway was to be constructed by several companies. Within the limits of California, the Central Pacific of California, already organized and well managed, was to have the privilege. Between the boundary line of California and Nevada and the hundredth meridian, the new Union Pacific was to be the constructing company. On the hundredth meridian, at some point between the Republican River in Kansas and the Platte River in Nebraska, radiating lines were to advance to various eastern frontier points, somewhat after the fashion of Benton's bill of 1855. Thus the Leavenworth, Pawnee, and Western of Kansas was authorized to connect this point with the Missouri River, south of the mouth of the Kansas, with a branch to Atchison and St. Joseph in connection with the Hannibal and St. Joseph of Missouri. The Union Pacific itself was required to build two more connections; one to run from the hundredth meridian to some point on the west boundary of

Iowa, to be fixed by the President of the United States, and another to Sioux City, Iowa, whenever a line from the east should reach that place.

The aid offered for the construction of these lines was more generous than any previously provided by Congress. In the first place, the roads were entitled to a right-of-way four hundred feet wide, with permission to take material for construction from adjacent parts of the public domain. Secondly, the roads were to receive ten sections of land for each mile of track on the familiar alternate section principle. Finally, the United States was to lend to the roads bonds to the amount of $16,000 per mile, on the level, $32,000 in the foothills, and $48,000 in the mountains, to facilitate construction. If not completed and open by 1876, the whole line was to be forfeited to the United States. If completed, the loan of bonds was to be repaid out of subsequent earnings.

The Central Pacific of California was prompt in its acceptance of the terms of the act of July 1, 1862. It proceeded with its organization, broke ground at Sacramento on February 22, 1863, and had a few miles of track in operation before the next year closed. But the Union Pacific was slow. "While fighting to retain eleven refractory states," wrote one irritated critic of the act, "the nation permitted itself to be cozened out of territory sufficient to form twelve new republics." Yet great as were the offered grants, eastern capital was reluctant to put life into the new route across the plains. That it could ever pay, was seriously doubted. Chances for more certain and profitable investment in the East were frequent in the years of war-time prosperity. Although the railroad organized according to the terms of the law, subscribers to the stock of the Union Pacific were hard to find, and the road lay dormant for two more years until Congress revised its offer and increased its terms.

In the session of 1863–1864 the general subject was again approached. Writes Davis, "The opinion was almost universal that additional legislation was needed to make the Act of 1862 effective, but the point where the limit of aid to patriotic capitalists should be set was difficult to determine." It was, and remained, the belief of the opponents of the bill now passed that "lobbyists, male and female, . . . shysters and adventurers" had much to do with the success of the measure. In its most essential parts, the new bill of 1864 increased the degree of government aid to the companies. The land grant was doubled from ten sections per mile of track to twenty, and the road was allowed to borrow of the general public, on first mortgage bonds, money to the amount of the United States loan, which was reduced by a self-denying ordinance to the status of a second mortgage. With these added inducements, the Union Pacific was finally begun.

The project at last under way in 1864–1865, as Davis graphically pictures it, "was thoroughly saturated and fairly dripping with the elements of adventure and romance." But he overstates his case when he goes on to remark that, "Before the building of the Pacific railway most of the wide expanse of territory west of the Missouri was *terra incognita* to the mass of Americans." For twenty years the railway had been under agitation; during the whole period population had crossed the great desert in increasing thousands; new states had banked up around its circumference, east, west, and south, while Kansas had been thrust into its middle; new camps had dotted its interior. The great West was by no means unknown, but with the construction of the railway the American frontier entered upon its final phase.

CHAPTER XIV

THE PLAINS IN THE CIVIL WAR

THAT the fate of the outlying colonies of the United States should have aroused grave concerns at the beginning of the Civil War is not surprising. California and Oregon, Carson City, Denver, and the other mining camps were indeed on the same continent with the contending factions, but the degree of their isolation was so great that they might as well have been separated by an ocean. Their inhabitants were more mixed than those of any portion of the older states, while in several of the communities the parties were so evenly divided as to raise doubts of the loyalty of the whole. "The malignant secession element of this Territory," wrote Governor Gilpin of Colorado, in October, 1861, "has numbered 7,500. It has been ably and secretly organized from November last, and requires extreme and extraordinary measures to meet and control its onslaught." At best, the western population was scanty and scattered over a frontier that still possessed its virgin character in most respects, though hovering at the edge of a period of transition. An English observer, hopeful for the worst, announced in the middle of the war that "When that 'late lamented institution,' the once United States, shall have passed away, and when, after this detestable and fratricidal war — the most disgraceful to human nature that civilization ever witnessed — the New World shall be restored to order and tranquility, our shikaris will not forget, that a single fortnight of comfortable travel suffices to transport them from fallow deer and pheasant shooting to the haunts of the bison and the grizzly bear. There is little chance of these animals being 'improved off' the Prairies, or even of their becoming rare during the lifetime of the present generation." The factors of most consequence in shaping the course of the great plains during the Civil War were those of mixed population, of ever present Indian danger, and of isolation. Though the plains had no effect upon the outcome of the war, the war furthered the work already under way of making known the West, clearing off the Indians, and preparing for future settlement.

Like the rest of the United States the West was organized into military divisions for whose good order commanding officers were made responsible. At times the burden of military control fell chiefly upon the shoulders of territorial governors; again, special divisions were organized to meet particular needs, and generals of experience were detached from the main armies to direct movements in the West.

Among the earliest of the episodes which drew attention to the western departments was the resignation of Albert Sidney Johnston, commanding the

Department of the Pacific, and his rather spectacular
flight across New Mexico, to join the confederate
forces. From various directions, federal troops were
sent to head him off, but he succeeded in evading all
these and reaching safety at the Rio Grande by
August 1. Here he could take an overland stage
for the rest of his journey. The department which
he abandoned included the whole West beyond
the Rockies except Utah and present New Mexico.
The country between the mountains and Missouri
constituted the Department of the West. As the
war advanced, new departments were created and
boundaries were shifted at convenience. The Department of the Pacific remained an almost constant
quantity throughout. A Department of the Northwest, covering the territory of the Sioux Indians,
was created in September, 1862, for the better defence of Minnesota and Wisconsin. To this command Pope was assigned after his removal from the
command of the Army of Virginia. Until the close
of the war, when the great leaders were distributed
and Sheridan received the Department of the Southwest, no detail of equal importance was made to a
western department.

The fighting on the plains was rarely important
enough to receive the dignified name of battle.
There were plenty of marching and reconnoitring,
much police duty along the trails, occasional skir-
mishes with organized troops or guerrillas, aggressive
campaigns against the Indians, and campaigns in

defence of the agricultural frontier. But the armies
so occupied were small and inexperienced. Commonly regiments of local volunteers were used in
these movements, or returned captives who were on
parole to serve no more against the confederacy.
Disciplined veterans were rarely to be found. As a
consequence of the spasmodic character of the plains
warfare and the inferior quality of the troops available, western movements were often hampered and
occasionally made useless.

The struggle for the Rio Grande was as important
as any of the military operations on the plains. At
the beginning of the war the confederate forces
seized the river around El Paso in time to make clear
the way for Johnston as he hurried east. The
Tucson country was occupied about the same time,
so that in the fall of 1861 the confederate outposts
were somewhat beyond the line of Texas and the
Rio Grande, with New Mexico, Utah, and Colorado
threatened. In December General Henry Hopkins
Sibley assumed command of the confederate troops
in the upper Rio Grande, while Colonel E. R. S.
Canby, from Fort Craig, organized the resistance
against further extension of the confederate power.

Sibley's manifest intentions against the upper Rio
Grande country, around Santa Fé and Albuquerque,
aroused federal apprehensions in the winter of 1862.
Governor Gilpin, at Denver, was already frightened
at the danger within his own territory, and scarcely
needed the order which came from Fort Leavenworth

through General Hunter to reënforce Canby and look after the Colorado forts. He took responsibility easily, drew upon the federal treasury for funds which had not been allowed him, and shortly had the first Colorado, and a part of the second Colorado volunteers marching south to join the defensive columns. It is difficult to define this march in terms applicable to movements of war. At least one soldier in the second Colorado took with him two children and a wife, the last becoming the historian of the regiment and praising the chivalry of the soldiers, apparently oblivious of the fact that it is not a soldier's duty to be child's nurse to his comrade's family. But with wife and children, and the degree of individualism and insubordination which these imply, the Pike's Peak frontiersmen marched south to save the territory. Their patriotism at least was sure.

As Sibley pushed up the river, passing Fort Craig and brushing aside a small force at Valverde, the Colorado forces reached Fort Union. Between Fort Union and Albuquerque, which Sibley entered easily, was the turning-point in the campaign. On March 26, 1862, Major J. M. Chivington had a successful skirmish at Johnson's ranch in Apache Cañon, about twenty miles southeast of Santa Fé. Two days later, at Pigeon's ranch, a more decisive check was given to the confederates, but Colonel John P. Slough, senior volunteer in command, fell back upon Fort Union after the engagement, while the confederates were left free to occupy Santa Fé.　A few days later Slough was deposed in the Colorado regiment, Chivington made colonel, and the advance on Santa Fé begun again.　Sibley, now caught between Canby advancing from Fort Craig and Chivington coming through Apache Cañon from Fort Union, evacuated Sante Fé on April 7, falling back to Albuquerque. The union troops, taking Santa Fé on April 12, hurried down the Rio Grande after Sibley in his final retreat.　New Mexico was saved, and its security brought tranquillity to Colorado.　The Colorado volunteers were back in Denver for the winter of 1862–1863, but Gilpin, whose vigorous and independent support had made possible their campaign, had been dismissed from his post as governor.

Along the frontier of struggle campaigns of this sort occurred from time to time, receiving little attention from the authorities who were directing weightier movements at the centre.　Less formal than these, and more provocative of bitter feeling, were the attacks of guerrillas along the central frontier, — chiefly the Missouri border and eastern Kansas.　Here the passions of the struggle for Kansas had not entirely cooled down, southern sympathizers were easily found, and communities divided among themselves were the more intense in their animosities.

The Department of Kansas, where the most aggravated of these guerrilla conflicts occurred, was organized in November, 1861, under Major-general

Hunter. From his headquarters at Leavenworth the commanding officer directed the affairs of Kansas, Nebraska, Dakota, Colorado, and "the Indian Territory west of Arkansas." The department was often shifted and reshaped to meet the needs of the frontier. A year later the Department of the Northwest was cut away from it, after the Sioux outbreak, its own name was changed to Missouri, and the states of Missouri and Arkansas were added to it. Still later it was modified again. But here throughout the war continued the troubles produced by the mixture of frontier and farm-lands, partisan whites and Indians.

Bushwhacking, a composite of private murder and public attack, troubled the Kansas frontier from an early period of the war. It was easily aroused because of public animosities, and difficult to suppress because its participating parties retired quickly into the body of peace-professing citizens. In it, asserted General Order No. 13, of June 26, 1862, "rebel fiends lay in wait for their prey to assassinate Union soldiers and citizens; it is therefore . . . especially directed that whenever any of this class of offenders shall be captured, they shall not be treated as prisoners of war but be summarily tried by drum-head court-martial, and if proved guilty, be executed . . . on the spot."

In August, 1863, occurred Quantrill's notable raid into Kansas to terrify the border which was already harassed enough. The old border hatred between

Kansas and Missouri had been intensified by the "murders, robberies, and arson" which had characterized the irregular warfare carried on by both sides. In western Missouri, loyal unionists were not safe outside the federal lines; here the guerrillas came and went at pleasure; and here, about August 18, Quantrill assembled a band of some three hundred men for a foray into Kansas. On the 20th he entered Kansas, heading at once for Lawrence, which he surprised on the 21st. Although the city arsenal contained plenty of arms and the town could have mustered 500 men on "half an hour's notice," the guerrilla band met no resistance. It "robbed most of the stores and banks, and burned one hundred and eighty-five buildings, including one-fourth of the private residences and nearly all of the business houses of the town, and, with circumstances of the most fiendish atrocity, murdered 140 unarmed men." The retreat of Quantrill was followed by a vigorous federal pursuit and a partial devastation of the adjacent Missouri counties. Kansas, indignant, was in arms at once, protesting directly to President Lincoln of the "imbecility and incapacity" of Major-general John M. Schofield, commanding the Department of the Missouri, "whose policy has opened Kansas to invasion and butchery." Instead of carrying out an unimpeded pursuit of the guerrillas, Schofield had to devote his strength to keeping the state of Kansas from declaring war against and wreaking indiscriminate vengeance upon the state of Missouri. A year after Quantrill's raid came Price's Missouri expedition, with its pitched battles near Kansas City and Westport, and its pursuit through southern Missouri, where confederate sympathizers and the partisan politics of this presidential year made punitive campaigns anything but easy.

Carleton's march into New Mexico has already been described in connection with the mining boom of Arizona. The silver mines of the Santa Cruz Valley had drawn American population to Tubac and Tucson several years before the war; while the confederate successes in the upper Rio Grande in the summer of 1861 had compelled federal evacuation of the district. Colonel E. R. S. Canby devoted the small force at his command to regaining the country around Albuquerque and Sante Fé, while the relief of the forts between the Rio Grande and the Colorado was intrusted to Carleton's California Column. After May, 1862, Carleton was firmly established in Tucson, and later he was given command of the whole Department of New Mexico. Of fighting with the confederates there was almost none. He prosecuted, instead, Apache and Navaho wars, and exploited the new gold fields which were now found. In much of the West, as in his New Mexico, occasional ebullitions of confederate sympathizers occurred, but the military task of the commanders was easy.

The military problem of the plains was one of police, with the extinction of guerrilla warfare and the pacification of Indians as its chief elements. The careers of Canby, Carleton, and Gilpin indicate the nature of the western strategic warfare, Schofield's illustrates that of guerrilla fighting, the Minnesota outbreak that of the Indian relations.

In the Northwest, where the agricultural expansion of the fifties had worked so great changes, the pressure on the tribes had steadily increased. In 1851 the Sioux bands had ceded most of their territory in Minnesota, and had agreed upon a reduced reserve in the St. Peter's, or Minnesota, Valley. But the terms of this treaty had been delayed in enforcement, while bad management on the part of the United States and the habitual frontier disregard of Indian rights created tense feelings, which might break loose at any time. No single grievance of the Indians caused more trouble than that over traders' claims. The improvident savages bought largely of the traders, on credit, at extortionate prices. The traders could afford the risk because when treaties of cession were made, their influence was generally able to get inserted in the treaty a clause for satisfying claims against individuals out of the tribal funds before these were handed over to the savages. The memory of the savage was short, and when he found that his allowance, the price for his lands, had gone into the traders' pockets, he could not realize that it had gone to pay his debts, but felt, somehow, defrauded. The answer would have been to prevent trade with the Indians on credit. But the traders' influence at Washington was great. It would be an interesting study to investigate the connection between traders' bills and agitation for new cessions, since the latter generally meant satisfaction of the former.

Among the Sioux there were factional feelings that had aroused the apprehensions of their agents before the war broke out. The "blanket" Indians continually mocked at the "farmers" who took kindly to the efforts of the United States for their agricultural civilization. There was civil strife among the progressives and irreconcilables which made it difficult to say what was the disposition of the whole nation. The condition was so unstable that an accidental row, culminating in the murder of five whites at Acton, in Meeker County, brought down the most serious Indian massacre the frontier had yet seen.

There was no more occasion for a general uprising in 1862 than there had been for several years. The wiser Indians realized the futility of such a course. Yet Little Crow, inclined though he was to peace, fell in with the radicals as the tribe discussed their policy; and he determined that since a massacre had been commenced they had best make it as thorough as possible. Retribution was certain whether they continued war or not, and the farmer Indians were unlikely to be distinguished from the blankets by angry frontiersmen. The attack fell first upon the stores at the lower agency, twenty miles above Fort Ridgely, whence refugee whites fled to Fort Ridgely with news of the outbreak. All day, on the 18th of August, massacres occurred along the St. Peter's, from near New Ulm to the Yellow Medicine River. The incidents of Indian war were all there, in surprise, slaughter of women and children, mutilation and torture.

The next day, Tuesday the 19th, the increasing bands fell upon the rambling village of New Ulm, twenty-eight miles above Mankato, where fugitives had gathered and where Judge Charles E. Flandrau hastily organized a garrison for defence. He had been at St. Peter's when the news arrived, and had led a relief band through the drenching rain, reaching New Ulm in the evening. On Wednesday afternoon Little Crow, his band still growing — the Sioux could muster some 1300 warriors — surprised Fort Ridgely, though with no success. On Thursday he renewed the attack with a force now dwindling because of individual plundering expeditions which drew his men to various parts of the neighboring country. On Friday he attacked once more.

On Saturday the 23d Little Crow came down the river again to renew his fight upon New Ulm, which, unmolested since Tuesday, had been increasing its defences. Here Judge Flandrau led out the whites in a pitched battle. A few of his men were old frontiersmen, cool and determined, of unerring aim; but most were German settlers, recently arrived, and often terrified by their new experiences. During the week of horrors the depredations covered the

Minnesota frontier and lapped over into Iowa and Dakota. Isolated families, murdered and violated, or led captive into the wilderness, were common. Stories of those who survived these dangers form a large part of the local literature of this section of the Northwest. At New Ulm the situation had become so desperate that on the 25th Flandrau evacuated the town and led its whole remaining population to safety at Mankato.

Long before the week of suffering was over, aid had been started to the harassed frontier. Governor Ramsey, of Minnesota, hurried to Mendota, and there organized a relief column to move up the Minnesota Valley. Henry Hastings Sibley, quite different from him of Rio Grande fame, commanded the column and reached St. Peter's with his advance on Friday. By Sunday he had 1400 men with whom to quiet the panic and restore peace and repopulate the deserted country. He was now joined by Ignatius Donnelly, Lieutenant-governor, sent to urge greater speed. The advance was resumed. By Friday, the 29th, they had reached Fort Ridgely, passing through country "abandoned by the inhabitants; the houses, in many cases, left with the doors open, the furniture undisturbed, while the cattle ranged about the doors or through the cultivated fields." The country had been settled up to the very edge of the Fort Ridgely reserve. It was entirely deserted, though only partially devastated. Donnelly commented in his report upon the prayer-books and old German trunks of

"Johann Schwartz," strewn upon the ground in one place; and upon bodies found, "bloated, discolored, and far gone in decomposition." The Indian agent, Thomas J. Galbraith, who was at Fort Ridgely during the trouble, reported in 1863, that 737 whites were known to have been massacred.

Sibley, having reached Fort Ridgely, proceeded at first to reconnoitre and bury the dead, then to follow the Indians and rescue the captives. More than once the tribes had found that it was wise to carry off prisoners, who by serving as hostages might mollify or prevent punishment for the original outbreak. Early in September there were pitched battles at Birch Coolie and Fort Abercrombie and Wood Lake. At this last engagement, on September 23, Sibley was able not only to defeat the tribes and take nearly 2000 prisoners, but to release 227 women and children, who had been the "prime object," from whose "pursuit nothing could drive or divert him." The Indians were handed over under arrest to Agent Galbraith to be conveyed first to the Lower Agency, and then, in November, to Fort Snelling.

The punishment of the Sioux was heavy. Inkpaduta's massacre at Spirit Lake was still remembered and unavenged. Sibley now cut them down in battle in 1862, though Little Crow and other leaders escaped. In 1863, Pope, who had been called to command a new department in the Northwest, organized a general campaign against the tribes, sending Sibley up the Minnesota River to drive them west, and Sully up the Missouri to head them off, planning to catch and crush them between the two columns. The manœuvre was badly timed and failed, while punishment drifted gradually into a prolonged war.

Civil retribution was more severe, and fell, with judicial irony, on the farmer Sioux who had been drawn reluctantly into the struggle. At the Lower Agency, at Redwood, the captives were held, while more than four hundred of their men were singled out for trial for murder. Nothing is more significant of the anomalous nature of the Indian relation than this trial for murder of prisoners of war. The United States held the tribes nationally to account, yet felt free to punish individuals as though they were citizens of the United States. The military commission sat at Redwood for several weeks with the missionary and linguist, Rev. S. R. Riggs, "in effect, the Grand Jury of the court." Three hundred and three were condemned to death by the court for murder, rape, and arson, their condemnation starting a wave of protest over the country, headed by the Indian Commissioner, W. P. Dole. To the indignation of the frontier, naturally revengeful and never impartial, President Lincoln yielded to the protests in the case of most of the condemned. Yet thirty-eight of them were hanged on a single scaffold at Mankato on December 26, 1862. The innocent and uncondemned were punished also, when Congress confiscated all their Minnesota reserve in 1863, and transferred the tribe to Fort Thompson on the

Missouri, where less desirable quarters were found for them.

All along the edge of the frontier, from Minnesota to the Rio Grande, were problems that drew the West into the movement of the Civil War. The situation was trying for both whites and Indians, but nowhere did the Indians suffer between the millstones as they did in the Indian Territory, where the Cherokee and Creeks, Choctaw and Chickasaw and Seminole, had been colonized in the years of creation of the Indian frontier. For a generation these nations had resided in comparative peace and advancing civilization, but they were undone by causes which they could not control.

The confederacy was no sooner organized than its commissioners demanded of the tribes colonized west of Arkansas their allegiance and support, professing to have inherited all the rights and obligations of the United States. To the Indian leaders, half civilized and better, this demand raised difficulties which would have been a strain on any diplomacy. If they remained loyal to the United States, the confederate forces, adjacent in Arkansas and Texas, and already coveting their lands, would cut them to pieces. If they adhered to the confederacy and the latter lost, they might anticipate the resentment of the United States. Yet they were too weak to stand alone and were forced to go one way or other. The resulting policy was temporizing and brought to them a large measure of punishment from both sides, and the heavy subsequent wrath of the United States.

John Ross, principal chief in the Cherokee nation, tried to maintain his neutrality at the commencement of the conflict, but the fiction of Indian nationality was too slight for his effort to be successful. During the spring and summer of 1861 he struggled against the confederate control to which he succumbed by August, when confederate troops had overrun most of Indian Territory, and disloyal Indian agents had surrendered United States property to the enemy. The war which followed resembled the guerrilla conflicts of Kansas, with the addition of the Indian element.

By no means all the Indians accepted the confederate control. When the Indian Territory forts — Gibson, Arbuckle, Washita, and Cobb — fell into the hands of the South, loyal Indians left their homes and sought protection within the United States lines. Almost the only way to fight a war in which a population is generally divided, is by means of depopulation and concentration. Along the Verdigris River, in southeast Kansas, these Indian refugees settled in 1861 and 1862, to the number of 6000. Here the Indian Commissioner fed them as best he could, and organized them to fight when that was possible. With the return of federal success in the occupation of Fort Smith and western Arkansas during the next two years, the natives began to return to their homes. But the relation of their

R

tribes to the United States was tainted. The compulsory cession of their western lands which came at the close of the conflict belongs to a later chapter and the beginnings of Oklahoma. Here, as elsewhere, the condition of the tribes was permanently changed.

The great plains and the Far West were only the outskirts of the Civil War. At no time did they shape its course, for the Civil War was, from their point of view, only an incidental sectional contest in the East, and merely an episode in the grander development of the United States. The way is opening ever wider for the historian who shall see in this material development and progress of civilization the central thread of American history, and in accordance with it, retail the story. But during the years of sectional strife the West was occasionally connected with the struggle, while toward their close it passed rapidly into a period in which it came to be the admitted centre of interest. The last stand of the Indians against the onrush of settlement is a warfare with an identity of its own.

CHAPTER XV

THE CHEYENNE WAR

IT has long been the custom to attribute the dangerous restlessness of the Indians during and after the Civil War to the evil machinations of the Confederacy. It has been plausible to charge that agents of the South passed among the tribes, inciting them to outbreak by pointing out the preoccupation of the United States and the defencelessness of the frontier. Popular narratives often repeat this charge when dealing with the wars and depredations, whether among the Sioux of Minnesota, or the Northwest tribes, or the Apache and Navaho, or the Indians of the plains. Indeed, had the South been able thus to harass the enemy it is not improbable that it would have done it. It is not impossible that it actually did it. But at least the charge has not been proved. No one has produced direct evidence to show the existence of agents or their connection with the Confederacy, though many have uttered a general belief in their reality. Investigators of single affairs have admitted, regretfully, their inability to add incitement of Indians to the charges against the South. If such a cause were needed to explain the increasing turbulence of the tribes, it might be worth while to search further in the hope of establishing it, but nothing occurred in these wars which cannot be accounted for, fully, in facts easily obtained and well authenticated.

Before 1861 the Indians of the West were commonly on friendly terms with the United States. Occasional wars broke this friendship, and frequent massacres aroused the fears of one frontier or another, for the Indian was an irresponsible child, and the frontiersman was reckless and inconsiderate. But the outbreaks were exceptional, they were easily put down, and peace was rarely hard to obtain. By 1865 this condition had changed over most of the West. Warfare had become systematic and widely spread. The frequency and similarity of outbreaks in remote districts suggested a harmonious plan, or at least similar reactions from similar provocations. From 1865, for nearly five years, these wars continued with only intervals of truce, or professed peace ; while during a long period after 1870, when most of the tribes were suppressed and well policed, upheavals occurred which were clearly to be connected with the Indian wars. The reality of this transition from peace to war has caused many to charge it to the South. It is, however, connected with the culmination of the westward movement, which more than explains it.

For a setting of the Indian wars some restatement of the events before 1861 is needed. By 1840 the agricultural frontier of the United States had reached the bend of the Missouri, while the Indian tribes, with plenty of room, had been pushed upon the plains. In the generation following appeared the heavy traffic along the overland trails, the advance of the frontier into the new Northwest, and the Pacific railway surveys. Each of these served to compress the Indians and restrict their range. Accompanying these came curtailing of reserves, shifting of residences to less desirable grounds, and individual maltreatment to a degree which makes marvellous the incapacity, weakness, and patience of the Indians. Occasionally they struggled, but always they lost. The scalped and mutilated pioneer, with his haystacks burning and his stock run off, is a vivid picture in the period, but is less characteristic than the long-suffering Indian, accepting the inevitable, and moving to let the white man in.

The necessary results of white encroachment were destruction of game and education of the Indian to the luxuries and vices of the white man. At a time when starvation was threatening because of the disappearance of the buffalo and other food animals, he became aware of the superior diet of the whites and the ease with which robbery could be accomplished. In the fifties the pressure continued, heavier than ever. The railway surveys reached nearly every corner of the Indian Country. In the next few years came the prospectors who started hundreds of mining camps beyond the line of settlements, while the engineers began to stick the advancing heads of railways out from the Missouri frontier and into the buffalo range.

Even the Indian could see the approaching end. It needed no confederate envoy to assure him that the United States could be attacked. His own hunger and the white peril were persuading him to defend his hunting-ground. Yet even now, in the widespread Indian wars of the later sixties, uniformity of action came without much previous coöperation. A general Indian league against the whites was never raised. The general war, upon dissection and analysis, breaks up into a multitude of little wars, each having its own particular causes, which, in many instances, if the word of the most expert frontiersmen is to be believed, ran back into cases of white aggression and Indian revenge.

The Sioux uprising of 1862 came a little ahead of the general wars, with causes rising from the treaties of Mendota and Traverse des Sioux in 1851. The plains situation had been clearly seen and succinctly stated in this year. "We are constrained to say," wrote the men who made these treaties, "that in our opinion *the time has come* when the extinguishment of the Indian title to this region should no longer be delayed, if government would not have the mortification, on the one hand, of confessing its inability to protect the Indian from encroachment; or be subject to the painful necessity, upon the other, of ejecting by force thousands of its citizens from a land which they desire to make their homes, and which, without their occupancy and labor, will be comparatively useless and waste." The other treaties concluded in this same year at Fort Laramie were equally the fountains of discontent which boiled over in the early sixties and gave rise at last to one of the most horrible incidents of the plains war.

In the Laramie treaties the first serious attempt to partition the plains among the tribes was made. The lines agreed upon recognized existing conditions to a large extent, while annuities were pledged in consideration of which the savages agreed to stay at peace, to allow free migration along the trails, and to keep within their boundaries. The Sioux here agreed that they belonged north of the Platte. The Arapaho and Cheyenne recognized their area as lying between the Platte and the Arkansas, the mountains and, roughly, the hundred and first meridian. For ten years after these treaties the last-named tribes kept the faith to the exclusion of attacks upon settlers or emigrants. They even allowed the Senate in its ratification of the treaty to reduce the term of the annuities from fifty years to fifteen.

In a way, the Arapaho and Cheyenne Indians lay off the beaten tracks and apart from contact with the whites. Their home was in the triangle between the great trails, with a mountain wall behind them that offered almost insuperable obstacles to those who would cross the continent through their domain. The Gunnison railroad survey, which was run along the thirty-ninth parallel and through the Cochetopa Pass, revealed the difficulty of penetrating the range at this point. Accordingly, a decade which built up Oregon and California made little impression on this section until in 1858 gold was discovered in Cherry Creek. Then came the deluge.

Nearly one hundred thousand miners and hangers-on crossed the plains to the Pike's Peak country in 1859 and settled unblushingly in the midst of the Indian lands. They "possessed nothing more than the right of transit over these lands," admitted the Peace Commissioners in 1868. Yet they "took possession of them for the purpose of mining, and, against the protest of the Indians, founded cities, established farms, and opened roads. Before 1861 the Cheyenne and Arapaho had been driven from the mountain regions down upon the waters of the Arkansas, and were becoming sullen and discontented because of this violation of their rights." The treaty of 1851 had guaranteed the Indians in their possession, pledging the United States to prevent depredations by the whites, but here, as in most similar cases, the guarantees had no weight in the face of a population under way. The Indians were brushed aside, the United States agents made no real attempts to enforce the treaty, and within a few months the settlers were demanding protection against the surrounding tribes. "The Indians saw their former homes and hunting grounds overrun by a greedy population, thirsting for gold," continued the

Commissioners. "They saw their game driven east to the plains, and soon found themselves the objects of jealousy and hatred. They too must go. The presence of the injured is too often painful to the wrong-doer, and innocence offensive to the eyes of guilt. It now became apparent that what had been taken by force must be retained by the ravisher, and nothing was left for the Indian but to ratify a treaty consecrating the act."

Instead of a war of revenge in which the Arapaho and Cheyenne strove to defend their lands and to drive out the intruders, a war in which the United States ought to have coöperated with the Indians, a treaty of cession followed. On February 18, 1861, at Fort Wise, which was the new name for Bent's old fort on the Arkansas, an agreement was signed by which these tribes gave up much of the great range reserved for them in 1851, and accepted in its place, with what were believed to be greater guarantees, a triangular tract bounded, east and northeast, by Sand Creek, in eastern Colorado; on the south by the Arkansas and Purgatory rivers; and extending west some ninety miles from the junction of Sand Creek and the Arkansas. The cessions made by the Ute on the other side of the range, not long after this, are another part of the same story of mining aggression. The new Sand Creek reserve was designed to remove the Arapaho and Cheyenne from under the feet of the restless prospectors. For years they had kept the peace in the face of great provocation.   For three years more they put up with white encroachment before their war began.

The Colorado miners, like those of the other boom camps, had been loud in their demand for transportation.   To satisfy this, overland traffic had been organized on a large scale, while during 1862 the stage and freight service of the plains fell under the control of Ben Holladay.   Early in August, 1864, Holladay was nearly driven out of business.   About the 10th of the month, simultaneous attacks were made along his mail line from the Little Blue River to within eighty miles of Denver.   In the forays, stations were sacked and burned, isolated farms were wiped out, small parties on the trails were destroyed. At Ewbank Station, a family of ten "was massacred and scalped, and one of the females, besides having suffered the latter inhuman barbarity, was pinned to the earth by a stake thrust through her person, in a most revolting manner; . . . at Plum Creek . . . nine persons were murdered, their train, consisting of ten wagons, burnt, and two women and two children captured. . . .   The old Indian traders . . . and the settlers . . . abandoned their habitations." For a distance of 370 miles, Holladay's general superintendent declared, every ranch but one was "deserted and the property abandoned to the Indians."

Fifteen years after the destruction of his stations, Holladay was still claiming damages from the United States and presenting affidavits from his men which revealed the character of the attacks.   George H.

Carlyle told how his stage was chased by Indians for twenty miles, how he had helped to bury the mutilated bodies of the Plum Creek victims, and how within a week the route had to be abandoned, and every ranch from Fort Kearney to Julesburg was deserted. The division agent told how property had been lost in the hurried flight. To save some of the stock, fodder and supplies had to be sacrificed, — hundreds of sacks of corn, scores of tons of hay, besides the buildings and their equipment. Nowhere were the Indians overbold in their attacks. In small bands they waited their time to take the stations by surprise. Well-armed coaches might expect to get through with little more than a few random shots, but along the hilltops they could often see the savages waiting in safety for them to pass. Indian warfare was not one of organized bodies and formal manœuvres. Only when cornered did the Indian stand to fight. But in wild, unexpected descents the tribes fell upon the lines of communication, reducing the frontier to an abject terror overnight.

The destruction of the stage route was not the first, though it was the most general hostility which marked the commencement of a new Indian war. Since the spring of 1864 events had occurred which in the absence of a more rigorous control than the Indian Department possessed, were likely to lead to trouble. The Cheyenne had been dissatisfied with the Fort Wise treaty ever since its conclusion. The Sioux were carrying on a prolonged war. The

Arapaho, Comanche, and Kiowa were ready to be started on the war-path. It was the old story of too much compression and isolated attacks going unpunished. Whatever the merits of an original controversy, the only way to keep the savages under control was to make fair retribution follow close upon the commission of an outrage. But the punishment needed to be fair.

In April, 1864, a ranchman named Ripley came into one of the camps on the South Platte and declared that some Indians had stolen his stock. Perhaps his statement was true; but it must be remembered that the ranchman whose stock strayed away was prone to charge theft against the Indians, and that there is only Ripley's own word that he ever had any stock. Captain Sanborn, commanding, sent out a troop of cavalry to recover the animals. They came upon some Indians with horses which Ripley claimed as his, and in an attempt to disarm them, a fight occurred in which the troop was driven off. Their lieutenant thought the Indians were Cheyenne.

A few weeks after this, Major Jacob Downing, who had been in Camp Sanborn inspecting troops, came into Denver and got from Colonel Chivington about forty men, with whom "to go against the Indians." Downing later swore that he found the Cheyenne village at Cedar Bluffs. "We commenced shooting; I ordered the men to commence killing them. . . . They lost . . . some twenty-six killed and thirty wounded. . . . I burnt up their lodges and everything I could get hold of. . . . We captured about one hundred head of stock, which was distributed among the boys."

On the 12th of June, a family living on Box Elder Creek, twenty miles east of Denver, was murdered by the Indians. Hungate, his wife, and two children were killed, the house burned, and fifty or sixty head of stock run off. When the "scalped and horribly mangled bodies" were brought into Denver, the population, already uneasy, was thrown into panic by this appearance of danger so close to the city. Governor Evans began at once to organize the militia for home defence and to appeal to Washington for help.

By the time of the attack upon the stage line it was clear that an Indian war existed, involving in varying degrees parts of the Arapaho, Cheyenne, Comanche, and Kiowa tribes. The merits of the causes which provoked it were considerably in doubt. On the frontier there was no hesitation in charging it all to the innate savagery of the tribes. Governor Evans was entirely satisfied that "while some of the Indians might yet be friendly, there was no hope of a general peace on the plains, until after a severe chastisement of the Indians for these depredations."

In restoring tranquillity the frontier had to rely largely upon its own resources. Its own Second Colorado was away doing duty in the Missouri campaign, while the eastern military situation presented no probability of troops being available to help out the West. Colonel Chivington and Governor John

Evans, with the long-distance aid of General Curtis, were forced to make their own plans and execute them.

As early as June, Governor Evans began his corrective measures, appealing first to Washington for permission to raise extra troops, and then endeavoring to separate the friendly and warlike Indians in order that the former "should not fall victims to the impossibility of soldiers discriminating between them and the hostile, upon whom they must, to do any good, inflict the most severe chastisement." To this end, and with the consent of the Indian Department, he sent out a proclamation, addressed to "the friendly Indians of the Plains," directing them to keep away from those who were at war, and as evidence of friendship to congregate around the agencies for safety. Forts Lyons, Laramie, Larned, and Camp Collins were designated as concentration points for the several tribes. "None but those who intend to be friendly with the whites must come to these places. The families of those who have gone to war with the whites must be kept away from among the friendly Indians. The war on hostile Indians will be continued until they are all effectually subdued." The Indians, frankly at war, paid no attention to this invitation. Two small bands only sought the cover of the agencies, and with their exception, so Governor Evans reported on October 15, the proclamation "met no response from any of the Indians of the plains."

The war parties became larger and more general as the summer advanced, driving whites off the plains between the two trails for several hundred miles. But as fall approached, the tribes as usual sought peace. The Indians' time for war was summer. Without supplies, they were unable to fight through the winter, so that autumn brought them into a mood well disposed to peace, reservations, and government rations. Major Colley, the agent on the Sand Creek reserve at Fort Lyon, received an overture early in September. In a letter written for them on August 29, by a trader, Black Kettle, of the Cheyenne, and other chiefs declared their readiness to make a peace if all the tribes were included in it. As an olive branch, they offered to give up seven white prisoners. They admitted that five war parties, three Cheyenne and two Arapaho, were yet in the field.

Upon receipt of Black Kettle's letter, Major E. W. Wynkoop, military commander at Fort Lyon, marched with 130 men to the Cheyenne camp at Bend of Timbers, some eighty miles northeast of Fort Lyons. Here he found "from six to eight hundred Indian warriors drawn up in line of battle and prepared to fight." He avoided fighting, demanded and received the prisoners, and held a council with the chiefs. Here he told them that he had no authority to conclude a peace, but offered to conduct a group of chiefs to Denver, for a conference with Governor Evans.

On September 28, Governor Evans held a council

with the Cheyenne and Arapaho chiefs brought in by Major Wynkoop; Black Kettle and White Antelope being the most important. Black Kettle opened the conference with an appeal to the governor in which he alluded to his delivery of the prisoners and Wynkoop's invitation to visit Denver. "We have come with our eyes shut, following his handful of men, like coming through the fire," Black Kettle went on. "All we ask is that we may have peace with the whites. We want to hold you by the hand. You are our father. We have been travelling through a cloud. The sky has been dark ever since the war began. These braves who are with me are all willing to do what I say. We want to take good tidings home to our people, that they may sleep in peace. I want you to give all these chiefs of the soldiers here to understand that we are for peace, and that we have made peace, that we may not be mistaken by them for enemies." To him Governor Evans responded that this submission was a long time coming, and that the nation had gone to war, refusing to listen to overtures of peace. This Black Kettle admitted.

"So far as making a treaty now is concerned," continued Governor Evans, "we are in no condition to do it. . . . You, so far, have had the advantage; but the time is near at hand when the plains will swarm with United States soldiers. I have learned that you understand that as the whites are at war among themselves, you think you can now drive the whites from this country; but this reliance is false. The Great Father at Washington has men enough to drive all the Indians off the plains, and whip the rebels at the same time. Now the war with the whites is nearly through, and the Great Father will not know what to do with all his soldiers, except to send them after the Indians on the plains. My proposition to the friendly Indians has gone out; [I] shall be glad to have them all come in under it. I have no new proposition to make. Another reason that I am not in a condition to make a treaty is that war is begun, and the power to make a treaty of peace has passed to the great war chief." He further counselled them to make terms with the military authorities before they could hope to talk of peace. No prospect of an immediate treaty was given to the chiefs. Evans disclaimed further powers, and Colonel Chivington closed the council, saying: "I am not a big war chief, but all the soldiers in this country are at my command. My rule of fighting white men or Indians is to fight them until they lay down their arms and submit." The same evening came a despatch from Major-general Curtis, at Fort Leavenworth, confirming the non-committal attitude of Evans and Chivington: "I want no peace till the Indians suffer more. . . . I fear Agent of the Interior Department will be ready to make presents too soon. . . . No peace must be made without my directions."

The chiefs were escorted home without their peace or any promise of it, Governor Evans believing that

s

the great body of the tribes was still hostile, and that a decisive winter campaign was needed to destroy their lingering notion that the whites might be driven from the plains.   Black Kettle had been advised at the council to surrender to the soldiers, Major Wynkoop at Fort Lyon being mentioned as most available.   Many of his tribe acted on the suggestion, so that on October 20 Agent Colley, their constant friend, reported that "nearly all the Arapahoes are now encamped near this place and desire to remain friendly, and make reparation for the damages committed by them."

The Indians unquestionably were ready to make peace after their fashion and according to their ability.   There is no evidence that they were reconciled to their defeat, but long experience had accustomed them to fighting in the summer and drawing rations as peaceful in the winter.   The young men, in part, were still upon the war-path, but the tribes and the head chiefs were anxious to go upon a winter basis.   Their interpreter who had attended the conference swore that they left Denver, "perfectly contented, deeming that the matter was settled," that upon their return to Fort Lyon, Major Wynkoop gave them permission to bring their families in under the fort where he could watch them better; and that "accordingly the chiefs went after their families and villages and brought them in, . . . satisfied that they were in perfect security and safety."

While the Indians gathered around the fort, Major Wynkoop sent to General Curtis for advice and orders respecting them. Before the orders arrived, however, he was relieved from command and Major Scott J. Anthony, of the First Colorado Cavalry, was detailed in his place. After holding a conference with the Indians and Anthony, in which the latter renewed the permission for the bands to camp near the fort, he left Fort Lyons on November 26. Anthony meanwhile had become convinced that he was exceeding his authority. First he disarmed the savages, receiving only a few old and worn-out weapons. Then he returned these and ordered the Indians away from Fort Lyons. They moved forty miles away and encamped on Sand Creek.

The Colorado authorities had no idea of calling it a peace. Governor Evans had scolded Wynkoop for bringing the chiefs in to Denver. He had received special permission and had raised a hundred-day regiment for an Indian campaign. If he should now make peace, Washington would think he had misrepresented the situation and put the government to needless expense. "What shall I do with the third regiment, if I make peace?" he demanded of Wynkoop. They were "raised to kill Indians, and they must kill Indians."

Acting on the supposition that the war was still on, Colonel Chivington led the Third Colorado, and a part of the First Colorado Cavalry, from 900 to 1000 strong, to Fort Lyons in November, arriving two days after Wynkoop departed. He picketed the fort, to prevent the news of his arrival from getting out, and conferred on the situation with Major Anthony, who, swore Major Downing, wished he would attack the Sand Creek camp and would have done so himself had he possessed troops enough. Three days before, Anthony had given a present to Black Kettle out of his own pocket. As the result of the council of war, Chivington started from Fort Lyon at nine o'clock, on the night of the 28th.

About daybreak on November 29 Chivington's force reached the Cheyenne village on Sand Creek, where Black Kettle, White Antelope, and some 500 of their band, mostly women and children, were encamped in the belief that they had made their peace. They had received no pledge of this, but past practice explained their confidence. The village was surrounded by troops who began to fire as soon as it was light. "We killed as many as we could; the village was destroyed and burned," declared Downing, who further professed, "I think and earnestly believe the Indians to be an obstacle to civilization, and should be exterminated." White Antelope was killed at the first attack, refusing to leave the field, stating that it was the fault of Black Kettle, others, and himself that occasioned the massacre, and that he would die. Black Kettle, refusing to leave the field, was carried off by his young men. The latter had raised an American flag and a white flag in his effort to stop the fight.

The firing began, swore interpreter Smith, on the northeast side of Sand Creek, near Black Kettle's lodge. Driven thence, the disorderly horde of savages retreated to War Bonnet's lodge at the upper end of the village, some few of them armed but most making no resistance. Up the dry bottom of Sand Creek they ran, with the troops in wild charge close behind. In the hollows of the banks they sought refuge, but the soldiers dragged them out, killing seventy or eighty with the worst barbarities Smith had seen: "All manner of depredations were inflicted on their persons; they were scalped, their brains knocked out; the men used their knives, ripped open women, clubbed little children, knocked them in the head with their guns, beat their brains out, mutilated their bodies in every sense of the word." The affidavits of soldiers engaged in the attack are printed in the government documents. They are too disgusting to be more than referred to elsewhere.

Here at last was the culmination of the plains war of 1864 in the "Chivington massacre," which has been the centre of bitter controversy ever since its heroes marched into Denver with their bloody trophies. It was without question Indian fighting at its worst, yet it was successful in that the Indian hostilities stopped and a new treaty was easily obtained by the whites in 1865. The East denounced Chivington, and the Indian Commissioner described the event in 1865 as a butchery "in cold blood by troops in the service of the United States." "Comment cannot magnify the horror," said the *Nation*. The heart of the question had to do with the matter of good faith. At no time did the military or Colorado authorities admit or even appear to admit that the war was over. They regarded the campaign as punitive and necessary for the foundation of a secure peace. The Indians, on the other hand, believed that they had surrendered and were anxious to be let alone. Too often their wish in similar cases had been gratified, to the prolongation of destructive wars. What here occurred was horrible from any standard of civilized criticism. But even among civilized nations war is an unpleasant thing, and war with savages is most merciful, in the long run, when it speaks the savages' own tongue with no uncertain accent. That such extreme measures could occur was the result of the impossible situation on the plains. "My opinion," said Agent Colley, "is that white men and wild Indians cannot live in the same country in peace." With several different and diverging authorities over them, with a white population wanting their reserves and anxious for a provocation that might justify retaliation upon them, little difficulties were certain to lead to big results. It was true that the tribes were being dispossessed of lands which they believed to belong to them. It was equally true that an Indian war could terrify a whole frontier and that stern repression was its best cure. The blame which was accorded to Chivington left out of account the terror in

Colorado, which was no less real because the whites were the aggressors. The slaughter and mutilation of Indian women and children did much to embitter Eastern critics, who did not realize that the only way to crush an Indian war is to destroy the base of supplies, — the camp where the women are busy helping to keep the men in the field; and who overlooked also the fact that in the mêlée the squaws were quite as dangerous as the bucks. Indiscriminate blame and equally indiscriminate praise have been accorded because of the Sand Creek affair. The terrible event was the result of the orderly working of causes over which individuals had little control.

In October, 1865, a peace conference was held on the Little Arkansas at which terms were agreed upon with Apache, Kiowa and Comanche, Arapaho and Cheyenne, while the last named surrendered their reserve at Sand Creek. For four years after this, owing to delays in the Senate and ambiguity in the agreements, they had no fixed abode. Later they were given room in the Indian Territory in lands taken from the civilized tribes.

CHAPTER XVI

THE SIOUX WAR

THE struggle for the possession of the plains worked the displacement of the Indian tribes. At the beginning, the invasion of Kansas had undone the work accomplished in erecting the Indian frontier. The occupation of Minnesota led surely to the downfall and transportation of the Sioux of the Mississippi. Gold in Colorado attracted multitudes who made peace impossible for the Indians of the southern plains. The Sioux of the northern plains came within the influence of the overland march in the same years with similar results.

The northern Sioux, commonly known as the Sioux of the plains, and distinguished from their relatives the Sioux of the Mississippi, had participated in the treaty of Fort Laramie in 1851, had granted rights of transit to the whites, and had been recognized themselves as nomadic bands occupying the plains north of the Platte River. Heretofore they had had no treaty relations with the United States, being far beyond the frontier. Their people, 16,000 perhaps, were grouped roughly in various bands: Brulé, Yankton, Yanktonai, Blackfoot, Hunkpapa, Sans

Arcs, and Miniconjou. Their dependence on the chase made them more dependent on the annuities provided them at Laramie. As the game diminished the annuity increased in relative importance, and scarcely made a fair equivalent for what they lost. Yet on the whole, they imitated their neighbors, the Cheyenne and Arapaho, and kept the peace.

Almost the only time that the pledge was broken was in the autumn of 1854. Continual trains of immigrants passing through the Sioux country made it nearly impossible to prevent friction between the races in which the blame was quite likely to fall upon the timorous homeseekers. On August 17, 1854, a cow strayed away from a band of Mormons encamped a few miles from Fort Laramie. Some have it that the cow was lame, and therefore abandoned; but whatever the cause, the cow was found, killed, and eaten by a small band of hungry Miniconjou Sioux. The charge of theft was brought into camp at Laramie, not by the Mormons, but by The Bear, chief of the Brulé, and Lieutenant Grattan with an escort of twenty-nine men, a twelve-pounder and a mountain howitzer, was sent out the next day to arrest the Indian who had slaughtered the animal. At the Indian village the culprit was not forthcoming, Grattan's drunken interpreter roughened a diplomacy which at best was none too tactful, and at last the troops fired into the lodge which was said to contain the offender. No one of the troops got away from the enraged Sioux, who, after their anger had led them to retaliate, followed it up by plundering the near-by post of the fur company. Commissioner Manypenny believed that this action by the troops was illegal and unnecessary from the start, since the Mormons could legally have been reimbursed from the Indian funds by the agent.

No general war followed this outbreak. A few braves went on the warpath and rumors of great things reached the East, but General Harney, sent out with three regiments to end the Sioux war in 1855, found little opposition and fought only one important battle. On the Little Blue Water, in September, 1855, he fell upon Little Thunder's band of Brulé Sioux and killed or wounded nearly a hundred of them. There is some doubt whether this band had anything to do with the Grattan episode, or whether it was even at war, but the defeat was, as Agent Twiss described it, "a thunderclap to them." For the first time they learned the mighty power of the United States, and General Harney made good use of this object lesson in the peace council which he held with them in March, 1856. The treaty here agreed upon was never legalized, and remained only a sort of *modus vivendi* for the following years. The Sioux tribes were so loosely organized that the authority of the chiefs had little weight; young braves did as they pleased regardless of engagements supposed to bind the tribes. But the lesson of the defeat lasted long in the memory of the plains tribes, so that they gave little trouble until the wars of 1864 broke out. Meanwhile Chouteau's old Fort Pierre on the Missouri was bought by the United States and made a military post for the control of these upper tribes.

Before the plains Sioux broke out again, the Minnesota uprising had led the Mississippi Sioux to their defeat. Some were executed in the fall of 1862, others were transported to the Missouri Valley; still others got away to the Northwest, there to continue a profitless war that kept up fighting for several years. Meanwhile came the plains war of 1864 in which the tribes south of the Platte were chiefly concerned, and in which men at the centre of the line thought there were evidences of an alliance between northern and southern tribes. Thus Governor Evans wrote of "information furnished me, through various sources, of an alliance of the Cheyenne and a part of the Arapahoe tribes with the Comanche, Kiowa, and Apache Indians of the south, and the great family of the Sioux Indians of the north upon the plains," and the Indian Commissioner accepted the notion. But, like the question of intrigue, this was a matter of belief rather than of proof; while local causes to account for the disorder are easily found. Yet it is true that during 1864 and 1865 the northern Sioux became uneasy.

During 1865, though the causes likely to lead to hostilities were in no wise changed, efforts were made to reach agreements with the plains tribes. The Cheyenne, humbled at Sand Creek, were readily handled at the Little Arkansas treaty in October. They there surrendered to the United States all their reserve in Colorado and accepted a new one, which they never actually received, south of the Arkansas, and bound themselves not to camp within ten miles of the route to Sante Fé. On the other side, "to heal the wounds caused by the Chivington affair," special appropriations were made by the United States to the widows and orphans of those who had been killed. The Apache, Kiowa, and Comanche joined in similar treaties. During the same week, in 1865, a special commission made treaties of peace with nine of the Sioux tribes, including the remnants of the Mississippi bands. " These treaties were made," commented the Commissioner, "and the Indians, in spite of the great suffering from cold and want of food endured during the very severe winter of 1865–66, and consequent temptation to plunder to procure the absolute necessaries of life, faithfully kept the peace."

In September, 1865, the steamer *Calypso* struggled up the shallow Missouri River, carrying a party of commissioners to Fort Sully, there to make these treaties with the Sioux. Congress had provided $20,000 for a special negotiation before adjourning in March, 1865, and General Sully, who was yet conducting the prolonged Sioux War, had pointed out the place most suitable for the conference. The first council was held on October 6.

The military authorities were far from eager to hold

this council. Already the breach between the military power responsible for policing the plains and the civilian department which managed the tribes was wide. Thus General Pope, commanding the Department of the Missouri, grumbled to Grant in June that whenever Indian hostilities occurred, the Indian Department, which was really responsible, blamed the soldiers for causing them. He complained of the divided jurisdiction and of the policy of buying treaties from the tribes by presents made at the councils. In reference to this special treaty he had "only to say that the Sioux Indians have been attacking everybody in their region of country; and only lately . . . attacked in heavy force Fort Rice, on the upper Missouri, well fortified and garrisoned by four companies of infantry with artillery. If these things show any desire for peace, I confess I am not able to perceive it."

In future years this breach was to become wider yet. At Sand Creek the military authorities had justified the attack against the criticism of the local Indian agents and Eastern philanthropists. There was indeed plenty of evidence of misconduct on both sides. If the troops were guilty on the charge of being over-ready to fight — and here the words of Governor Evans were prophetic, "Now the war . . . is nearly through, and the Great Father will not know what to do with all his soldiers, except to send them after the Indians on the plains," — the Indian agents often succumbed to the opportunity for petty thieving. The case of one of the agents of the Yankton Sioux illustrates this. It was his custom each year to have the chiefs of his tribe sign general receipts for everything sent to the agency. Thus at the end of the year he could turn in Indians' vouchers and report nothing on hand. But the receipt did not mean that the Indian had got the goods; although signed for, these were left in the hands of the agent to be given out as needed. The inference is strong that many of the supplies intended for and signed for by the Indians went into the pocket of the agent. During the third quarter of 1863 this agent claimed to have issued to his charges: "One pair of bay horses, 7 years old; . . . 1 dozen 17-inch mill files; . . . 6 dozen Seidlitz powders; 6 pounds compound syrup of squills; 6 dozen Ayer's pills; . . . 3 bottles of rose water; . . . 1 pound of wax; . . . 1 ream of vouchers; . . . $\frac{1}{2}$ M 6434 8$\frac{1}{2}$-inch official envelopes; . . . 4 bottles 8-ounce mucilage." So great was this particular agent's power that it was nearly impossible to get evidence against him. "If I do, he will fix it so I'll never get anything in the world and he will drive me out of the country," was typical of the attitude of his neighbors.

With jurisdiction divided, and with claimants for it quarrelling, it is no wonder that the charges suffered. But the ill results came more from the impossible situation than from abuse on either side. It needs often to be reiterated that the heart of the Indian question was in the infiltration of greedy, timorous, enterprising, land-hungry whites who could not be restrained by any process known to American government. In the conflict between two civilizations, the lower must succumb. Neither the War Department nor the Indian Office was responsible for most of the troubles; yet of the two, the former, through readiness to fight and to hold the savage to a standard of warfare which he could not understand, was the greater offender. It was not so great an offender, however, as the selfish interests of those engaged in trading with the Indians would make it out to be.

The Fort Sully conference, terminating in a treaty signed on October 10, 1865, was distinctly unsatisfactory. Many of the western Sioux did 'not come at all. Even the eastern were only partially represented. And among tribes in which the central authority of the chiefs was weak, full representation was necessary to secure a binding peace. The commissioners, after most pacific efforts, were "unable to ascertain the existence of any really amicable feeling among these people towards the government." The chiefs were sullen and complaining, and the treaty which resulted did little more than repeat the terms of the treaty of 1851, binding the Indians to permit roads to be opened through their country and to keep away from the trails.

It is difficult to show that the northern Sioux were bound by the treaty of Fort Sully. The Laramie treaty of 1851 had never had full force of law because the Senate had added amendments to it, which all the signatory Indians had not accepted. Although Congress had appropriated the annuities specified in the treaty the binding force of the document was not great on savages. The Fort Sully treaty was deficient in that it did not represent all of the interested tribes. In making Indian treaties at all, the United States acted upon a convenient fiction that the Indians had authorities with power to bind; whereas the leaders had little control over their followers and after nearly every treaty there were many bands that could claim to have been left out altogether. Yet such as they were, the treaties existed, and the United States proceeded in 1865 and 1866 to use its specified rights in opening roads through the hunting-grounds of the Sioux.

The mines of Montana and Idaho, which had attracted notice and emigration in the early sixties, were still the objective points of a large traffic. They were somewhat off the beaten routes, being accessible by the Missouri River and Fort Benton, or by the Platte trail and a northern branch from near Fort Hall to Virginia City. To bring them into more direct connection with the East an available route from Fort Laramie was undertaken in 1865. The new trail left the main road near Fort Laramie, crossed to the north side of the Platte, and ran off to the northwest. Shortly after leaving the Platte the road got into the charming foothill country where the slopes "are all covered with a fine growth of grass, and in every valley there is either a rushing stream or some quiet babbling brook of pure, clear snow-water filled with trout, the banks lined with trees — wild cherry, quaking asp, some birch, willow, and cottonwood." To the left, and not far distant, were the Big Horn Mountains. To the right could sometimes be seen in the distance the shadowy billows of the Black Hills. Running to the north and draining the valley were the Powder and Tongue rivers, both tributaries of the Yellowstone. Here were water, timber, and forage, coal and oil and game. It was the garden spot of the Indians, "the very heart of their hunting-grounds." In a single day's ride were seen "bear, buffalo, elk, deer, antelope, rabbits, and sage-hens." With little exaggeration it was described as a "natural source of recuperation and supply to moving, hunting, and roving bands of all tribes, and their lodge trails cross it in great numbers from north to south." Through this land, keeping east of the Big Horn Mountains and running around their northern end into the Yellowstone Valley, was to run the new Powder River road to Montana. The Sioux treaties were to have their severest testing in the selection of choice hunting-grounds for an emigrant road, for it was one of the certainties in the opening of new roads that game vanished in the face of emigration.

While the commissioners were negotiating their treaty at Fort Sully, the first Powder River expedition, in its attempt to open this new road by the short

T

and direct route from Fort Laramie to Bozeman and
the Montana mines, was undoing their work. In the
summer of 1865 General Patrick E. Connor, with a
miscellaneous force of 1600, including a detachment
of ex-Confederate troops who had enlisted in the
United States army to fight Indians, started from
Fort Laramie for the mouth of the Rosebuds on the
Yellowstone, by way of the Powder River. Old Jim
Bridger, the incarnation of this country, led them,
swearing mightily at "these damn paper-collar
soldiers," who knew so little of the Indians. There
was plenty of fighting as Connor pushed into the
Yellowstone, but he was relieved from command in
September and the troops were drawn back, so that
there were no definitive results of the expedition of
1865.

In 1866, in spite of the fact that the Sioux of this
region, through their leader Red Cloud, had refused
to yield the ground or even to treat concerning it,
Colonel Henry B. Carrington was ordered by General
Pope to command the Mountain District, Department of the Platte, and to erect and garrison posts
for the control of the Powder River road. On December 21 of this year, Captain W. J. Fetterman,
of his command, and seventy-eight officers and men
were killed near Fort Philip Kearney in a fight whose
merits aroused nearly as much acrimonious discussion as the Sand Creek massacre.

The events leading up to the catastrophe at Fort
Philip Kearney, a catastrophe so complete that none

of its white participants escaped to tell what happened, were connected with Carrington's work in building forts. He had been detailed for the work in the spring, and after a conference at Fort Kearney, Nebraska, with General Sherman, had marched his men in nineteen days to Fort Laramie. He reached Fort Reno, which became his headquarters, on June 28. On the march, if his orders were obeyed, his soldiers were scrupulous in their regard for the Indians. His orders issued for the control of emigrants passing along the Powder River route were equally careful. Thirty men were to constitute the minimum single party; these were to travel with a military pass, which was to be scrutinized by the commanding officer of each post. The trains were ordered to hold together and were warned that "nearly all danger from Indians lies in the recklessness of travellers. A small party, when separated, either sell whiskey to or fire upon scattering Indians, or get into disputes with them, and somebody is hurt. An insult to an Indian is resented by the Indians against the first white men they meet, and innocent travellers suffer."

Carrington's orders were to garrison Fort Reno and build new forts on the Powder, Big Horn, and Yellowstone rivers, and cover the road. The last-named fort was later cut away because of his insufficient force, but Fort Philip Kearney and Fort C. F. Smith were located during July and August. The former stood on a little plateau formed between the two Pineys as they emerge from the Big Horn Mountains.   Its site was surveyed and occupied on July 15. Already Carrington was complaining that he had too few men for his work.   With eight companies of eighty men each, and most of these new recruits, he had to garrison his long line, all the while building and protecting his stockades and fortifications.   " I am my own engineer, draughtsman, and visit my pickets and guards nightly, with scarcely a day or night without attempts to steal stock."   Worse than this, his military equipment was inadequate.   Only his band, specially armed for the expedition, had Spencer carbines and enough ammunition.   His main force, still armed with Springfield rifles, had under fifty rounds to the man.

The Indians, Cheyenne and Sioux, were, all through the summer, showing no sign of accepting the invasion of the hunting-grounds without a fight.   Yet Carrington reported on August 29 that he was holding them off; that Fort C. F. Smith on the Big Horn had been occupied; that parties of fifty well-armed men could get through safely if they were careful. The Indians, he said, "are bent on robbery; they only fight when assured of personal security and remunerative stealings; they are divided among themselves."

With the sites for forts C. F. Smith and Philip Kearney selected, the work of construction proceeded during the autumn.   A sawmill, sent out from the states, was kept hard at work.   Wood was cut on the adjacent hills and speedily converted into cabins and palisades which approached completion before winter set in. It was construction during a state of siege, however. Instead of pacifying the valley the construction of the forts aggravated the Sioux hostility so that constant watchfulness was needed. That the trains sent out to gather wood were not seriously injured was due to rigorous discipline. The wagons moved twenty or more at a time, with guards, and in two parallel columns. At first sight of Indians they drove into corral and signalled back to the lookouts at the fort for help. Occasionally men were indeed cut out by the Indians, who in turn suffered considerable loss; but Carrington reduced his own losses to a minimum. Friendly Indians were rarely seen. They were allowed to come to the fort, by the main road and with a white flag, but few availed themselves of the privilege. The Sioux were up in arms, and in large numbers hung about the Tongue and Powder river valleys waiting for their chance.

Early in December occurred an incident revealing the danger of annihilation which threatened Carrington's command. At one o'clock on the afternoon of the sixth a messenger reported to the garrison at Fort Philip Kearney that the wood train was attacked by Indians four miles away. Carrington immediately had every horse at the post mounted. For the main relief he sent out a column under Brevet Lieutenant-colonel Fetterman, who had just arrived at the fort, while he led in person a flanking party to cut off the Indians' retreat. The mercury was below zero. Carrington was thrown into the water of Peno Creek when his horse stumbled through breaking ice. Fetterman's party found the wood train in corral and standing off the attack with success. The savages retreated as the relief approached and were pursued for five miles, when they turned and offered battle. Just as the fighting began, most of the cavalry broke away from Fetterman, leaving him and some fourteen others surrounded by Indians and attacked on three sides. He held them off, however, until Carrington came in sight and the Indians fled. Why Lieutenant Bingham retreated with his cavalry and left Fetterman in such danger was never explained, for the Indians killed him and one of his non-commissioned officers, while several other privates were wounded. The Indians, once the fight was over, disappeared among the hills, and Carrington had no force with which to follow them. In reporting the battle that night he renewed his requests for men and officers. He had but six officers for the six companies at Fort Philip Kearney. He was totally unable to take the aggressive because of the defences which had constantly to be maintained.

In this fashion the fall advanced in the Powder River Valley. The forts were finished. The Indian hostilities increased. The little, overworked force of Carrington, chopping, building, guarding, and fighting, struggled to fulfil its orders. If one should criticise Carrington, the attack would be chiefly that he looked to defensive measures in the Indian war. He did indeed ask for troops, officers, and equipment, but his despatches and his own vindication show little evidence that he realized the need for large reënforcements for the specific purpose of a punitive campaign. More skilful Indian fighters knew that the Indians could and would keep up indefinitely this sort of filibustering against the forts, and that a vigorous move against their own villages was the surest means to secure peace. In Indian warfare, even more perhaps than in civilized, it is advantageous to destroy the enemy's base of supplies.

The wood train was again attacked on December 21. About eleven o'clock that morning the pickets reported the train "corralled and threatened by Indians on Sullivant Hills, a mile and a half from the fort." The usual relief party was at once organized and sent out under Fetterman, who claimed the right to command it by seniority, and who was not highest in the confidence of Colonel Carrington. He had but recently joined the command, was full of enthusiasm and desire to hunt Indians, and needed the admonition with which he left the fort: that he was "fighting brave and desperate enemies who sought to make up by cunning and deceit all the advantage which the white man gains by intelligence and better arms." He was ordered to support and bring in the wood train, this being all Carrington believed himself strong enough to do and keep on doing.   Any one could have had a fight at any time, and Carrington was wise to issue the "peremptory and explicit" orders to avoid pursuit beyond the summit of Lodge Trail Ridge, as needless and unduly dangerous.   Three times this order was given to Fetterman; and after that, "fearing still that the spirit of ambition might override prudence," says Carrington, "I crossed the parade and from a sentry platform halted the cavalry and again repeated my precise orders."

With these admonitions, Fetterman started for the relief, leading a party of eighty-one officers and men, picked and all well armed.   He crossed the Lodge Trail Ridge as soon as he was out of sight of the fort and disappeared.   No one of his command came back alive.   The wood train, before twelve o'clock, broke corral and moved on in safety, while shots were heard beyond the ridge.   For half an hour there was a constant volleying; then all was still.   Meanwhile Carrington, nervous at the lack of news from Fetterman, had sent a second column, and two wagons to relieve him, under Captain Ten Eyck. The latter, moving along cautiously, with large bands of Sioux retreating before him, came finally upon forty-nine bodies, including that of Fetterman.   The evidence of arrows, spears, and the position of bodies was that they had been surrounded, surprised, and overwhelmed in their defeat.   The next day the rest of the bodies were reached and brought back. Naked, dismembered, slashed, visited with indescribable indignities, they were buried in two great graves; seventy-nine soldiers and two civilians.

The Fetterman massacre raised a storm in the East similar in volume to that following Sand Creek, two years before. Who was at fault, and why, were the questions indignantly asked. Judicious persons were well aware, wrote the *Nation*, that "our whole Indian policy is a system of mismanagement, and in many parts one of gigantic abuse." The military authorities tried to place the blame on Carrington, as plausible, energetic, and industrious, but unable to maintain discipline or inspire his officers with confidence. Unquestionably a part of this was true, yet the letter which made the charge admitted that often the Indians were better armed than the troops, and the critic himself, General Cooke, had ordered Carrington: "You can only defend yourself and trains, and emigrants, the best you can." The Indian Commissioner charged it on the bad disposition of the troops, always anxious to fight.

The issue broke over the number of Indians involved. Current reports from Fort Philip Kearney indicated from 3000 to 5000 hostile warriors, chiefly Sioux and led by Red Cloud of the Oglala tribe. The Commissioner pointed out that such a force must imply from 21,000 to 35,000 Indians in all — a number that could not possibly have been in the Powder River country. It is reasonable to believe that Fetterman was not overwhelmed by any multitude like this, but that his own rash disobedience led

to ambush and defeat by a force well below 3000.
Upon him fell the immediate responsibility; above
him, the War Department was negligent in detail-
ing so few men for so large a task; and ultimately
there was the impossibility of expecting savage Sioux
to give up their best hunting-grounds as a result of
a treaty signed by others than themselves.

The fight at Fort Philip Kearney marked a point of
transition in Indian warfare.   Even here the Indians
were mostly armed with bows and arrows, and were
relying upon their superior numbers for victory.
Yet a change in Indian armament was under way,
which in a few years was to convert the Indian from
a savage warrior into the "finest natural soldier in
the world."   He was being armed with rifles.   As
the game diminished the tribes found that the old
methods of hunting were inadequate and began the
pressure upon the Indian Department for better
weapons.   The department justified itself in issuing
rifles and ammunition, on the ground that the laws
of the United States expected the Indians to live
chiefly upon game, which they could not now procure by the older means.   Hence came the anomalous situation in which one department of the
United States armed and equipped the tribes for
warfare against another.   If arms were cut down,
the tribes were in danger of extinction; if they
were issued, hostilities often resulted.   After the
Fetterman massacre the Indian Office asserted that
the hostile Sioux were merely hungry, because the

War Department had caused the issuing of guns to be stopped. It was all an unsolvable problem, with bad temper and suspicion on both sides.

A few months after the Fetterman affair Red Cloud tried again to wreck a wood train near Fort Philip Kearney. But this time the escort erected a barricade with the iron, bullet-proof bodies of a new variety of army wagon, and though deserted by most of his men, Major James Powell, with one other officer, twenty-six privates, and four citizens, lay behind their fortification and repelled charge after charge from some 800 Sioux and Cheyenne. With little loss to himself he inflicted upon the savages a lesson that lasted many years.

The Sioux and Cheyenne wars were links in the chain of Indian outbreaks that stretched across the path of the westward movement, the overland traffic and the continental railways. The Pacific railways had been chartered just as the overland telegraph had been opened to the Pacific coast. With this last, perhaps from reverence for the nearly supernatural, the Indians rarely meddled. But as the railway advanced, increasing compression and repression stirred the tribes to a series of hostilities. The first treaties which granted transit — meaning chiefly wagon transit — broke down. A new series of conferences and a new policy were the direct result of these wars.

CHAPTER XVII

THE PEACE COMMISSION AND THE OPEN WAY

THE crisis in the struggle for the control of the great plains may fairly be said to have been reached about the time of the slaughter of Fetterman and his men at Fort Philip Kearney.   During the previous fifteen years the causes had been shaping through the development of the use of the trails, the opening of the mining territories, and the agitation for a continental railway.   Now the railway was not only authorized and begun, but Congress had put a premium upon its completion by an act of July, 1866, which permitted the Union Pacific to build west and the Central Pacific to build east until the two lines should meet.   In the ensuing race for the land grants the roads were pushed with new vigor, so that the crisis of the Indian problem was speedily reached.   In the fall of 1866 Ben Holladay saw the end of the overland freighting and sold out.   In November the terminus of the overland mail route was moved west to Fort Kearney, Nebraska, whither the Union Pacific had now arrived in its course of construction.   No wonder the tribes realized their danger and broke out in protest.

As the crisis drew near radical differences of opinion among those who must handle the tribes became apparent. The question of the management by the War Department or the Interior was in the air, and was raised again and again in Congress. More fundamental was the question of policy, upon which the view of Senator John Sherman was as clear as any. " I agree with you," he wrote to his brother William, in 1867, " that Indian wars will not cease until all the Indian tribes are absorbed in our population, and can be controlled by constables instead of soldiers." Upon another phase of management Francis A. Walker wrote a little later : "There can be no question of national dignity involved in the treatment of savages by a civilized power. The proudest Anglo-Saxon will climb a tree with a bear behind him. . . . With wild men, as with wild beasts, the question whether to fight, coax, or run is a question merely of what is safest or easiest in the situation given." That responsibility for some decided action lay heavily upon the whites may be implied from the admission of Colonel Henry Inman, who knew the frontier well — "that, during more than a third of a century passed on the plains and in the mountains, he has never known of a war with the hostile tribes that was not caused by broken faith on the part of the United States or its agents." A professional Indian fighter, like Kit Carson, declared on oath that "as a general thing, the difficulties arise from aggressions on the part of the whites."

In Congress all the interests involved in the Indian

problem found spokesmen. The War and Interior departments had ample representation; the Western members commonly voiced the extreme opinion of the frontier; Eastern men often spoke for the humanitarian sentiment that saw much good in the Indian and much evil in his treatment. But withal, when it came to special action upon any situation, Congress felt its lack of information. The departments best informed were partisan and antagonistic. Even to-day it is a matter of high critical scholarship to determine, with the passions cooled off, truth and responsibility in such affairs as the Minnesota outbreak, and the Chivington or the Fetterman massacre. To lighten in part its feeling of helplessness in the midst of interested parties Congress raised a committee of seven, three of the Senate and four of the House, in March, 1865, to investigate and report on the condition of the Indian tribes. The joint committee was resolved upon during a bitter and ill-informed debate on Chivington; while it sat, the Cheyenne war ended and the Sioux broke out; the committee reported in January, 1867. To facilitate its investigation it divided itself into three groups to visit the Pacific Slope, the southern plains, and the northern plains. Its report, with the accompanying testimony, fills over five hundred pages. In all the storm centres of the Indian West the committee sat, listened, and questioned.

The *Report on the Condition of the Indian Tribes* gave a doleful view of the future from the Indians'

standpoint. General Pope was quoted to the effect
that the savages were rapidly dying off from wars,
cruel treatment, unwise policy, and dishonest administration, "and by steady and resistless encroachments of the white emigration towards the west, which
is every day confining the Indians to narrower limits,
and driving off or killing the game, their only means
of subsistence." To this catalogue of causes General
Carleton, who must have believed his war of Apache
and Navaho extermination a potent handmaid of
providence, added: "The causes which the Almighty
originates, when in their appointed time He wills
that one race of man — as in races of lower animals —
shall disappear off the face of the earth and give place
to another race, and so on, in the great cycle traced
out by Himself, which may be seen, but has reasons
too deep to be fathomed by us. The races of mam-
moths and mastodons, and the great sloths, came
and passed away; the red man of America is passing away!"

The committee believed that the wars with their
incidents of slaughter and extermination by both sides,
as occasion offered, were generally the result of white
encroachments. It did not fall in with the growing
opinion that the control of the tribes should be passed
over to the War Department, but recommended instead a system of visiting boards, each including a
civilian, a soldier, and an Assistant Indian Commissioner, for the regular inspection of the tribes. The
recommendation of the committee came to naught

in Congress, but the information it gathered, supplementing the annual reports of the Commissioner of Indian Affairs and the special investigations of single wars, gave much additional weight to the belief that a crisis was at hand.

Meanwhile, through 1866 and 1867, the Cheyenne and Sioux wars dragged on. The Powder River country continued to be a field of battle, with Powell's fight coming in the summer of 1867. In the spring of 1867 General Hancock destroyed a Cheyenne village at Pawnee Fork. Eastern opinion came to demand more forcefully that this fighting should stop. Western opinion was equally insistent that the Indian must go, while General Sherman believed that a part of its bellicose demand was due to a desire for "the profit resulting from military occupation." Certain it was that war had lasted for several years with no definite results, save to rouse the passions of the West, the revenge of the Indians, and the philanthropy of the East. The army had had its chance. Now the time had come for general, real attempts at peace.

The fortieth Congress, beginning its life on March 4, 1867, actually began its session at that time. Ordinarily it would have waited until December, but the prevailing distrust of President Johnson and his reconstruction ideas induced it to convene as early as the law allowed. Among the most significant of its measures in this extra session was "Mr. Henderson's bill for establishing peace with certain Indian tribes now at war with the United States," which, in the view of the *Nation*, was a "practical measure for the security of travel through the territories and for the selection of a new area sufficient to contain all the unsettled tribes east of the Rocky Mountains." Senator Sherman had informed his brother of the prospect of this law, and the General had replied: "The fact is, this contact of the two races has caused universal hostility, and the Indians operate in small, scattered bands, avoiding the posts and well-guarded trains and hitting little parties who are off their guard. I have a much heavier force on the plains, but they are so large that it is impossible to guard at all points, and the clamor for protection everywhere has prevented our being able to collect a large force to go into the country where we believe the Indians have hid their families; viz. up on the Yellowstone and down on the Red River." Sherman believed more in fighting than in treating at this time, yet he went on the commission erected by the act of July 20, 1867. By this law four civilians, including the Indian Commissioner, and three generals of the army, were appointed to collect and deal with the hostile tribes, with three chief objects in view: to remove the existing causes of complaint, to secure the safety of the various continental railways and the overland routes, and to work out some means for promoting Indian civilization without impeding the advance of the United States. To this last end they were to hunt for permanent homes for the tribes, which were to be off the lines of all

U

the railways then chartered, — the Union Pacific, the Northern Pacific, and the Atlantic and Pacific.

The Peace Commission, thus organized, sat for fifteen months. When it rose at last, it had opened the way for the railways, so far as treaties could avail. It had persuaded many tribes to accept new and more remote reserves, but in its debates and negotiations the breach between military and civil control had widened, so that the Commission was at the end divided against itself.

On August 6, 1867, the Commission organized at St. Louis and discussed plans for getting into touch with the tribes with whom it had to treat. "The first difficulty presenting itself was to secure an interview with the chiefs and leading warriors of these hostile tribes. They were roaming over an immense country, thousands of miles in extent, and much of it unknown even to hunters and trappers of the white race. Small war parties constantly emerging from this vast extent of unexplored country would suddenly strike the border settlements, killing the men and carrying off into captivity the women and children. Companies of workmen on the railroads, at points hundreds of miles from each other, would be attacked on the same day, perhaps in the same hour. Overland mail coaches could not be run without military escort, and railroad and mail stations unguarded by soldiery were in perpetual danger. All safe transit across the plains had ceased. To go without soldiers was hazardous in the extreme; to go with them forbade reasonable hope of securing peaceful interviews with the enemy." Fortunately the Peace Commission contained within itself the most useful of assistants.   General Sherman and Commissioner Taylor sent out word to the Indians through the military posts and Indian agencies, notifying the tribes that the Commissioners desired to confer with them near Fort Laramie in September and Fort Larned in October.

The Fort Laramie conference bore no fruit during the summer of 1867.   After inspecting conditions on the upper Missouri the Commissioners proceeded to Omaha in September and thence to North Platte station on the Union Pacific Railroad.   Here they met Swift Bear of the Brulé Sioux and learned that the Sioux would not be ready to meet them until November.   The Powder River War was still being fought by chiefs who could not be reached easily and whose delegations must be delayed. When the Commissioners returned to Fort Laramie in November, they found matters little better.   Red Cloud, who was the recognized leader of the Oglala and Brulé Sioux and the hostile northern Cheyenne, refused even to see the envoys, and sent them word: "that his war against the whites was to save the valley of the Powder River, the only hunting ground left to his nation, from our intrusion.   He assured us that whenever the military garrisons at Fort Philip Kearney and Fort C. F. Smith were withdrawn, the war on his part would cease."   Regretfully, the

Commissioners left Fort Laramie, having seen no savages except a few non-hostile Crows, and having summoned Red Cloud to meet them during the following summer, after asking " a truce or cessation of hostilities until the council could be held."

The southern plains tribes were met at Medicine Lodge Creek some eighty miles south of the Arkansas River. Before the Commissioners arrived here General Sherman was summoned to Washington, his place being taken by General C. C. Augur, whose name makes the eighth signature to the published report. For some time after the Commissioners arrived the Cheyenne, sullen and suspicious, remained in their camp forty miles away from Medicine Lodge. But the Kiowa, Comanche, and Apache came to an agreement, while the others held off. On the 21st of October these ceded all their rights to occupy their great claims in the Southwest, the whole of the two panhandles of Texas and Oklahoma, and agreed to confine themselves to a new reserve in the southwestern part of Indian Territory, between the Red River and the Washita, on lands taken from the Choctaw and Chickasaw in 1866.

The Commissioners could not greatly blame the Arapaho and Cheyenne for their reluctance to treat. These had accepted in 1861 the triangular Sand Creek reserve in Colorado, where they had been massacred by Chivington in 1864. Whether rightly or not, they believed themselves betrayed, and the

Indian Office sided with them.   In 1865, after Sand
Creek, they exchanged this tract for a new one in
Kansas and Indian Territory, which was amended
to nothingness when the Senate added to the treaty
the words, "no part of the reservation shall be within
the state of Kansas."   They had left the former reserve; the new one had not been given them; yet
for two years after 1865 they had generally kept the
peace.   Sherman travelled through this country in
the autumn of 1866 and " met no trouble whatever,"
although he heard rumors of Indian wars.   In 1867,
General Hancock had destroyed one of their villages
on the Pawnee Fork of the Arkansas, without provocation, the Indians believed.   After this there had
been admitted war.   The Indians had been on the
war-path all the time, plundering the frontier and
dodging the military parties, and were unable for
some weeks to realize that the Peace Commissioners
offered a change of policy.   Yet finally these yielded
to blandishment and overture, and signed, on October 28, a treaty at Medicine Lodge.   The new reserve was a bit of barren land nearly destitute of
wood and water, and containing many streams that
were either brackish or dry during most of the year.
It was in the Cherokee Outlet, between the Arkansas
and Cimarron rivers.

   The Medicine Lodge treaties were the chief result of
the summer's negotiations.   The Peace Commission
returned to Fort Laramie in the following spring to
meet the reluctant northern tribes.   The Sioux, the

Crows, and the Arapaho and Cheyenne who were allied with them, made peace after the Commissioners had assented to the terms laid down by Red Cloud in 1867. They had convinced themselves that the occupation of the Powder River Valley was both illegal and unjust, and accordingly the garrisons had been drawn out of the new forts. Much to the anger of Montana was this yielding. "With characteristic pusillanimity," wrote one of the pioneers, years later, denouncing the act, "the government ordered all the forts abandoned and the road closed to travel." In the new Fort Laramie treaty of April 29, 1868, it was specifically agreed that the country east of the Big Horn Mountains was to be considered as unceded Indian territory; while the Sioux bound themselves to occupy as their permanent home the lands west of the Missouri, between the parallels of 43° and 46°, and east of the 104th meridian — an area coinciding to-day with the western end of South Dakota. Thus was begun the actual compression of the Sioux of the plains.

The treaties made by the Peace Commissioners were the most important, but were not the only treaties of 1867 and 1868, looking towards the relinquishment by the Indians of lands along the railroad's right of way. It had been found that rights of transit through the Indian Country, such as those secured at Laramie in 1851, were insufficient. The Indian must leave even the vicinity of the route of travel, for peace and his own good.

Most important of the other tribes shoved away from the route were the Ute, Shoshoni, and Bannock, whose country lay across the great trail just west of the Rockies. The Ute, having given their name to the territory of Utah, were to be found south of the trail, between it and the lower waters of the Colorado. Their western bands were earliest in negotiation and were settled on reserves, the most important being on the Uintah River in northeast Utah, after 1861. The Colorado Ute began to treat in 1863, but did not make definite cessions until 1868, when the southwestern third of Colorado was set apart for them. Active life in Colorado territory was at the start confined to the mountains in the vicinity of Denver City, while the Indians were pushed down the slopes of the range on both sides. But as the eastern Sand Creek reserve soon had to be abolished, so Colorado began to growl at the western Ute reserve and to complain that indolent savages were given better treatment than white citizens. The Shoshoni and Bannock ranged from Fort Hall to the north and were visited by General Augur at Fort Bridger in the summer of 1868. As the results of his gifts and diplomacy the former were pushed up to the Wind River reserve in Wyoming territory, while the latter were granted a home around Fort Hall.

The friction with the Indians was heaviest near the line of the old Indian frontier and tended to be lighter towards the west. It was natural enough that on the eastern edge of the plains, where the tribes had been colonized and where Indian population was most dense, the difficulties should be greatest. Indeed the only wars which were sufficiently important to count as resistance to the westward movement were those of the plains tribes and were fought east of the continental divide. The mountain and western wars were episodes, isolated from the main movements. Yet these great plains that now had to be abandoned had been set aside as a permanent home for the race in pursuance of Monroe's policy. In the report of the Peace Commissioners all agreed that the time had come to change it.

The influence of the humanitarians dominated the report of the Commissioners, which was signed in January, 1868. Wherever possible, the side of the Indian was taken. The Chivington massacre was an "indiscriminate slaughter," scarcely paralleled in the "records of the Indian barbarity"; General Hancock had ruthlessly destroyed the Cheyenne at Pawnee Fork, though himself in doubt as to the existence of a war: Fetterman had been killed because "the civil and military departments of our government cannot, or will not, understand each other." Apologies were made for Indian hostility, and the "revolting" history of the removal policy was described. It had been the result of this policy to promote barbarism rather than civilization. "But one thing then remains to be done with honor to the nation, and that is to select a district, or districts of country, as indicated by Congress, on which all the tribes east of the Rocky mountains may be gathered. For each district let a territorial government be established, with powers adapted to the ends designed. The governor should be a man of unquestioned integrity and purity of character; he should be paid such salary as to place him above temptation." He should be given adequate powers to keep the peace and enforce a policy of progressive civilization. The belief that under American conditions the Indian problem was insoluble was confirmed by this report of the Peace Commissioners, well informed and philanthropic as they were. After their condemnation of an existing removal policy, the only remedy which they could offer was another policy of concentration and removal.

The Commissioners recommended that the Indians should be colonized on two reserves, north and south of the railway lines respectively. The southern reserve was to be the old territory of the civilized tribes, known as Indian Territory, where the Commissioners thought a total of 86,000 could be settled within a few years. A northern district might be located north of Nebraska, within the area which they later allotted to the Sioux; 54,000 could be colonized here. Individual savages might be allowed to own land and be incorporated among the citizens of the Western states, but most of the tribes ought to be settled in the two Indian territories, while this removal policy should be the last.

Upon the vexed question of civilian or military control the Commissioners were divided. They believed that both War and Interior departments were too busy to give proper attention to the wards, and recommended an independent department for the Indians. In October, 1868, they reversed this report and, under military influence, spoke strongly for the incorporation of the Indian Office in the War Department. "We have now selected and provided reservations for all, off the great roads," wrote General Sherman to his brother in September, 1868. "All who cling to their old hunting-grounds are hostile and will remain so till killed off. We will have a sort of predatory war for years, every now and then be shocked by the indiscriminate murder of travellers and settlers, but the country is so large, and the advantage of the Indians so great, that we cannot make a single war and end it. From the nature of things we must take chances and clean out Indians as we encounter them." Although it was the tendency of military control to provoke Indian wars, the army was near the truth in its notion that Indians and whites could not live together.

The way across the continent was opened by these treaties of 1867 and 1868, and the Union Pacific hurried to take advantage of it. The other Pacific railways, Northern Pacific and Atlantic and Pacific, were so slow in using their charters that hope in their

construction was nearly abandoned, but the chief
enterprise neared completion before the inauguration
of President Grant.   The new territory of Wyoming,
rather than the statue of Columbus which Benton
had foreseen, was perched upon the summit of the
Rockies as its monument.

Intelligent easterners had difficulty in keeping
pace with western development during the decade
of the Civil War.   The United States itself had made
no codification of Indian treaties since 1837, and
allowed the law of tribal relations to remain scattered
through a thousand volumes of government documents.   Even Indian agents and army officers were
often as ignorant of the facts as was the general
public.   "All Americans have some knowledge of
the country west of the Mississippi," lamented the
Nation in 1868, but "there is no book of travel relat-
ing to those regions which does more than add to a
mass of very desultory information.   Few men have
more than the most unconnected and unmethodical
knowledge of the vast expanse of territory which
lies beyond Kansas . . . [By] this time Leavenworth
must have ceased to be in the West; probably,
as we write, Denver has become an Eastern city,
and day by day the Pacific Railroad is abolishing the
marks that distinguish Western from Eastern life. . . .
A man talks to us of the country west of the Rocky
Mountains, and while he is talking, the Territory
of Wyoming is established, of which neither he nor
his auditors have before heard."

In that division of the plains which was sketched out in the fifties, the great amorphous eastern territories of Kansas and Nebraska met on the summit of the Rockies the great western territories of Washington, Utah, and New Mexico. The gold

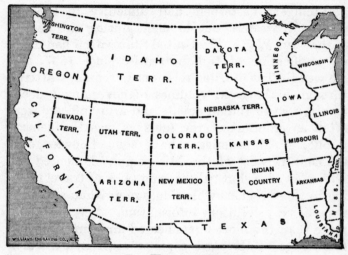

THE WEST IN 1863

The mining booms had completed the territorial divisions of the Southwest. In 1864 Idaho was reduced and Montana created. Wyoming followed in 1868.

booms had broken up all of these. Arizona, Nevada, Idaho, Montana, Dakota, Colorado, had found their excuses for existence, while Kansas and Nevada entered the Union, with Nebraska following in 1867. Between the thirty-seventh and forty-first parallels Colorado fairly straddled the divide.

To the north, in the region of the great river valleys, — Green, Big Horn, Powder, Platte, and Sweetwater, — the precious metals were not found in quantities which justified exploitation earlier than 1867. But in that year moderate discoveries on the Sweetwater and the arrival of the terminal camps of the Union Pacific gave plausibility to a scheme for a new territory.

The Sweetwater mines, without causing any great excitement, brought a few hundred men to the vicinity of South Pass. A handful of towns was established, a county was organized, a newspaper was brought into life at Fort Bridger. If the railway had not appeared at the same time, the foundation for a territory would probably have been too slight. But the Union Pacific, which had ended at Julesburg early in 1867, extended its terminus to a new town, Cheyenne, in the summer, and to Laramie City in the spring of 1868.

Cheyenne was laid out a few weeks before the Union Pacific advanced to its site. It had a better prospect of life than had most of the mushroom cities that accompanied the westward course of the railroad, because it was the natural junction point for Denver trade. Colorado had been much disappointed at its own failure to induce the Union Pacific managers to put Denver City on the main line of the road, and felt injured when compelled to do its business through Cheyenne. But just because of this, Cheyenne grew in the autumn of 1867 with a rapidity unusual even in the West. It was not an orderly or reputable population that it had during the first months of its existence, but, to its good fortune, the advance of the road to Laramie drew off the worst of the floating inhabitants early in 1868. Cheyenne was left with an overlarge town site, but with some real excuse for existence. Most of the terminal towns vanished completely when the railroad moved on.

A new territory for the country north of Colorado had been talked about as early as 1861. Since the creation of Montana territory in 1864, this area had been attached, obviously only temporarily, to Dakota. Now, with the mining and railway influences at work, the population made appeal to the Dakota legislature and to Congress for independence. "Without opposition or prolonged discussion," as Bancroft puts it, the new territory was created by Congress in July, 1868. It was called Wyoming, just escaping the names of Lincoln and Cheyenne, and received as bounds the parallels of 41° and 45°, and the meridians of 27° and 34°, west of Washington.

For several years after the Sioux treaties of 1868 and the erection of Wyoming territory, the Indians of the northern plains kept the peace. The routes of travel had been opened, the white claim to the Powder River Valley had been surrendered, and a great northern reserve had been created in the Black Hills country of southern Dakota. All these, by lessening contact, removed the danger of

Indian friction. But the southern tribes were still uneasy, — treacherous or ill-treated, according as the sources vary, — and one more war was needed before they could be compelled to settle down.

CHAPTER XVIII

OF the four classes of persons whose interrelations determined the condition of the frontier, none admitted that it desired to provoke Indian wars. The tribes themselves consistently professed a wish to be allowed to remain at peace. The Indian agents lost their authority and many of their perquisites during war time. The army and the frontiersmen denied that they were belligerent. "I assert," wrote Custer, "and all candid persons familiar with the subject will sustain the assertion, that of all classes of our population the army and the people living on the frontier entertain the greatest dread of an Indian war, and are willing to make the greatest sacrifices to avoid its horrors." To fix the responsibility for the wars which repeatedly occurred, despite the protestations of amiability on all sides, calls for the examination of individual episodes in large number. It is easier to acquit the first two classes than the last two. There are enough instances in which the tribes were persuaded to promise and keep the peace to establish the belief that a policy combining benevolence, equity, and relentless firmness in punishing wrong-doers, white or red, could have maintained friendly relations with ease. The Indian agents were hampered most by their inability to enforce the laws intrusted to them for execution, and by the slowness of the Senate in ratifying agreements and of Congress in voting supplies. The frontiersmen, with their isolated homesteads lying open to surprise and destruction, would seem to be sincere in their protestations; yet repeatedly they thrust themselves as squatters upon lands of unquieted Indian title, while their personal relations with the red men were commonly marked by fear and hatred. The army, with greater honesty and better administration than the Indian Bureau, overdid its work, being unable to think of the Indians as anything but public enemies and treating them with an arbitrary curtness that would have been dangerous even among intelligent whites. The history of the southwest Indians, after the Sand Creek massacre, illustrates well how tribes, not specially ill-disposed, became the victims of circumstances which led to their destruction.

After the battle at Sand Creek, the southwest tribes agreed to a series of treaties in 1865 by which new reserves were promised them on the borderland of Kansas and Indian Territory. These treaties were so amended by the Senate that for a time the tribes had no admitted homes or rights save the guaranteed hunting privileges on the plains south of the Platte. They seem generally to have been peaceful during 1866, in spite of the rather shabby treatment which the neglect of Congress procured for them. In 1867 uneasiness became apparent. Agent E. W. Wynkoop, of Sand Creek fame, was now in charge of the Arapaho, Cheyenne, and Apache tribes in the vicinity of Fort Larned, on the Santa Fé trail in Kansas. In 1866 they had "complained of the government not having fulfilled its promises to them, and of numerous impositions practised upon them by the whites." Some of their younger braves had gone on the war-path. But Wynkoop claimed to have quieted them, and by March, 1867, thought that they were "well satisfied and quiet, and anxious to retain the peaceful relations now existing."

The military authorities at Fort Dodge, farther up the Arkansas and near the old Santa Fé crossing, were less certain than Wynkoop that the Indians meant well. Little Raven, of the Arapaho, and Satanta, "principal chief" of the Kiowa, were reported as sending in insulting messages to the troops, ordering them to cut no more wood, to leave the country, to keep wagons off the Santa Fé trail. Occasional thefts of stock and forays were reported along the trail. Custer thought that there was "positive evidence from the agents themselves" that the Indians were guilty, the trouble only being that Wynkoop charged the guilt on the Kiowa and Comanche, while J. H. Leavenworth, agent for these tribes, asserted their innocence and accused the wards of Wynkoop.

The Department of the Missouri, in which these

tribes resided, was under the command of Major-general Winfield Scott Hancock in the spring of 1867. With a desire to promote the tranquillity of his command, Hancock prepared for an expedition on the plains as early as the roads would permit. He wrote of this intention to both of the agents, asking them to accompany him, "to show that the officers of the government are acting in harmony." His object was not necessarily war, but to impress upon the Indians his ability "to chastise any tribes who may molest people who are travelling across the plains." In each of the letters he listed the complaints against the respective tribes — failure to deliver murderers, outrages on the Smoky Hill route in 1866, alliances with the Sioux, hostile incursions into Texas, and the specially barbarous Box murder. In this last affair one James Box had been murdered by the Kiowas, and his wife and five daughters carried off. The youngest of these, a baby, died in a few days, the mother stated, and they "took her from me and threw her into a ravine." Ultimately the mother and three of the children were ransomed from the Kiowas after Mrs. Box and her eldest daughter, Margaret, had been passed around from chief to chief for more than two months. Custer wrote up this outrage with much exaggeration, but the facts were bad enough.

With both agents present, Hancock advanced to Fort Larned. "It is uncertain whether war will be the result of the expedition or not," he declared

in general orders of March 26, 1867, thus admitting
that a state of war did not at that time exist. "It
will depend upon the temper and behavior of the
Indians with whom we may come in contact. We go
prepared for war and will make it if a proper occasion
presents." The tribes which he proposed to visit
were roaming indiscriminately over the country
traversed by the Santa Fé trail, in accordance with
the treaties of 1865, which permitted them, until they
should be settled upon their reserves, to hunt at
will over the plains south of the Platte, subject only
to the restriction that they must not camp within ten
miles of the main roads and trails. It was Hancock's
intention to enforce this last provision, and more,
to insist "upon their keeping off the main lines of
travel, where their presence is calculated to bring
about collisions with the whites."

The first conference with the Indians was held at
Fort Larned, where the "principal chiefs of the Dog
Soldiers of the Cheyennes" had been assembled by
Agent Wynkoop. Leavenworth thought that the
chiefs here had been very friendly, but Wynkoop
criticised the council as being held after sunset,
which was contrary to Indian custom and calculated
"to make them feel suspicious." At this council
General Hancock reprimanded the chiefs and told
them that he would visit their village, occupied by
themselves and an almost equal number of Sioux;
which village, said Wynkoop, "was 35 miles from
any travelled road." "Why don't he confine the

troops to the great line of travel?" demanded Leavenworth, whose wards had the same privilege of hunting south of the Arkansas that those of Wynkoop
had between the Arkansas and the Platte.   So long
as they camped ten miles from the roads, this was
their right.

Contrary to Wynkoop's urgings, Hancock led his
command from Fort Larned on April 13, 1867,
moving for the main Arapaho, Cheyenne, and Sioux
village on Pawnee Fork, thirty-five miles west of the
post.   With cavalry, infantry, artillery, and a pon-
toon train, it was hard for him to assume any
other appearance than that of war.   Even the
General's particular assurance, as Custer puts it,
"that he was not there to make war, but to promote
peace," failed to convince the chiefs who had attended the night council.   It was not a pleasant
march.   The snow was nearly a foot deep, fodder was
scarce, and the Indian disposition was uncertain.
Only a few had come in to the Fort Larned conference,
and none appeared at camp after the first day's
march.   After this refusal to meet him, Hancock
marched on to the village, in front of which he
found some three hundred Indians drawn up in
battle array.   Fighting seemed imminent, but at
last Roman Nose, Bull Bear, and other chiefs met
Hancock between the lines and agreed upon an evening conference.   It developed that the men alone
were left at the Indian camp.   Women and children,
with all the movables they could handle, had fled out

upon the snowy plains at the approach of the troops. Fear of another Sand Creek had caused it, said Wynkoop. But Hancock chose to regard this as evidence of a treacherous disposition, demanded that the fugitives return at once, and insisted upon encamping near the village against the protest of the chiefs. Instead of bringing back their people, the men themselves abandoned the village that evening, while Hancock, learning of the flight, surrounded and took possession of it. The next morning, April 15, Custer was sent with cavalry in pursuit of the flying bands. Depredations occurring to the north of Pawnee Fork within a day or two, Hancock burned the village in retaliation and proceeded to Fort Dodge. Wynkoop insisted that the Cheyenne and Arapaho had been entirely innocent and that these injuries had been committed by the Sioux. "I have no doubt," he wrote, "but that they think that war has been forced upon them."

When Hancock started upon the plains, there was no war, but there was no doubt about its existence as the spring advanced. When the Peace Commissioners of this year came with their protestations of benevolence for the Great Father, it was small wonder that the Cheyenne and Arapaho had to be coaxed into the camp on the Medicine Lodge Creek. And when the treaties there made failed of prompt execution by the United States, the war naturally dragged on in a desultory way during 1868 and 1869.

In the spring of 1868 General Sheridan, who

had succeeded Hancock in command of the Department of the Missouri, visited the posts at Fort Larned and Fort Dodge. Here on Pawnee and Walnut creeks most of the southwest Indians were congregated. Wynkoop, in February and April, reported them as happy and quiet. They were destitute, to be sure, and complained that the Commissioners at Medicine Lodge had promised them arms and ammunition which had not been delivered. Indeed, the treaty framed there had not yet been ratified. But he believed it possible to keep them contented and wean them from their old habits. To Sheridan the situation seemed less happy. He declined to hold a council with the complaining chiefs on the ground that the whole matter was yet in the hands of the Peace Commission, but he saw that the young men were chafing and turbulent and that frontier hostilities would accompany the summer buffalo hunt.

There is little doubt of the destitution which prevailed among the plains tribes at this time. The rapid diminution of game was everywhere observable. The annuities at best afforded only partial relief, while Congress was irregular in providing funds. Three times during the spring the Commissioner prodded the Secretary of the Interior, who in turn prodded Congress, with the result that instead of the $1,000,000 asked for $500,000 were, in July, 1868, granted to be spent not by the Indian Office, but by the War Department. Three weeks later General Sherman created an organization for distributing this charity, placing the district south of Kansas in command of General Hazen. Meanwhile, the time for making the spring issues of annuity goods had come. It was ordered in June that no arms or ammunition should be given to the Cheyenne and Arapaho because of their recent bad conduct; but in July the Commissioner, influenced by the great dissatisfaction on the part of the tribes, and fearing "that these Indians, by reason of such non-delivery of arms, ammunition, and goods, will commence hostilities against the whites in their vicinity, modified the order and telegraphed Agent Wynkoop that he might use his own discretion in the matter: "If you are satisfied that the issue of the arms and ammunition is necessary to preserve the peace, and that no evil will result from their delivery, let the Indians have them." A few days previously on July 20, Wynkoop had issued the ordinary supplies to his Arapaho and Apache, his Cheyenne refusing to take anything until they could have the guns as well. "They felt much disappointed, but gave no evidence of being angry . . . and would wait with patience for the Great Father to take pity upon them." The permission from the Commissioner was welcomed by the agent, and approved by Thomas Murphy, his superintendent. Murphy had been ordered to Fort Larned to reënforce Wynkoop's judgment. He held a council on August 1 with Little Raven and the Arapaho and Apache, and issued them their arms. "Raven and the other chiefs then promised that these arms should never be used against the whites, and Agent Wynkoop then delivered to the Arapahoes 160 pistols, 80 Lancaster rifles, 12 kegs of powder, $1\frac{1}{2}$ keg of lead, and 15,000 caps; and to the Apaches he gave 40 pistols, 20 Lancaster rifles, 3 kegs of powder, $\frac{1}{2}$ keg of lead, and 5000 caps." The Cheyenne came in a few days later for their share, which Wynkoop handed over on the 9th. "They were delighted at receiving the goods," he reported, "particularly the arms and ammunition, and never before have I known them to be better satisfied and express themselves as being so well contented." The fact that within three days murders were committed by the Cheyenne on the Solomon and Saline forks throws doubt upon the sincerity of their protestations.

The war party which commenced the active hostilities of 1868 at a time so well calculated to throw discredit upon the wisdom of the Indian Office, had left the Cheyenne village early in August, "smarting under their *supposed* wrongs," as Wynkoop puts it. They were mostly Cheyenne, with a small number of Arapaho and a few visiting Sioux, about 200 in all. Little Raven's son and a brother of White Antelope, who died at Sand Creek, were with them; Black Kettle is said to have been their leader. On August 7 some of them spent the evening at Fort Hays, where they held a powwow at the post. "Black Kettle loves his white

soldier brothers, and his heart feels glad when he
meets them and shakes their hands in friendship,"
is the way the post-trader, Hill P. Wilson, reported
his speech. "The white soldiers ought to be glad
all the time, because their ponies are so big and so
strong, and because they have so many guns and
so much to eat. . . . All other Indians may take
the war trail, but Black Kettle will forever keep
friendship with his white brothers." Three nights
later they began to kill on Saline River, and on the
11th they crossed to the Solomon. Some fifteen
settlers were killed, and five women were carried off.
Here this particular raid stopped, for the news
had got abroad, and the frontier was instantly in
arms. Various isolated forays occurred, so that
Sheridan was sure he had a general war upon his
hands. He believed nearly all the young men of
the Cheyenne, Kiowa, Arapaho, and Comanche to
be in the war parties, the old women, men, and
children remaining around the posts and professing solicitous friendship. There were 6000 potential warriors in all, and that he might better devote
himself to suppressing them, Sheridan followed the
Kansas Pacific to its terminus at Fort Hays and there
established his headquarters in the field.

The war of 1868 ranged over the whole frontier
south of the Platte trail. It influenced the Peace
Commission, at its final meeting in October, 1868,
to repudiate many of the pacific theories of January
and recommend that the Indians be handed over

to the War Department. Sheridan, who had led the Commission to this conclusion, was in the field directing the movement. His policy embraced a concentration of the peaceful bands south of the Arkansas, and a relentless war against the rest. It is fairly clear that the war need not have come, had it not been for the cross-purposes ever apparent between the Indian Office and the War Department, and even within the War Department itself.

At Fort Hays, Sheridan prepared for war. He had, at the start, about 2600 men, nearly equally divided among cavalry and infantry. Believing his force too small to cover the whole plains between Fort Hays and Denver, he called for reënforcements, receiving a part of the Fifth Cavalry and a regiment of Kansas volunteers. With enthusiasm this last addition was raised among the frontiersmen, where Indian fighting was popular; the governor of the state resigned his office to become its colonel. September and October were occupied in getting the troops together, keeping the trails open for traffic, and establishing, about a hundred miles south of Fort Dodge, a rendezvous which was known as Camp Supply. It was the intention to protect the frontier during the autumn, and to follow up the Indian villages after winter had fallen, catching the tribes when they would be concentrated and at a disadvantage.

On October 15, 1868, Sherman, just from the Chicago meeting of the Peace Commissioners

and angry because he had there been told that the
army wanted war, gave Sheridan a free hand for the
winter campaign. "As to 'extermination,' it is
for the Indians themselves to determine. We don't
want to exterminate or even to fight them. . . .
The present war . . . was begun and carried on by
the Indians in spite of our entreaties and in spite
of our warnings, and the only question to us is,
whether we shall allow the progress of our western
settlements to be checked, and leave the Indians
free to pursue their bloody career, or accept their
war and fight them. . . . We . . . accept the war
. . . and hereby resolve to make its end final. . . .
I will say nothing and do nothing to restrain our
troops from doing what they deem proper on the
spot, and will allow no mere vague general charges
of cruelty and inhumanity to tie their hands, but
will use all the powers confided to me to the end
that these Indians, the enemies of our race and of our
civilization, shall not again be able to begin and
carry on their barbarous warfare on any kind of pre-
text that they may choose to allege."

The plan of campaign provided that the main
column, Custer in immediate command, should
march from Fort Hays directly against the Indians,
by way of Camp Supply; two smaller columns
were to supplement this, one marching in on Indian
Territory from New Mexico, and the other from
Fort Lyon on the old Sand Creek reserve. Detachments of the chief column began to move in the

middle of November, Custer reaching the depot at
Camp Supply ahead of the rest, while the Kansas
volunteers lost themselves in heavy snow-storms.
On November 23 Custer was ordered out of Camp
Supply, on the north fork of the Canadian, to follow
a fresh trail which led southwest towards the Washita
River, near the eastern line of Texas. He pushed on
as rapidly as twelve inches of snow would allow,
discovering in the early morning of November 27 a
large camp in the valley of the Washita.

It was Black Kettle's camp of Cheyenne and
Arapaho that they had found in a strip of heavy
timber along the river. After reconnoitring Custer
divided his force into four columns for simultaneous
attacks upon the sleeping village. At daybreak
"my men charged the village and reached the lodges
before the Indians were aware of our presence. The
moment the charge was ordered the band struck
up 'Garry Owen,' and with cheers that strongly
reminded me of scenes during the war, every trooper,
led by his officer, rushed towards the village." For
several hours a promiscuous fight raged up and down
the ravine, with Indians everywhere taking to cover,
only to be prodded out again. Fifty-one lodges in all
fell into Custer's hands; 103 dead Indians, including Black Kettle himself, were found later. "We
captured in good condition 875 horses, ponies, and
mules; 241 saddles, some of very fine and costly
workmanship; 573 buffalo robes, 390 buffalo skins
for lodges, 160 untanned robes, 210 axes, 140

hatchets, 35 revolvers, 47 rifles, 535 pounds of powder, 1050 pounds of lead, 4000 arrows and arrow-heads, 75 spears, 90 bullet moulds, 35 bows and quivers, 12 shields, 300 pounds of bullets, 775 lariats, 940 buckskin saddle-bags, 470 blankets, 93 coats, 700 pounds of tobacco.''

As the day advanced, Custer's triumph seemed likely to turn into defeat. The Cheyenne village proved to be only the last of a long string of villages that extended down the Washita for fifteen miles or more, and whose braves rode up by hundreds to see the fight. A general engagement was avoided, how-ever, and with better luck and more discretion than he was one day to have, Custer marched back to Camp Supply on December 3, his band playing gayly the tune of battle, "Garry Owen." The commander in his triumphal procession was followed by his scouts and trailers, and the captives of his prowess — a long train of Indian widows and orphans.

The decisive blow which broke the power of the southwest tribes had been struck, and Black Kettle had carried on his last raid, — if indeed he had carried on this one at all — but as the reports came in it became evident that the merits of the triumph were in doubt. The Eastern humanitarians were shocked at the cold-blooded attack upon a camp of sleeping men, women, and children, forgetting that if Indians were to be fought this was the most successful way to do it, and was no shock to the Indians' own ideals of warfare and attack. The deeper question was

whether this camp was actually hostile, whether the
tribes had not abandoned the war-path in good faith,
whether it was fair to crush a tribe that with apparent
earnestness begged peace because it could not control
the excesses of some of its own braves. It became
certain, at least, that the War Department itself
had fallen victim to that vice with which it had so
often reproached the Indian Office — failure to
produce a harmony of action among several branches
of the service.

The Indian Office had no responsibility for the
battle of the Washita. It had indeed issued arms
to the Cheyenne in August, but only with the approval of the military officer commanding Forts
Larned and Dodge, General Alfred Sully, "an
officer of long experience in Indian affairs." In the
early summer all the tribes had been near these forts
and along the Santa Fé trail. After Congress had
voted its half million to feed the hungry, Sherman
had ordered that the peaceful hungry among the
southern tribes should be moved from this locality
to the vicinity of old Fort Cobb, in the west end of
Indian Territory on the Washita River.

During September, while Sheridan was gathering
his armament at Fort Hays, Sherman was ordering
the agents to take their peaceful charges to Fort
Cobb. With the major portion of the tribes at war
it would be impossible for the troops to make any
discrimination unless there should be an absolute
separation between the well-disposed and the war-

like. He proposed to allow the former a reasonable time to get to their new abode and then beg the President for an order "declaring all Indians who remain outside of their lawful reservations" to be outlaws. He believed that by going to war these tribes had violated their hunting rights. Superintendent Murphy thought he saw another Sand Creek in these preparations. Here were the tribes ordered to Fort Cobb; their fall annuity goods were on the way thither for distribution; and now the military column was marching in the same direction.

In the meantime General W. B. Hazen had arrived at Fort Cobb on November 7 and had immediately voiced his fear that "General Sheridan, acting under the impression of hostiles, may attack bands of Comanche and Kiowa before they reach this point." He found, however, most of these tribes, who had not gone to war this season, encamped within reach on the Canadian and Washita rivers, — 5000 of the Comanche and 1500 of the Kiowa. Within a few days Cheyenne and Arapaho began to join the settlements in the district, Black Kettle bringing in his band to the Washita, forty miles east of Antelope Hills, and coming in person to Fort Cobb for an interview with General Hazen on November 20.

"I have always done my best," he protested, "to keep my young men quiet, but some will not listen, and since the fighting began I have not been able to keep them all at home. But we all want peace." To which added Big Mouth, of the Arapaho: "I came to you because I wish to do right. . . . I do not want war, and my people do not, but although we have come back south of the Arkansas, the soldiers follow us and continue fighting, and we want you to send out and stop these soldiers from coming against us."

To these, General Hazen, fearful as he was of an unjust attack, responded with caution. Sherman had spoken of Fort Cobb in his orders to Sheridan, as "aimed to hold out the olive branch with one hand and the sword in the other. But it is not thereby intended that any hostile Indians shall make use of that establishment as a refuge from just punishment for acts already done. Your military control over that reservation is as perfect as over Kansas, and if hostile Indians retreat within that reservation, . . . they may be followed even to Fort Cobb, captured, and punished." It is difficult to see what could constitute the fact of peaceful intent if coming in to Fort Cobb did not. But Hazen gave to Black Kettle cold comfort: "I am sent here as a peace chief; all here is to be peace; but north of the Arkansas is General Sheridan, the great war chief, and I do not control him; and he has all the soldiers who are fighting the Arapahoes and Cheyennes. . . . If the soldiers come to fight, you must remember they are not from me, but from that great war chief, and with him you must make peace. . . . I cannot stop the war. . . . You must not come in again unless I send for you, and you must keep well out beyond

ᴙ

the friendly Kiowas and Comanches." So he sent the suitors away and wrote, on November 22, to Sherman for more specific instructions covering these cases. He believed that Black Kettle and Big Mouth were themselves sincere, but doubted their control over their bands. These were the bands which Custer destroyed before the week was out, and it is probable that during the fight they were reënforced by braves from the friendly lodges of Satanta's Kiowa and Little Raven's Arapaho.

Whatever might have been a wise policy in treating semi-hostile Indian tribes, this one was certainly unsatisfactory. It is doubtful whether the war was ever so great as Sherman imagined it. The injured tribes were unquestionably drawn to Fort Cobb by a desire for safety; the army was in the position of seeming to use the olive branch to assemble the Indians in order that the sword might the better disperse them. There is reasonable doubt whether Black Kettle had anything to do with the forays. Murphy believed in him and cited many evidences of his friendly disposition, while Wynkoop asserted positively that he had been encamped on Pawnee Fork all through the time when he was alleged to have been committing depredations on the Saline. The army alone had been no more successful in producing obvious justice than the army and Indian Office together had been. Yet whatever the merits of the case, the power of the Cheyenne and their neighbors was permanently gone.

During the winter of 1868–1869 Sheridan's army

remained in the vicinity of Fort Cobb, gathering the remnants of the shattered tribes in upon their reservation. The Kiowa and Comanche were placed at last on the lands awarded them at the Medicine Lodge treaties, while the Arapaho and Cheyenne once more had their abiding-place changed in August, 1869, and were settled down along the upper waters of the Washita, around the valley of their late defeat.

The long controversy between the War and Interior departments over the management of the tribes entered upon a new stage with the inauguration of Grant in 1869. One of the earliest measures of his administration was a bill erecting a board of civilian Indian commissioners to advise the Indian Department and promote the civilization of the tribes. A generous grant of two millions accompanied the act. More care was used in the appointment of agents than had hitherto been taken, and the immediate results seemed good when the Commissioner wrote his annual report in December, 1869. But the worst of the troubles with the Indians of the plains was over, so that without special effort peace could now have been the result.

CHAPTER XIX

THE FIRST OF THE RAILWAYS

TWENTY years before the great tribes of the plains made their last stand in front of the invading white man overland travel had begun; ten years before, Congress, under the inspiration of the prophetic Whitney and the leadership of more practical men, had provided for a survey of railroad routes along the trails; on the eve of the struggle the earliest continental railway had received its charter; and the struggle had temporarily ceased while Congress, in 1867, sent out its Peace Commission to prepare an open way. That the tribes must yield was as inevitable as it was that their yielding must be ungracious and destructive to them. Too weak to compel their enemy to respect their rights, and uncertain what their rights were, they were too low in intelligence to realize that the more they struggled, the worse would be their suffering. So they struggled on, during the years in which the iron band was put across the continent. Its completion and their subjection came in 1869.

After years of tedious debate the earliest of the Pacific railways was chartered in 1862. The withdrawal of southern claims had made possible an agreement upon a route, while the spirit of nationality engendered by the Civil War gave to the project its final impetus. Under the management of the Central Pacific of California, the Union Pacific, and two or three border railways, provision was made for a road from the Iowa border to California. Land grants and bond subsidies were for two years dangled before the capitalists of America in the vain attempt to entice them to construct it. Only after these were increased in 1864 did active organization begin, while at the end of 1865 but forty miles of the Union Pacific had been built.

Building a railroad from the Missouri River to the Pacific Ocean was easily the greatest engineering feat that America had undertaken. In their day the Cumberland Road, and the Erie Canal, and the Pennsylvania Portage Railway had ranked among the American wonders, but none of these had been accompanied by the difficult problems that bristled along the eighteen hundred miles of track that must be laid across plain and desert, through hostile Indian country and over mountains. Worse yet, the road could hope for little aid from the country through which it ran. Except for the small colonies at Carson, Salt Lake, and Denver, the last of which it missed by a hundred miles, its course lay through unsettled wilderness for nearly the whole distance. Like the trusses of a cantilever, its advancing ends projected themselves across the continent, relying, up to the moment of joining, upon the firm anchorage of the termini in the settled lands of Iowa and California.

Equally trying, though different in variety, were the difficulties attendant upon construction at either end.

The impetus which Judah had given to the Central Pacific had started the western end of the system two years ahead of the eastern, but had not produced great results at first. It was hard work building east into the Sierra Nevadas, climbing the gullies, bridging, tunnelling, filling, inch by inch, to keep the grade down and the curvature out. Twenty miles a year only were completed in 1863, 1864, and 1865, thirty in 1866, and forty-six in 1867 — one hundred and thirty-six miles during the first five years of work. Nature had done her best to impede the progress of the road by thrusting mountains and valleys across its route. But she had covered the mountains with timber and filled them with stone, so that materials of construction were easily accessible along all of the costliest part of the line. Bridges and trestles could be built anywhere with local material. The labor problem vexed the Central Pacific managers at the start. It was a scanty and inefficient supply of workmen that existed in California when construction began. Like all new countries, California possessed more work than workmen. Economic independence was to be had almost for the asking. Free land and fertile soil made it unnecessary for men to work for hire. The slight results of the first five years were due as much to lack of labor as to refractory roadway or political opposition. But by 1865 the employment of Chinese laborers began. Coolies imported by the thousand and ably directed by Charles Crocker, who was the most active constructor, brought a new rapidity into construction. "I used to go up and down that road in my car like a mad bull," Crocker dictated to Bancroft's stenographer, "stopping along wherever there was anything amiss, and raising Old Nick with the boys that were not up to time." With roadbed once graded new troubles began. California could manufacture no iron. Rolling stock and rails had to be imported from Europe or the East, and came to San Francisco after the costly sea voyage, *via* Panama or the Horn. But the men directing the Central Pacific — Stanford, Crocker, Huntington, and the rest — rose to the difficulties, and once they had passed the mountains, fairly romped across the Nevada desert in the race for subsidies.

The eastern end started nearer to a base of supplies than did the California terminus, yet until 1867 no railroad from the East reached Council Bluffs, where the President had determined that the Union Pacific should begin. There had been railway connection to the Missouri River at St. Joseph since 1859, and various lines were hurrying across Iowa in the sixties, but for more than two years of construction the Union Pacific had to get rolling stock and iron from the Missouri steamers or the laborious prairie schooners. Until its railway connection was established its difficulty in this respect was only less great than that of the Central Pacific. The compensation of the

Union Pacific came, however, in its roadbed. Following the old Platte trail, flat and smooth as the best highways, its construction gangs could do the light grading as rapidly as the finished single track could deliver the rails at its growing end. But for the needful culverts and trestles there was little material at hand. The willows and cottonwood lining the river would not do. The Central Pacific could cut its wood as it needed it, often within sight of its track. The Union Pacific had to haul much of its wood and stone, like its iron, from its eastern terminus.

The labor problem of the Union Pacific was intimately connected with the solution of its Indian problem. The Central Pacific had almost no trouble with the decadent tribes through whom it ran, but the Union Pacific was built during the very years when the great plains were most disturbed and hostile forays were most frequent. Its employees contained large elements of the newly arrived Irish and of the recently discharged veterans of the Civil War. General Dodge, who was its chief engineer, has described not only the military guards who "stacked their arms on the dump and were ready at a moment's warning to fall in and fight," but the military capacity of the construction gangs themselves. The "track train could arm a thousand men at a word," and from chief constructor down to chief spiker "could be commanded by experienced officers of every rank, from general to a captain. They had served five years at the front, and over half of the men had

shouldered a musket in many battles. An illustration of this came to me after our track had passed
Plum Creek, 200 miles west of the Missouri River.
The Indians had captured a freight train and were
in possession of it and its crews." Dodge came to
the rescue in his car, "a travelling arsenal," with
twenty-odd men, most of whom were strangers to
him; yet "when I called upon them to fall in, to go
forward and retake the train, every man on the train
went into line, and by his position showed that he
was a soldier. . . . I gave the order to deploy as
skirmishers, and at the command they went forward
as steadily and in as good order as we had seen the
old soldiers climb the face of Kenesaw under fire."

By an act passed in July, 1866, Congress did much
to accelerate the construction of the road. Heretofore
the junction point had been in the Nevada Desert,
a hundred and fifty miles east of the California line.
It was now provided that each road might build until
it met the other. Since the mountain section, with
the highest accompanying subsidies, was at hand,
each of the companies was spurred on by its desire
to get as much land and as many bonds as possible.
The race which began in the autumn of 1866 ended
only with the completion of the track in 1869. A
mile a day had seemed like quick work at the start;
seven or eight a day were laid before the end.

The English traveller, Bell, who published his
New Tracks in North America in 1869, found somewhere an enthusiastic quotation admirably descrip-

tive of the process. "Track-laying on the Union
Pacific is a science," it read, "and we pundits of the
Far East stood upon that embankment, only about
a thousand miles this side of sunset, and backed
westward before that hurrying corps of sturdy opera-
tives with mingled feelings of amusement, curiosity,
and profound respect. On they came. A light car,
drawn by a single horse, gallops up to the front with
its load of rails. Two men seize the end of a rail and
start forward, the rest of the gang taking hold by twos
until it is clear of the car. They come forward at a
run. At the word of command, the rail is dropped in
its place, right side up, with care, while the same
process goes on at the other side of the car. Less
than thirty seconds to a rail for each gang, and so four
rails go down to the minute! Quick work, you say,
but the fellows on the U. P. are tremendously in
earnest. The moment the car is empty it is tipped
over on the side of the track to let the next loaded car
pass it, and then it is tipped back again; and it is a
sight to see it go flying back for another load, pro-
pelled by a horse at full gallop at the end of 60
or 80 feet of rope, ridden by a young Jehu, who
drives furiously. Close behind the first gang come
the gaugers, spikers, and bolters, and a lively time
they make of it. It is a grand Anvil Chorus that
these sturdy sledges are playing across the plains.
It is in a triple time, three strokes to a spike.
There are ten spikes to a rail, four hundred rails to
a mile, eighteen hundred miles to San Francisco.

That's the sum, what is the quotient? Twenty-one million times are those sledges to be swung — twenty-one million times are they to come down with their sharp punctuation, before the great work of modern America is complete!"

Handling, housing, and feeding the thousands of laborers who built the road was no mean problem. Ten years earlier the builders of the Illinois Central had complained because their road from Galena and Chicago to Cairo ran generally through an uninhabited country upon which they could not live as they went along. Much more the continental railways, building rapidly away from the settlements, were forced to carry their dwellings with them. Their commissariat was as important as their general offices.

An acquaintance of Bell told of standing where Cheyenne now is and seeing a long freight train arrive "laden with frame houses, boards, furniture, palings, old tents, and all the rubbish" of a mushroom city. "The guard jumped off his van, and seeing some friends on the platform, called out with a flourish, 'Gentlemen, here's Julesburg.'" The head of the serpentine track, sometimes indeed "crookeder than the horn that was blown around the walls of Jericho," was the terminal town; its tongue was the stretch of track thrust a few miles in advance of the head; repeatedly as the tongue darted out the head followed, leaving across the plains a series of scars, marking the spots where it had rested for a time.

Every few weeks the town was packed upon a freight train and moved fifty or sixty miles to the new end of the track. Its vagrant population followed it. It was at Julesburg early in 1867; at Cheyenne in the end of the year; at Laramie City the following spring. Always it was the most disreputably picturesque spot on the anatomy of the railroad.

In the fall of 1868 "Hell on Wheels," as Samuel Bowles, editor of the *Springfield Republican*, appropriately designated the terminal town, was at Benton, Wyoming, six hundred and ninety-eight miles from Omaha and near the military reservation at Fort Steele. In the very midst of the gray desert, with sand ankle-deep in its streets, the town stood dusty white — "a new arrival with black clothes looked like nothing so much as a cockroach struggling through a flour barrel." A less promising location could hardly have been found, yet within two weeks there had sprung up a city of three thousand people with ordinances and government suited to its size, and facilities for vice ample for all. The needs of the road accounted for it: to the east the road was operating for passengers and freight; to the west it was yet constructing track. Here was the end of rail travel and the beginning of the stage routes to the coast and the mines. Two years earlier the similar point had been at Fort Kearney, Nebraska.

The city of tents and shacks contained, according to the count of John H. Beadle, a peripatetic journalist, twenty-three saloons and five dance houses. It had all the worst details of the mining camp. Gambling and rowdyism were the order of day and night. Its great institution was the "'Big Tent,' sometimes, with equal truth but less politeness, called the 'Gamblers' Tent.'" This resort was a hundred feet long by forty wide, well floored, and given over to drinking, dancing, and gambling. The sumptuous bar provided refreshment much desired in a dry alkali country; all the games known to the professional gambler were in full blast; women, often fair and well-dressed, were there to gather in what the bartender and faro-dealer missed. Whence came these people, and how they learned their trade, was a mystery to Bowles. "Hell would appear to have been raked to furnish them," he said, "and to it they must have naturally returned after graduating here, fitted for its highest seats and most diabolical service."

Behind the terminal town real estate disappointments, like beads, were strung along the cord of rails. In advance of the construction gangs land companies would commonly survey town sites in preparation for a boom. Brisk speculation in corner lots was a form of gambling in which real money was often lost and honest hopes were regularly shattered. Each town had its advocates who believed it was to be the great emporium of the West. Yet generally, as the railroad moved on, the town relapsed into a condition of deserted prairie, with only the street lines and débris to remind it of its past. Omaha, though Beadle thought in 1868 that no other "place in America had been so well lied about," and Council Bluffs retained a share of greatness because of their strategic position at the commencement of the main line. Tied together in 1872 by the great iron bridge of the Union Pacific, their relations were as harmonious as those of the cats of Kilkenny, as they quarrelled over the claims of each to be the real terminus. But the future of both was assured when the eastern roads began to run in to get connections with the West. Cheyenne, too, remained a city of some consequence because the Denver Pacific branched off at this point to serve the Pike's Peak region. But the names of most of the other one-time terminal towns were writ in sand.

The progress of construction of the road after 1866 was rapid enough. At the end of 1865, though the Central Pacific had started two years before the Union Pacific, it had completed only sixty miles of track, to the latter's forty. During 1866 the Central Pacific built thirty laborious miles over the mountains, and in 1867, forty-six miles, while in the same two years the Union Pacific built five hundred. In 1868, the western road, now past its worst troubles, added more than 360 to its mileage; the Union Pacific, unchecked by the continental divide, making a new record of 425. By May 10, 1869, the line was done, 1776 miles from Omaha to Sacramento. For the last sixteen months of the continental race the two roads together had built more than two and a half miles for every working day. Never before had construction been systematized so highly or the rewards for speed been so great.

Whether regarded as an economic achievement or a national work, the building of the road deserved the attention it received; yet it was scarcely finished before the scandal-monger was at work. Beadle had written a chapter full of "floridly complimentary notices" of the men who had made possible the feat, but before he went to press their reputations were blasted, and he thought it safest "to mention no names." "Never praise a man," he declared in disgust, "or name your children after him, till he is dead." Before the end of Grant's first administration the *Crédit Mobilier* scandal proved that men, high in the national government, had speculated in the project whose success depended on their votes. That many of them had been guilty of indiscretion, was perfectly clear, but they had done only what many of their greatest predecessors had done. Their real fault was made more prominent by their misfortune in being caught by an aroused national conscience which suddenly awoke to heed a call that it had ever disregarded in the past.

The junction point for the Union Pacific and Central Pacific had been variously fixed by the acts of 1862 and 1864. In 1866 it was left open to fortune or enterprise, and had not Congress intervened in 1869 it might never have existed. In their rush for the land grants the two rivals hurried on their surveys to the vicinity of Great Salt Lake, where their advancing ends began to overlap, and continued parallel for scores of miles. Congress, noticing their indisposition to agree upon a junction, intervened in the spring of 1869, ordering the two to bring their race to an end at Promontory Point, a few miles northwest of Ogden on the shore of the lake. Here in May, 1869, the junction was celebrated in due form.

Since the "Seneca Chief" carried DeWitt Clinton from Buffalo to the Atlantic in 1825, it has been the custom to make the completion of a new road an occasion for formal celebration. On the 10th of May, 1869, the whole United States stood still to signalize the junction of the tracks. The date had been agreed upon by the railways on short notice, and small parties of their officials, Governor Stanford for the Central Pacific and President Dillon for the Union Pacific, had come to the scene of activities. The latter wrote up the "Driving the Last Spike" for one of the magazines twenty years later, telling how General Dodge worked all night of the 9th, laying his final section, and how at noon on the appointed day the last two rails were spiked to a tie of California laurel. The immediate audience was small, including few beyond the railway officials, but within hearing of the telegraphic taps that told of the last blows of the sledge-hammer was much of the United States. President Dillon told the story as it was given in the leading paragraph of the *Nation* of the Thursday after. "So far as we have seen them," wrote Godkin's censor of American morals, "the speeches, prayers, and congratulatory telegrams . . . all broke down under the weight of the occasion, and it is a relief to turn from them to the telegrams which passed between the various operators, and to get their flavor of business and the West. 'Keep quiet,' the Omaha man says, when the operators all over the Union begin to pester him with questions. 'When the last spike is driven at Promontory Point, we will say "Done."' By-and-by he sends the word, 'Hats off! Prayer is being offered.' Then at the end of thirteen minutes he says, apparently with a sense of having at last come to business: 'We have got done praying. The spike is about to be presented.' . . . Before sunset the event was celebrated, not very noisily but very heartily, throughout the country. Chicago made a procession seven miles long; New York hung out bunting, fired a hundred guns, and held thanksgiving services in Trinity; Philadelphia rang the old Liberty Bell; Buffalo sang the 'Star-spangled Banner'; and many towns burnt powder in honor of the consummation of a work which, as all good Americans believe, gives us a road to the Indies, a means of making the United States a halfway house between the East and West, and last, but not least, a new guarantee of the perpetuity of the Union as it is."

No single event in the struggle for the last frontier

z

had a greater significance for the immediate audience, or for posterity, than this act of completion.   Bret Harte, poet of the occasion, asked the question that all were framing: —

> "What was it the Engines said,
> Pilots touching, head to head
> Facing on the single track,
> Half a world behind each back?"

But he was able to answer only a part of it.   His western engine retorted to the eastern: —

> "'You brag of the East!   *You* do?
> Why, *I* bring the East to *you!*
> All the Orient, all Cathay,
> Find through me the shortest way;
> And the sun you follow here
> Rises in my hemisphere.
> Really, — if one must be rude, —
> Length, my friend, ain't longitude.'"

The oriental trade of Whitney and Benton yet dazzled the eyes of the men who built the road, blinding them to the prosaic millions lying beneath their feet.   The East and West were indeed united; but, more important, the intervening frontier was ceasing to divide.   When the road was undertaken, men thought naturally of the East and the Pacific Coast, unhappily separated by the waste of the mountains and the desert and the Indian Country.   The mining flurries of the early sixties raised a hope that this intervening land might not all be waste. As the railway had advanced, settlement had marched with it, the two treading upon the heels of the Peace Commissioners sent out to lure away the Indians. With the opening of the road the new period of national assimilation of the continent had begun. In fifteen years more, as other roads followed, there had ceased to be any unbridgeable gap between the East and West, and the frontier had disappeared.

CHAPTER XX

THROUGH the negotiations of the Peace Commissioners of 1867 and 1868, and the opening of the Pacific railway in 1869, the Indians of the plains had been cleanly split into two main groups which had their centres in the Sioux reserve in southwest Dakota and the old Indian Territory. The advance of a new wave of population had followed along the road thus opened, pushing settlements into central Nebraska and Kansas. Through the latter state the Union Pacific, Eastern Division, better known as the Kansas Pacific, had been thrust west to Denver, where it arrived before 1870 was over. With this advance of civilized life upon the plains it became clear that the old Indian policy was gone for good, and that the idea of a permanent country, where the tribes, free from white contact, could continue their nomadic existence, had broken down. The old Indian policy had been based upon the permanence of this condition, but with the white advance troops for police had been added, while the loud bickerings between the military authorities, thus superimposed, and the Indian Office, which regarded itself as the

340

rightful custodian of the problem, proved to be the overture to a new policy. Said Grant, in his first annual message in 1869: "No matter what ought to be the relations between such [civilized] settlements and the aborigines, the fact is they do not harmonize well, and one or the other has to give way in the end. A situation which looks to the extinction of a race is too horrible for a nation to adopt without entailing upon itself the wrath of all Christendom and engendering in the citizen a disregard for human life and the rights of others, dangerous to society. I see no substitute for such a system, except in placing all the Indians on large reservations, as rapidly as it can be done, and giving them absolute protection there."

The vexed question of civilian or military control had reached the bitterest stage of its discussion when Grant became President. For five years there had been general wars in which both departments seemed to be badly involved and for which responsibility was hard to place. There were many things to be said in favor of either method of control. Beginning with the establishment of the Bureau of Indian Affairs in 1832, the office had been run by the War Department for seventeen years. In this period the idea of a permanent Indian Country had been carried out; the frontier had been established in an unbroken line of reserves from Texas to Green Bay; and the migration across the plains had begun. But with the creation of the Interior Department in 1849 the Indian Bureau had been transferred to civilian hands. As yet the Indian war was so exceptional that it was easy to see the arguments in favor of a peace policy. It was desired, and honestly too, though the results make this conviction hard to hold, to treat the Indian well, to keep the peace, and to elevate the savages as rapidly as they would permit it. However the government failed in practice and in controlling the men of the frontier, there is no doubt about the sincerity of its general intent. Had there been no Oregon and no California, no mines and no railways, and no mixture of slavery and politics, the hope might not have failed of realization. Even as it was, the civilian bureau had little trouble with its charges for nearly fifteen years after its organization. In general the military power was called upon when disorder passed beyond the control of the agent; short of that time the agent remained in authority.

As a means of introducing civilization among the tribes the agents were more effective than army officers could be. They were, indeed, underpaid, appointed for political reasons, and often too weak to resist the allurements of immorality or dishonesty; but they were civilians. Their ideals were those of industry and peace. Their terms of service were often too short for them to learn the business, but they were not subject to the rapid shifting and transfer which made up a large part of army life. Army officers were better picked and trained than the agents, but their ambitions were military, and they were frequently unable to understand why breaches of formal discipline were not always matters of importance.

The strong arguments in favor of military control were founded largely on the permanency of tenure in the army. Political appointments were fewer, the average of personal character and devotion was higher. Army administration had fewer scandals than had that of the Indian Bureau. The partisan on either side in the sixties was prone to believe that his favorite branch of the service was honest and wise, while the other was inefficient, foolish, and corrupt. He failed to see that in the earliest phase of the policy, when there was no friction, and consequently little fighting, the problem was essentially civilian; that in the next period, when constant friction was provoking wars, it had become military; and that finally, when emigration and transportation had changed friction into overwhelming pressure, the wars would again cease. A large share of the disputes were due to the misunderstandings as to whether, in particular cases, the tribes should be under the bureau or the army. On the whole, even when the tribes were hostile, army control tended to increase the cost of management and the chance of injustice. There never was a time when a few thousand Indian police, with the ideals of police rather than those of soldiers, could not have done better than the army did. But the student, attacking the problem from afar, is as unable to solve it fully and justly as were its immediate custodians. He can at most steer in between the badly biassed "Century of Dishonor" of Mrs. Jackson, and the outrageous cry of the radical army and the frontier, that the Indian must go.

The demand of the army for the control of the Indians was never gratified. Around 1870 its friends were insistent that since the army had to bear the knocks of the Indian policy, — knocks, they claimed, generally due to mistakes of the bureau, — it ought to have the whole responsibility and the whole credit. The inertia which attaches to federal reforms held this one back, while the Indian problem itself changed in the seventies so as to make it unnecessary. Once the great wars of the sixties were done the tribes subsided into general peace. Their vigorous resistance was confined to the years when the last great wave of the white advance was surging over them. Then, confined to their reservations, they resumed the march to civilization.

From the commencement of his term, Grant was willing to aid in at once reducing the abuses of the Indian Bureau and maintaining a peace policy on the plains. The Peace Commission of 1867 had done good work, which would have been more effective had coöperation between the army and the bureau been possible. Congress now, in April, 1869, voted two millions to be used in maintaining peace on the plains, "among and with the several tribes . . .

to promote civilization among said Indians, bring them, where practicable, upon reservations, relieve their necessities, and encourage their efforts at self-support." The President was authorized at the same time to erect a board of not more than ten men, "eminent for their intelligence and philanthropy," who should, with the Secretary of the Interior, and without salary, exercise joint control over the expenditures of this or any money voted for the use of the Indian Department.

The Board of Indian Commissioners was designed to give greater wisdom to the administration of the Indian policy and to minimize peculation in the bureau. It represented, in substance, a triumph of the peace party over the army. "The gentlemen who wrote the reports of the Commissioners revelled in riotous imaginations and discarded facts," sneered a friend of military control; but there was, more or less, a distinct improvement in the management of the reservation tribes after 1869; although, as the exposures of the Indian ring showed, corruption was by no means stopped. One way in which the Commissioners and Grant sought to elevate the tone of agency control was through the religious, charitable, and missionary societies. These organizations, many of which had long maintained missionary schools among the more civilized tribes, were invited to nominate agents, teachers, and physicians for appointment by the bureau. On the whole these appointments were an improvement over the men whom political influence had heretofore brought to power. Fifteen years later the Commissioner and the board were again complaining of the character of the agents; but there was an increasing standard of criticism.

In its annual reports made to the Secretary of the Interior in 1869, and since, the board gave much credit to the new peace policy. In 1869 it looked forward with confidence "to success in the effort to civilize the nomadic tribes." In 1871 it described "the remarkable spectacle seen this fall, on the plains of western Nebraska and Kansas and eastern Colorado, of the warlike tribes of the Sioux of Dakota, Montana, and Wyoming, hunting peacefully for buffalo without occasioning any serious alarm among the thousands of white settlers whose cabins skirt the borders of both sides of these plains." In 1872, "the advance of some of the tribes in civilization and Christianity has been rapid, the temper and inclination of all of them has greatly improved. . . . They show a more positive intention to comply with their own obligations, and to accept the advice of those in authority over them, and are in many cases disproving the assertion, that adult Indians cannot be induced to work." In 1906, in its *38th Annual Report*, there was still most marked improvement, "and for the last thirty years the legislation of Congress concerning Indians, their education, their allotment and settlement on lands of their own, their admission to citizenship, and the protection of their rights makes, upon the whole, a chapter of political history of which Americans may justly be proud."

The board of Indian Commissioners believed that most of the obvious improvement in the Indian condition was due to the substitution of a peace policy for a policy of something else. It made a mistake in assuming that there had ever been a policy of war. So far as the United States government had been concerned the aim had always been peace and humanity, and only when over-eager citizens had pushed into the Indian Country to stir up trouble had a war policy been administered. Even then it was distinctly temporary. The events of the sixties had involved such continuous friction and necessitated such severe repression that contemporaries might be pardoned for thinking that war was the policy rather than the cure. But the resistance of the tribes would generally have ceased by 1870, even without the new peace policy. Every mile of western railway lessened the Indians' capacity for resistance by increasing the government's ability to repress it. The Union Pacific, Northern Pacific, Atlantic and Pacific, Texas Pacific, and Southern Pacific, to say nothing of a multitude of private roads like the Chicago, Burlington, and Quincy, the Denver and Rio Grande, the Atchison, Topeka, and Santa Fé, and the Missouri, Kansas, and Texas, were the real forces which brought peace upon the plains. Yet the board was right in that its influence in bringing closer harmony between public opinion and the Indian Bureau, and in improving the tone of the bureau, had made the transformation of the savage into the citizen farmer more rapid.

Two years after the erection of the Board of Indian Commissioners Congress took another long step towards a better condition by ordering that no more treaties with the Indian tribes should be made by President and Senate. For more than two years before 1871 no treaty had been made and ratified, and now the policy was definitely changed. For ninety years the Indians had been treated as independent nations. Three hundred and seventy treaties had been concluded with various tribes, the United States only once repudiating any of them. In 1863, after the Sioux revolt, it abrogated all treaties with the tribes in insurrection; but with this exception, it had not applied to Indian relations the rule of international law that war terminates all existing treaties. The relation implied by the treaty had been anomalous. The tribes were at once independent and dependent. No foreign nation could treat with them; hence they were not free. No state could treat with them, and the Indian could not sue in United States courts; hence they were not Americans. The Supreme Court in the Cherokee cases had tried to define their unique status, but without great success. It was unfortunate for the Indians that the United States took their tribal existence seriously. The agreements had always a greater sanctity in appearance than in fact. Indians honestly unable to comprehend the meaning of the agreement, and often denying that they were in any wise bound by it, were held to fulfilment by the power of the United States. The United States often believed that treaty violation represented deliberate hostility of the tribes, when it signified only the unintelligence of the savage and his inclination to follow the laws of his own existence. Attempts to enforce treaties thus violated led constantly to wars whose justification the Indian could not see.

The act of March 3, 1871, prohibited the making of any Indian treaty in the future. Hereafter when agreements became necessary, they were to be made, much as they had been in the past, but Congress was the ratifying power and not the Senate. The fiction of an independence which had held the Indians to a standard which they could not understand was here abandoned; and quite as much to the point, perhaps, the predominance of the Senate in Indian affairs was superseded by control by Congress as a whole. In no other branch of internal administration would the Senate have been permitted to make binding agreements, but here the fiction had given it a dominance ever since the organization of the government.

In the thirty-five years following the abandonment of the Indian treaties the problems of management changed with the ascending civilization of the national wards. General Francis A. Walker, Indian Commissioner in 1872, had seen the dawn of the "the day of deliverance from the fear of Indian hostilities," while his successors in office saw his prophecy fulfilled. Five years later Carl Schurz, as Secretary of the Interior, gave his voice and his aid to the improvement of management and the drafting of a positive policy. His application of the merit system to Indian appointments, which was a startling innovation in national politics, worked a great change after the petty thievery which had flourished in the presidency of General Grant. Grant had indeed desired to do well, and conditions had appreciably bettered, yet his guileless trust had enabled practical politicians to continue their peculations in instances which ranged from humble agents up to the Cabinet itself. Schurz not only corrected much of this, but the first report of his Commissioner, E. A. Hayt, outlined the preliminaries to a well-founded civilization. Besides the continuance of concentration and education there were four policies which stood out in this report — economy in the administration of rations, that the Indians might not be pauperized; a special code of law for the Indian reserves; a well-organized Indian police to enforce the laws; and a division of reserve lands into farms which should be assigned to individual Indians in severalty. The administration of Secretary Schurz gave substance to all these policies.

The progress of Indian education and civilization began to be a real thing during Hayes's presidency.

Most of the wars were over, permanency in residence could be relied on to a considerable degree, the Indians could better be counted, tabulated, and handled. In 1880, the last year of Schurz in the Interior Department, the Indian Office reported an Indian population of 256,127 for the United States, excluding Alaska. Of these, 138,642 were described as wearing citizen's dress, while 46,330 were able to read. Among them had been erected both boarding and day schools, 72 of the former and 321 of the latter. "Reports from the reservations" were "full of encouragement, showing an increased and more regular attendance of pupils and a growing interest in education on the part of parents." Interest in the problem of Indian education had been aroused in the East as well as among the tribes during the preceding year or two, because of the experiment with which the name of R. H. Pratt was closely connected. The non-resident boarding school, where the children could be taken away from the tribe and educated among whites, had become a factor in Carlisle, Hampton, and Forest Grove. Lieutenant Pratt had opened the first of these with 147 students in November, 1879. His design had been to give to the boys and girls the rudiments of education and training in farming and mechanic arts. His experience had already, in 1880, shown this to be entirely practicable. The boys, uniformed and drilled as soldiers, under their own sergeants and corporals, marched to the music of their own band. Both sexes had exhibited at the Cumberland County Agricultural Fair, where prizes were awarded to many of them for quilts, shirts, pantaloons, bread, harness, tinware, and penmanship. Many of the students had increased their knowledge of white customs by going out in the summers to work in the fields or kitchens of farmers in the East. Here, too, they had shown the capacity for education and development which their bitterest frontier enemies had denied. In 1906 there were twenty-five of these schools with more than 9000 students in attendance.

It was one thing, however, to take the brighter Indian children away from home and teach them the ways of white men, and quite another to persuade the main tribe to support itself by regular labor. The ration system was a pauperizing influence that removed the incentive to work. Trained mechanics, coming home from Carlisle, or Hampton, or Haskell, found no work ready for them, no customers for their trade, and no occupation but to sit around with their relatives and wait for rations. Too much can be made of the success of Indian education, but the progress was real, if not rapid or great. The Montana Crows, for instance, were, in 1904, encouraged into agricultural rivalry by a county fair. Their congenital love for gambling was converted into competition over pumpkins and live stock. In 1906 they had not been drawing rations for nearly two years. While their settling down was but a single incident in tribal education and not a general reform, it indicated at least a change in emphasis in Indian conditions since the warlike sixties.   The brilliant green placard which announced their county fair for 1906 bears witness to this: —

"CROWS, WAKE UP!

"Your Big Fair Will Take Place Early in October.
"Begin Planting for it Now.
"Plant a Good Garden.
"Put in Wheat and Oats.
Get Your Horses, Cattle, Pigs, and Chickens in Shape to Bring to the Fair.
Cash Prizes and Badges will be awarded to Indians Making Best Exhibits.
"Get Busy.   Tell Your Neighbor to Go Home and Get Busy, too.
"Committee."

A great practical obstruction in the road of economic independence for the Indians was the absence of a legal system governing their relations, and more particularly securing to them individual owner-ship of land.   Treated as independent nations by the United States, no attempt had been made to pass civil or even criminal laws for them, while the tribal organizations had been too primitive to do much of this on their own account.   Individual attempts at progress were often checked by the fact that crime went unpunished in the Indian Country.   An Indian police, embracing 815 officers and men, had existed in 1880, but the law respecting trespassers on Indian lands was inadequate, and Congress was slow in providing codes and courts for the reservations. The Secretary of the Interior erected agency courts on his own authority in 1883; Congress extended certain laws over the tribes in 1885; and a little

2 A

later provided salaries for the officials of the agency courts.

An act passed in 1887 for the ownership of lands in severalty by Indians marked a great step towards solidifying Indian civilization. There had been no greater obstacle to this civilization than communal ownership of land. The tribal standard was one of hunting, with agriculture as an incidental and rather degrading feature. Few of the tribes had any recognition of individual ownership. The educated Indian and the savage alike were forced into economic stagnation by the system. Education could accomplish little in face of it. The changes of the seventies brought a growing recognition of the evil and repeated requests that Congress begin the breaking down of the tribal system through the substitution of Indian ownership.

In isolated cases and by special treaty provisions a few of the Indians had been permitted to acquire lands and be blended in the body of American citizens. But no general statute existed until the passage of the Dawes bill in February, 1887. In this year the Commissioner estimated that there were 243,299 Indians in the United States, occupying a total of 213,117 square miles of land, nearly a section apiece. By the Dawes bill the President was given authority to divide the reserves among the Indians located on them, distributing the lands on the basis of a quarter section or 160 acres to each head of a family, an eighth section to single adults and orphans, and a sixteenth to each dependent child.   It was provided also that when the allotments had been made, tribal owner-ship should cease, and the title to each farm should rest in the individual Indian or his heirs.   But to forestall the improvident sale of this land the owner was to be denied the power to mortgage or dispose of it for at least twenty-five years.   The United States was to hold it in trust for him for this time.

Besides allowing the Indian to own his farm and thus take his step toward economic independence, the Dawes bill admitted him to citizenship.   Once the lands had been allotted, the owners came within the full jurisdiction of the states or territories where they lived, and became amenable to and protected by the law as citizens of the United States.

The policy which had been recommended since the time of Schurz became the accepted policy of the United States in 1887.   "I fail to comprehend the full import of the allotment act if it was not the pur-pose of the Congress which passed it and the Exec-utive whose signature made it a law ultimately to dissolve all tribal relations and to place each adult Indian on the broad platform of American citizen-ship," wrote the Commissioner in 1887.   For the next twenty years the reports of the office were filled with details of subdivision of reserves and the adjust-ment of the legal problems arising from the process. And in the twenty-first year the old Indian Country ceased to exist as such, coming into the Union as the state of Oklahoma.

The progress of allotment under the Dawes bill steadily broke down the reserves of the so-called Indian Territory. Except the five civilized tribes, Cherokees, Creeks, Choctaws, Chickasaws, and Seminoles, the inhabitants who had been colonized there since the Civil War wanted to take advantage of the act. The civilized tribes preferred a different and more independent system for themselves, and retained their tribal identity until 1906. In the transition it was found that granting citizenship to the Indian in a way increased his danger by opening him to the attack of the liquor dealer and depriving him of some of the special protection of the Indian Office. To meet this danger, as the period of tribal extinction drew near, the Burke act of 1906 modified and continued the provisions of the Dawes bill. The new statute postponed citizenship until the expiration of the twenty-five-year period of trust, while giving complete jurisdiction over the allottee to the United States in the interim. In special cases the Secretary of the Interior was allowed to release from the period of guardianship and trusteeship individual Indians who were competent to manage their own affairs, but for the generality the period of twenty-five years was considered "not too long a time for most Indians to serve their apprenticeship in civic responsibilities."

Already the opening up to legal white settlement had begun. In the Dawes bill it was provided that after the lands had been allotted in severalty the undivided surplus might be bought by the United States and turned into the public domain for entry and settlement. Following this, large areas were purchased in 1888 and 1889, to be settled in 1890. The territory of Oklahoma, created in this year in the western end of Indian Territory, and "No Man's Land," north of Texas, marked the political beginning of the end of Indian Territory. It took nearly twenty years to complete it, through delays in the process of allotment and sale; but in these two decades the work was done thoroughly, the five civilized tribes divided their own lands and abandoned tribal government, and in November, 1908, the state of Oklahoma was admitted by President Roosevelt.

The Indian relations, which were most belligerent in the sixties, had changed completely in the ensuing forty years. In part the change was due to a greater and more definite desire at Washington for peace, but chiefly it was environmental, due to the progress of settlement and transportation which overwhelmed the tribes, destroying their capacity to resist and embedding them firmly in the white population. Oklahoma marked the total abandonment of Monroe's policy of an Indian Country.

CHAPTER XXI

THE LAST STAND OF CHIEF JOSEPH AND SITTING BULL

THE main defence of the last frontier by the Indians ceased with the termination of the Indian wars of the sixties. Here the resistance had most closely resembled a general war with the tribes in close alliance against the invader. With this obstacle overcome, the work left to be done in the conquest of the continent fell into two main classes: terminating Indian resistance by the suppression of sporadic outbreaks in remote byways and letting in the population. The new course of the Indian problem after 1869 led it speedily away from the part it had played in frontier advance until it became merely one of many social or race problems in the United States. It lost its special place as the great illustration of the difficulties of frontier life. But although the new course tended toward chronic peace, there were frequent relapses, here and there, which produced a series of Indian flurries after 1869. Never again do these episodes resemble, however remotely, a general Indian war.

Human nature did not change with the adoption of the so-called peace policy. The government had constantly to be on guard against the dishonest agent, while improved facilities in communication increased the squatters' ability to intrude upon valuable lands. The Sioux treaty of 1868, whereby the United States abandoned the Powder River route and erected the great reserve in Dakota, west of the Missouri River, was scarcely dry before rumors of the discovery of gold in the Black Hills turned the eyes of prospectors thither.

Early in 1870 citizens of Cheyenne and the territory of Wyoming organized a mining and prospecting company that professed an intention to explore the Big Horn country in northern Wyoming, but was believed by the Sioux to contemplate a visit to the Black Hills within their reserve. The local Sioux agent remonstrated against this, and General C. C. Augur was sent to Cheyenne to confer with the leaders of the expedition. He found Wyoming in a state of irritation against the Sioux treaty, which left the Indians in control of their Powder River country — the best third of the territory. He sympathized with the frontiersmen, but finally was forced by orders from Washington to prevent the expedition from starting into the field. Four years later this deferred reconnoissance took place as an official expedition under General Custer, with "great excitement among the whole Sioux." The approach from the northeast of the Northern Pacific, which had reached a landing at Bismarck on the Missouri before the panic of 1873, still further increased the apprehension of the tribes that they were to be dispossessed. The Indian Commissioner, in the end of 1874, believed that no harm would come of the expedition since no great gold finds had been made, but the Montana historian was nearer the truth when he wrote: "The whole Sioux nation was successfully defied." It was a clear violation of the tribal right, and necessarily emboldened the frontiersmen to prospect on their own account.

Still further to disquiet the Sioux, and to give countenance to the disgruntled warrior bands that resented the treaties already made, came the mismanagement of the Red Cloud agency. Professor O. C. Marsh, of Yale College, was stopped by Red Cloud, while on a geological visit to the Black Hills, in November, 1874, and was refused admission to the Indian lands until he agreed to convey to Washington samples of decayed flour and inferior rations which the Indian agent was issuing to the Oglala Sioux. With some time at his disposal, Professor Marsh proceeded to study the new problem thus brought to his notice, and accumulated a mass of evidence which seemed to him to prove the existence of big plots to defraud the government, and mismanagement extending even to the Secretary of the Interior. He published his charges in pamphlet form, and wrote letters of protest to the President, in which he maintained that the Indian officials were trying harder to suppress his evidence than to correct the grievances of the Sioux. He managed to stir up so much interest in the East that the Board of Indian Commissioners finally appointed a committee to investigate the affairs of the Red Cloud agency. The report of the committee in October, 1875, whitewashed many of the individuals attacked by Professor Marsh, and exonerated others of guilt at the expense of their intelligence, but revealed abuses in the Indian Office which might fully justify uneasiness among the Sioux.

To these tribes, already discontented because of their compression and sullen because of mismanagement, the entry of miners into the Black Hills country was the last straw. Probably a thousand miners were there prospecting in the summer of 1875, creating disturbances and exaggerating in the Indian mind the value of the reserve, so that an attempt by the Indian Bureau to negotiate a cession in the autumn came to nothing. The natural tendency of these forces was to drive the younger braves off the reserve, to seek comfort with the non-treaty bands that roamed at will and were scornful of those that lived in peace. Most important of the leaders of these bands was Sitting Bull.

In December the Indian Commissioner, despite the Sioux privilege to pursue the chase, ordered all the Sioux to return to their reserves before February 1, 1876, under penalty of being considered hostile. As yet the mutterings had not broken out in war, and the evidence does not show that conflict was inevitable. The tribes could not have got back on time had they wanted to; but their failure to return led the Indian Office to turn the Sioux over to the War Department. The army began by destroying a friendly village on the 17th of March, a fact attested not by an enemy of the army, but by General H. H. Sibley, of Minnesota, who himself had fought the Sioux with marked success in 1862.

With war now actually begun, three columns were sent into the field to arrest and restrain the hostile Sioux. Of the three commanders, Cook, Gibbon, and Custer, the last-named was the most romantic of fighters. He was already well known for his Cheyenne campaigns and his frontier book. Sherman had described him in 1867 as "young, *very* brave, even to rashness, a good trait for a cavalry officer," and as "ready and willing now to fight the Indians." La Barge, who had carried some of Custer's regiment on his steamer *De Smet*, in 1873, saw him as "an officer . . . clad in buckskin trousers from the seams of which a large fringe was fluttering, red-topped boots, broad sombrero, large gauntlets, flowing hair, and mounted on a spirited animal." His showy vanity and his admitted courage had already got him into more than one difficulty; now on June 25, 1876, his whole column of five companies, excepting only his battle horse, Comanche, and a half-breed scout, was destroyed in a battle on the Little Big Horn. If Custer had lived, he might perhaps have been cleared of the charge of disobedience, as Fetterman might ten years before, but, as it turned out, there were many to lay his death to his own rashness. The war ended before 1876 was over, though Sitting Bull with a small band escaped to Canada, where he worried the Dominion Government for several years. "I know of no instance in history," wrote Bishop Whipple of Minnesota, "where a great nation has so shamelessly violated its solemn oath." The Sioux were crushed, their Black Hills were ceded, and the disappointed tribes settled down to another decade of quiescence.

In 1877 the interest which had made Sitting Bull a hero in the Centennial year was transferred to Chief Joseph, leader of the non-treaty Nez Percés, in the valley of the Snake. This tribe had been a friendly neighbor of the overland migrations since the expedition of Lewis and Clark. Living in the valleys of the Snake and its tributaries, it could easily have hindered the course of travel along the Oregon trail, but the disposition of its chiefs was always good. In 1855 it had begun to treat with the United States and had ceded considerable territory at the conference held by Governor Stevens with Chief Lawyer and Chief Joseph.

The exigencies of the Civil War, failure of Congress to fulfil treaty stipulations, and the discovery of gold along the Snake served to change the character of the Nez Percés. Lawyer's annuity of five hundred dollars, as Principal Chief, was at best not royal, and when its vouchers had to be cashed in greenbacks at from forty-five to fifty cents on the dollar, he complained of hardship. It was difficult to persuade the savage that a depreciated greenback was as good as money. Congress was slow with the annuities promised in 1855. In 1861, only one Indian in six could have a blanket, while the 4393 yards of calico issued allowed under two yards to each Indian. The Commissioner commented mildly upon this, to the effect that "Giving a blanket to one Indian works no satisfaction to the other five, who receive none." The gold boom, with the resulting rise of Lewiston, in the heart of the reserve, brought in so many lawless miners that the treaty of 1855 was soon out of date.

In 1863 a new treaty was held with Chief Lawyer and fifty other headmen, by which certain valleys were surrendered and the bounds of the Lapwai reserve agreed upon. Most of the Nez Percés accepted this, but Chief Joseph refused to sign and gathered about him a band of unreconciled, non-treaty braves who continued to hunt at will over the Wallowa Valley, which Lawyer and his followers had professed to cede. It was an interesting legal point as to the right of a non-treaty chief to claim to own lands ceded by the rest of his tribe. But Joseph, though discontented, was not dangerous, and there was little friction until settlers began to penetrate into his hunting-grounds. In 1873, President Grant created a Wallowa reserve for Joseph's Nez Percés, since they claimed this chiefly as their home. But when they showed no disposition to confine them·

selves to its limits, he revoked the order in 1875.   The
next year a commission, headed by the Secretary of
the Interior, Zachary Chandler, was sent to persuade
Joseph to settle down, but returned without success.
Joseph stood upon his right to continue to occupy
at pleasure the lands which had always belonged
to the Nez Percés, and which he and his followers
had never ceded.   The commission recommended
the segregation of the medicine-men and dreamers,
especially Smohalla, who seemed to provide the
inspiration for Joseph, and the military occupation
of the Wallowa Valley in anticipation of an outbreak
by the tribe against the incoming white settlers.
These things were done in part, but in the spring of
1877, "it becoming evident to Agent Monteith that
all negotiations for the peaceful removal of Joseph
and his band, with other non-treaty Nez Percé
Indians, to the Lapwai Indian reservation in Idaho
must fail of a satisfactory adjustment," the Indian
Office gave it up, and turned the affair over to
General O. O. Howard and the War Department.

The conferences held by Howard with the leaders,
in May, made it clear to them that their alternatives
were to emigrate to Lapwai or to fight.   At first
Howard thought they would yield.   Looking Glass
and White Bird picked out a site on the Clearwater
to which the tribe agreed to remove at once; but
just before the day fixed for the removal, the murder
of one of the Indians near Mt. Idaho led to revenge
directed against the whites and the massacre of

several. War immediately followed, for the next two months covering the borderland of Idaho and Montana with confusion. A whole volume by General Howard has been devoted to its details. Chief Joseph himself discussed it in the *North American Review* in 1879. Dunn has treated it critically in his *Massacres of the Mountains*, and the Montana Historical Society has published many articles concerning it. Considerably less is known of the more important wars which preceded it than of this struggle of the Nez Percés. In August the fighting turned to flight, Chief Joseph abandoning the Salmon River country and crossing into the Yellowstone Valley. In seventy-five days Howard chased him 1321 miles, across the Yellowstone Park toward the Big Horn country and the Sioux reserve. Along the swift flight there were running battles from time to time, while the fugitives replenished their stores and stock from the country through which they passed. Behind them Howard pressed; in their front Colonel Nelson A. Miles was ordered to head them off. Miles caught their trail in the end of September after they had crossed the Missouri River and had headed for the refuge in Canada which Sitting Bull had found. On October 3, 1877, he surprised the Nez Percé camp on Snake Creek, capturing six hundred head of stock and inflicting upon Joseph's band the heaviest blow of the war. Two days later the stubborn chief surrendered to Colonel Miles.

"What shall be done with them?" Commissioner Hayt asked at the end of 1877. For once an Indian band had conducted a war on white principles, obeying the rules of war and refraining from mutilation and torture. Joseph had by his sheer military skill won the admiration and respect of his military opponents. But the murders which had inaugurated the war prevented a return of the tribe to Idaho. To exile they were sent, and Joseph's uprising ended as all such resistances must. The forcible invasion of the territory by the whites was maintained; the tribe was sent in punishment to malarial lands in Indian Territory, where they rapidly dwindled in number. There has been no adequate defence of the policy of the United States from first to last.

The Modoc of northern California, and the Apache of Arizona and New Mexico fought against the inevitable, as did the Sioux and the Nez Percés. The former broke out in resistance in the winter of 1872–1873, after they had long been proscribed by California opinion. In March of 1873 they made their fate sure by the treacherous murder of General E. R. S. Canby and other peace commissioners sent to confer with them. In the war which resulted the Modoc, under Modoc Jack and Scar-Faced Charley, were pursued from cave to ravine among the lava beds of the Modoc country until regular soldiers finally corralled them all. Jack was hanged for murder at Fort Klamath in October, but Charley lived to settle down and reform with a portion of the tribe in Indian Territory.

The Apache had always been a thorn in the flesh of the trifling population of Arizona and New Mexico, and a nuisance to both army and Indian Office. The Navaho, their neighbors, after a hard decade with Carleton and the Bosque Redondo, had quieted down during the seventies and advanced towards economic independence. But the Apache were long in learning the virtues of non-resistance. Bell had found in Arizona a young girl whose adventures as a fifteen-year-old child served to explain the attitude of the whites. She had been carried off by Indians who, when pressed by pursuers, had stripped her naked, knocked her senseless with a tomahawk, pierced her arms with three arrows and a leg with one, and then rolled her down a ravine, there to abandon her. The child had come to, and without food, clothes, or water, had found her way home over thirty miles of mountain paths. Such episodes necessarily inspired the white population with fear and hatred, while the continued residence of the sufferers in the Indians' vicinity illustrates the persistence of the pressure which was sure to overwhelm the tribes in the end. Tucson had retaliated against such excesses of the red men by equal excesses of the whites. Without any immediate provocation, fourscore Arivapa Apache, who had been concentrated under military supervision at Camp Grant, were massacred in cold blood.

General George Crook alone was able to bring order 'nto the Arizona frontier. From 1871 to 1875 he was there in command, — "the beau-ideal Indian fighter," Dunn calls him. For two years he engaged in constant campaigns against the "incorrigibly hostile," but before 1873 was over he had most of his Apache pacified, checked off, and under police supervision. He enrolled them and gave to each a brass identification check, so that it might be easier for his police to watch them. The tribes were passed back to the Indian Office in 1874, and Crook was transferred to another command in 1875. Immediately the Indian Commissioner commenced to concentrate the scattered tribes, but was hindered by hostilities among the Indians themselves quite as bitter as their hatred for the whites. First Victorio, and then Geronimo was the centre of the resistance to the concentration which placed hereditary enemies side by side. They protested against the sites assigned them, and successfully defied the Commissioner to carry out his orders. Crook was brought back to the department in 1882, and after another long war gradually established peace.

Sitting Bull, who had fled to Canada in 1876, returned to Dakota in the early eighties in time to witness the rapid settlement of the northern plains and the growth of the territories towards statehood. After his revolt the Black Hills had been taken away from the tribe, as had been the vague hunting rights over northern Wyoming. Now as statehood advanced in the later eighties, and as population piled up around the edges of the reserve, the time was

2 B

ripe for the medicine-men to preach the coming of a Messiah, and for Sitting Bull to increase his personal following.   Bad crops which in these years produced populism in Kansas and Nebraska, had even greater menace for the half-civilized Indians.   Agents and army officers became aware of the undercurrent of danger some months before trouble broke out.

The state of South Dakota was admitted in November, 1889.   Just a year later the Bureau turned the Sioux country over to the army, and General Nelson A. Miles proceeded to restore peace, especially in the vicinity of the Rosebud and Pine Ridge agencies. The arrest of Sitting Bull, who claimed miraculous powers for himself, and whose "ghost shirts" were supposed to give invulnerability to his followers, was attempted in December.   The troops sent out were resisted, however, and in the mêlée the prophet was killed.   The war which followed was much noticed, but of little consequence.   General Miles had plenty of troops and Hotchkiss guns.   Heliograph stations conveyed news easily and safely. But when orders were issued two weeks after the death of Sitting Bull to disarm the camp at Wounded Knee, the savages resisted.   The troops within reach, far outnumbered, blazed away with their rapid-fire guns, regardless of age or sex, with such effect that more than two hundred Indian bodies, mostly women and children, were found dead upon the field.

With the death of Sitting Bull, turbulence among

the Indians, important enough to be called resistance, came to an end. There had been many other isolated cases of outbreak since the adoption of the peace policy in 1869. There were petty riots and individual murders long after 1890. But there were, and could be, no more Indian wars. Many of the tribes had been educated to half-civilization, while lands in severalty had changed the point of view of many tribesmen. The relative strength of the two races was overwhelmingly in favor of the whites.

CHAPTER XXII

LETTING IN THE POPULATION *

" VEIL them, cover them, wall them round —
Blossom, and creeper, and weed —
Let us forget the sight and the sound,
The smell and the touch of the breed ! "

Thus Kipling wrote of "Letting in the Jungle," upon the Indian village. The forces of nature were turned loose upon it. The gentle deer nibbled at the growing crops, the elephant trampled them down, and the wild pig rooted them up. The mud walls of the thatched huts dissolved in the torrents, and "by the end of the Rains there was roaring Jungle in full blast on the spot that had been under plough not six months before." The white man worked the opposite of this on what remained of the American desert in the last fifteen years of the history of the old frontier. In a decade and a half a greater change came over it than the previous fifty years had seen, and before 1890, it is fair to say that the frontier was no more.

The American frontier, the irregular, imaginary line separating the farm lands and the unused West,

* This chapter follows, in part, F. L. Paxson, "The Pacific Railroads and the Disappearance of the Frontier in America," in Ann. Rep. of the Am. Hist. Assn., 1907, Vol. I, pp. 105–118.

had become nearly a circle before the compromise of 1850. In the form of a wedge with receding flanks it had come down the Ohio and up the Missouri in the last generation. The flanks had widened out in the thirties as Arkansas, and Missouri, and Iowa had received their population. In the next ten years Texas and the Pacific settlements had carried the line further west until the circular shape of the frontier was clearly apparent by the middle of the century. And thus it stood, with changes only in detail, for a generation more. In whatever sense the word "frontier" is used, the fact is the same. If it be taken as the dividing line, as the area enclosed, or as the domain of the trapper and the rancher, the frontier of 1880 was in most of its aspects the frontier of 1850.

The pressure on the frontier line had increased steadily during these thirty years. Population moved easily and rapidly after the Civil War. The agricultural states abutting on the line had grown in size and wealth, with a recognition of the barrier that became clearer as more citizens settled along it. East and south, it was close to the rainfall line which divides easy farming country from the semi-arid plains; west, it was a mountain range. In either case the country enclosed was too refractory to yield to the piecemeal process which had conquered the wilderness along other frontiers, while its check to expansion and hindrance to communication became of increasing consequence as population grew.

Yet the barrier held. By 1850 the agricultural frontier was pressing against it. By 1860 the railway frontier had reached it. The former could not cross it because of the slight temptation to agriculture offered by the lands beyond; the latter was restrained by the prohibitive cost of building railways through an entirely unsettled district. Private initiative had done all it could in reclaiming the continent; the one remaining task called for direct national aid.

The influences operating upon this frontier of the Far·West, though not making it less of a barrier, made it better known than any of the earlier frontiers. In the first place, the trails crossed it, with the result that its geography became well known throughout the country. No other frontier had been the site of a thoroughfare for many years before its actual settlement. Again, the mining discoveries of the later fifties and sixties increased general knowledge of the West, and scattered groups of inhabitants here and there, without populating it in any sense. Finally the Indian friction produced the series of Indian wars which again called the wild West to the centre of the stage for many years.

All of these forces served to advertise the existence of this frontier and its barrier character. They had coöperated to enlarge the railway movement, as it respected the Pacific roads, until the Union Pacific was authorized to meet the new demand; and while the Union Pacific was under construction, other roads to meet the same demands were chartered and promoted. These roads bridged and then dispelled the final barrier.

Congress provided the legal equipment for the annihilation of the entire frontier between 1862 and 1871. The charter acts of the Northern Pacific, the Atlantic and Pacific, the Texas Pacific, and the Southern Pacific at once opened the way for some five new continental lines and closed the period of direct federal aid to railway construction. The Northern Pacific received its charter on the same day that the Union Pacific was given its double subsidy in 1864. It was authorized to join the waters of Lake Superior and Puget Sound, and was to receive a land grant of twenty sections per mile in the states and forty in the territories through which it should run. In the summer of 1866 a third continental route was provided for in the South along the line of the thirty-fifth parallel survey. This, the Atlantic and Pacific, was to build from Springfield, Missouri, by way of Albuquerque, New Mexico, to the Pacific, and to connect, near the eastern line of California, with the Southern Pacific, of California. It likewise was promised twenty sections of land in the states and forty in the territories. The Texas Pacific was chartered March 3, 1871, as the last of the land grant railways. It received the usual grant, which was applicable only west of Texas; within that state, between Texarkana and El Paso, it could receive no federal aid since in Texas there were no public lands. Its charter called

for construction to San Diego, but the Southern
Pacific, building across Arizona and New Mexico,
headed it off at El Paso, and it got no farther.

To these deliberate acts in aid of the Pacific railways, Congress added others in the form of local
or state grants in the same years, so that by 1871 all
that the companies could ask for the future was
lenient interpretation of their contracts. For the
first time the federal government had taken an active initiative in providing for the destruction of a
frontier. Its resolution, in 1871, to treat no longer
with the Indian tribes as independent nations is evidence of a realization of the approaching frontier
change.

The new Pacific railways began to build just as the
Union Pacific was completed and opened to traffic.
In the cases of all, the development was slow, since
the investing public had little confidence in the existence of a business large enough to maintain four
systems, or in the fertility of the semi-arid desert.
The first period of construction of all these roads ter-
minated in 1873, when panic brought transportation
projects to an end, and forbade revival for a period of
five years.

Jay Cooke, whose Philadelphia house had done
much to establish public credit during the war and
had created a market of small buyers for investment securities on the strength of United States
bonds, popularized the Northern Pacific in 1869
and 1870. Within two years he is said to have

raised thirty millions for the construction of the road, making its building a financial possibility. And although he may have distorted the isotherm several degrees in order to picture his farm lands as semitropical in their luxuriance, as General Hazen charged, he established Duluth and Tacoma, gave St. Paul her opportunity, and had run the main line of track through Fargo, on the Red, to Bismarck, on the Missouri, more than three hundred and fifty miles from Lake Superior, before his failure in 1873 brought expansion to an end.

For the Northwest, the construction of the Northern Pacific was of fundamental importance. The railway frontier of 1869 left Minnesota, Dakota, and much of Wisconsin beyond its reach. The potential grain fields of the Red River region were virgin forest, and on the main line of the new road, for two thousand miles, hardly a trace of settled habitation existed. The panic of 1873 caught the Union Pacific at Bismarck, with nearly three hundred miles of unprofitable track extending in advance of the railroad frontier. The Atlantic and Pacific and Texas Pacific were less seriously overbuilt, but not less effectively checked. The former, starting from Springfield, had constructed across southwestern Missouri to Vinita, in Indian Territory, where it arrived in the fall of 1871. It had meanwhile acquired some of the old Missouri state-aided roads, so as to get track into St. Louis. The panic forced it to default, Vinita remained its terminus for several years, and when it emerged from the receiver's hands, it bore the new name of St. Louis and San Francisco.

The Texas Pacific represented a consolidation of local lines which expected, through federal incorporation, to reach the dignity of a continental railroad. It began its construction towards El Paso from Shreveport, Louisiana, and Texarkana, on the state line, and reached the vicinity of Dallas and Fort Worth before the panic. It planned to get into St. Louis over the St. Louis, Iron Mountain, and Southern, and into New Orleans over the New Orleans Pacific. The borderland of Texas, Arkansas, and Missouri became through these lines a centre of railway development, while in the near-by grazing country the meat-packing industries shortly found their sources of supply.

The panic which the failure of Jay Cooke precipitated in 1873 could scarcely have been deferred for many years. The waste of the Civil War period, and the enthusiasm for economic development which followed it, invited the retribution that usually follows continued and widespread inflation. Already the completion of a national railway system was foreshadowed. Heretofore the western demand had been for railways at any cost, but the Granger activities following the panic gave warning of an approaching period when this should be changed into a demand for regulation of railroads. But as yet the frontier remained substantially intact, and until its railway system should be completed the

Granger demand could not be translated into an effective movement for federal control. It was not until 1879 that the United States recovered from the depression following the crisis. In that year resumption marked the readjustment of national currency, reconstruction was over, and the railways entered upon the last five years of the culminating period in the history of the frontier. When the five years were over, five new continental routes were available for transportation.

The Texas and Pacific had hardly started its progress across Texas when checked by the panic in the vicinity of Fort Worth. When it revived, it pushed its track towards Sierra Blanca and El Paso, aided by a land grant from the state. Beyond Texas it never built. Corporations of California, Arizona, and New Mexico, all bearing the name of Southern Pacific, constructed the line across the Colorado River and along the Gila, through lands acquired by the Gadsden Purchase of 1853. Trains were running over its tracks to St. Louis by January, 1882, and to New Orleans by the following October. In the course of this Southern Pacific construction, connection had been made with the Atchison, Topeka, and Santa Fé at Deming, New Mexico, in March, 1881, but through lack of harmony between the roads their junction was of little consequence.

The owners of the Southern Pacific opened an additional line through southern Texas in the beginning of 1883. Around the Galveston, Harrisburg,

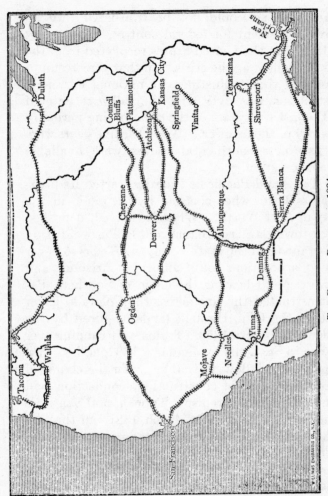

THE PACIFIC RAILROADS, 1884

This map shows only the main lines of the continental railroads in 1884, and omits the branch lines and local roads which existed everywhere and were specially thick in the Mississippi and lower Missouri valleys.

and San Antonio, of Texas, they had grouped other lines and begun double construction from San Antonio west, and from El Paso, or more accurately Sierra Blanca, east. Between El Paso and Sierra Blanca, a distance of about ninety miles, this new line and the Texas and Pacific used the same track. In later years the line through San Antonio and Houston became the main line of the Southern Pacific.

A third connection of the Southern Pacific across Texas was operated before the end of 1883 over its Mojave extension in California and the Atlantic and Pacific from the Needles to Albuquerque. The old Atlantic and Pacific had built to Vinita, gone into receivership, and come out as St. Louis and San Francisco. But its land grant had remained unused, while the Atchison, Topeka, and Santa Fé had reached Albuquerque and had exhausted its own land grant, received through the state of Kansas and ceasing at the Colorado line. Entering Colorado, the latter had passed by Las Animas and thrown a branch along the old Santa Fé trail to Santa Fé and Albuquerque. Here it came to an agreement with the St. Louis and San Francisco, by which the two roads were to build jointly under the Atlantic and Pacific franchise, from Albuquerque into California. They built rapidly; but the Southern Pacific, not relishing a rival in its state, had made use of its charter privilege to meet the new road on the eastern boundary of California. Hence its Mojave branch was waiting at the Needles when the Atlantic and Pacific arrived there; and the latter built no farther.   Upon the completion of bridges over the Colorado and Rio Grande this third eastern connection of the Southern Pacific was completed so that Pullman cars were running through into St. Louis on October 21, 1883.

The names of Billings and Villard are most closely connected with the renascence of the Northern Pacific.   The panic had stopped this line at the Missouri River, although it had built a few miles in Washington territory, around its new terminal city of Tacoma.   The illumination of crisis times had served to discredit the route as effectively as Jay Cooke had served to boom it with advertisements in his palmy days.   The existence of various land grant railways in Washington and Oregon made the revival difficult to finance since its various rivals could offer competition by both water and rail along the Columbia River, below Walla Walla.   Under the presidency of Frederick Billings construction revived about 1879, from Mandan, opposite Bismarck on the Missouri, and from Wallula, at the junction of the Columbia and Snake.   From these points lines were pushed over the Pend d'Oreille and Missouri divisions towards the continental divide.   Below Wallula, the Columbia Valley traffic was shared by agreement with the Oregon Railway and Navigation Company, which, under the presidency of Henry Villard, owned the steamship and railway lines of Oregon.   As the time for opening the through lines approached, the question of Columbia River competition increased in serious aspect. Villard solved the problem through the agency of his famous blind pool, which still stands remarkable in railway finance. With the proceeds of the pool he organized the Oregon and Transcontinental as a holding company, and purchased a controlling interest in the rival roads. With harmony of plan thus insured, he assumed the presidency of the Northern Pacific in 1881, in time to complete and celebrate the opening of its main line in 1883. His celebration was elaborate, yet the *Nation* remarked that the "mere achievement of laying a continuous rail across the continent has long since been taken out of the realm of marvels, and the country can never feel again the thrill which the joining of the Central and Union Pacific lines gave it."

The land grant railways completed these four eastern connections across the frontier in the period of culmination. Private capital added a fifth in the new route through Denver and Ogden, controlled by the Chicago, Burlington, and Quincy and the Denver and Rio Grande. The Burlington, built along the old Republican River trail to Denver, had competed with the Union Pacific for the traffic of that point since June, 1882. West of Denver the narrow gauge of the Denver and Rio Grande had been advancing since 1870.

General William J. Palmer and a group of Philadelphia capitalists had, in 1870, secured a Colorado

charter for their Denver and Rio Grande. Started
in 1871, it had reached the new settlement at
Colorado Springs that autumn, and had continued
south in later years. Like other roads it had progressed slowly in the panic years. In 1876 it had
been met at Pueblo by the Atchison, Topeka, and
Santa Fé. From Pueblo it contested successfully
with this rival for the grand cañon of the Arkansas,
and built up that valley through the Gunnison
country and across the old Ute reserve, to Grand
Junction. From the Utah line it had been continued to Ogden by an allied corporation. A
through service to Ogden, inaugurated in the summer
of 1883, brought competition to the Union Pacific
throughout its whole extent.

The continental frontier, whose isolation the Union
Pacific had threatened in 1869, was easily accessible
by 1884. Along six different lines between New
Orleans and St. Paul it had been made possible to
cross the sometime American desert to the Pacific
states. No longer could any portion of the republic
be considered as beyond the reach of civilization.
Instead of a waste that forbade national unity in its
presence, a thousand plains stations beckoned for
colonists, and through lines of railway iron bound
the nation into an economic and political unit. "As
the railroads overtook the successive lines of isolated
frontier posts, and settlements spread out over
country no longer requiring military protection,"
wrote General P. H. Sheridan in 1882, "the army

vacated its temporary shelters and marched on into remote regions beyond, there to repeat and continue its pioneer work. In rear of the advancing line of troops the primitive 'dug-outs' and cabins of the frontiersmen, were steadily replaced by the tasteful houses, thrifty farms, neat villages, and busy towns of a people who knew how best to employ the vast resources of the great West. The civilization from the Atlantic is now reaching out toward that rapidly approaching it from the direction of the Pacific, the long intervening strip of territory, extending from the British possessions to Old Mexico, yearly growing narrower; finally the dividing lines will entirely disappear and the mingling settlements absorb the remnants of the once powerful Indian nations who, fifteen years ago, vainly attempted to forbid the destined progress of the age." The deluge of population realized by Sheridan, and let in by the railways, had, by 1890, blotted the uninhabited frontier off the map. Local spots yet remained unpeopled, but the census of 1890 revealed no clear division between the unsettled West and the rest of the United States.

New states in plains and mountains marked the abolition of the last frontier as they had the earlier. In less than ten years the gap between Minnesota and Oregon was filled in: North Dakota and South Dakota, Montana, Idaho, Wyoming, and Washington. In 1890, for the first time, a solid band of states connected the Atlantic and Pacific. Farther

2 c

south, the Indian Country succumbed to the new pressure. The Dawes bill released a fertile acreage to be distributed to the land hungry who had banked up around the borders of Kansas, Arkansas, and Texas. Oklahoma, as a territory, appeared in 1890, while in eighteen more years, swallowing up the whole Indian Country, it had taken its place as a member of the Union. Between the northern tier of states and Oklahoma, the middle West had grown as well. Kansas, Nebraska, and Colorado, the last creating eleven new counties in its eastern third in 1889, had seen their population densify under the stimulus of easy transportation. Much of the settlement had been premature, inviting failure, as populism later showed, but it left no area in the United States unreclaimed, inaccessible, and large enough to be regarded as a national frontier. The last frontier, the same that Long had described as the American Desert in 1820, had been won.

NOTE ON THE SOURCES

THE fundamental ideas upon which all recent careful work in western history has been based were first stated by Frederick J. Turner, in his paper on *The Significance of the Frontier in American History*, in the *Annual Report of the Am. Hist. Assn.*, 1893. No comprehensive history of the trans-Mississippi West has yet appeared; Randall Parrish, *The Great Plains* (2d ed., Chicago, 1907), is at best only a brief and superficial sketch; the histories of the several far western states by Hubert Howe Bancroft remain the most useful collection of secondary materials upon the subject. R. G. Thwaites, *Rocky Mountain Exploration* (N.Y., 1904); O. P. Austin, *Steps in the Expansion of our Territory* (N.Y., 1903); H. Gannett, *Boundaries of the United States and of the Several States and Territories* (*Bulletin of the U.S. Geological Survey*, No. 226, 1904); and *Organic Acts for the Territories of the United States with Notes thereon* (56th Cong., 1st sess., Sen. Doc. 148), are also of use.

The local history of the West must yet be collected from many varieties of sources. The state historical societies have been active for many years, their more important collections comprising: *Publications of the Arkansas Hist. Assn., Annals of Iowa, Iowa Hist. Record, Iowa Journal of Hist. and Politics, Collections of the Minnesota Hist. Soc., Trans. of the Kansas State Hist. Soc., Trans. and Rep. of the Nebraska Hist. Soc., Proceedings of the Missouri Hist. Soc., Contrib. to the Hist. Soc. of Montana, Quart. of the Oregon Hist. Soc., Quart. of the Texas State Hist. Assn., Collections of the Wisconsin State Hist. Soc.* The scattered but valuable fragments to be found in these files are to be supplemented by the narratives contained in the histories of the single states or sections, the more important of these being:

T. H. Hittell, *California;* F. Hall, *Colorado;* J. C. Smiley, *Denver* (an unusually accurate and full piece of local history); W. Upham, *Minnesota in Three Centuries;* G. P. Garrison, *Texas;* E. H. Meany, *Washington;* J. Schafer, *Hist. of the Pacific Northwest;* R. G. Thwaites, *Wisconsin,* and the *Works* of H. H. Bancroft.

The comprehensive collection of geographic data for the West is the *Reports of Explorations and Surveys for a Railroad from the Mississippi River to the Pacific Ocean,* made by the War Department and published by Congress in twelve huge volumes, 1855 –. The most important official predecessors of this survey left the following reports: E. James, *Account of an Expedition from Pittsburg to the Rocky Mountains, performed in the Years 1819, 1820, . . . under the Command of Maj. S. H. Long* (Phila., 1823); J. C. Frémont, *Report of the Exploring Expeditions to the Rocky Mountains in the Year 1842, and to Oregon and North California in the Years 1843–'44* (28th Cong., 2d sess., Sen. Doc. 174); W. H. Emory, *Notes of a Military Reconnoissance from Ft. Leavenworth . . . to San Diego . . .* (30th Cong., 1st sess., Ex. Doc. 41); H. Stansbury, *Exploration and Survey of the Valley of the Great Salt Lake of Utah . . .* (32d Cong., 1st sess., Sen. Ex. Doc. 3). From the great number of personal narratives of western trips, those of James O. Pattie, John B. Wyeth, John K. Townsend, and Joel Palmer may be selected as typical and useful. All of these, as well as the James narrative of the Long expedition, are reprinted in the monumental R. G. Thwaites, *Early Western Travels,* which does not, however, give any aid for the period after 1850. Later travels of importance are J. I. Thornton, *Oregon and California in 1848 . . .* (N.Y., 1849); Horace Greeley, *An Overland Journey from New York to San Francisco in the Summer of 1859* (N.Y., 1860); R. F. Burton, *The City of the Saints, and across the Rocky Mountains to California* (N.Y., 1862); R. B. Marcy, *The Prairie Traveller, a Handbook for Overland Expeditions* (edited by R. F. Burton, London, 1863); F. C. Young, *Across the Plains in '65* (Denver, 1905); Samuel Bowles, *Across the Continent* (Springfield, 1861); Samuel

Bowles, *Our New West, Records of Travels between the Mississippi River and the Pacific Ocean* (Hartford, 1869); W. A. Bell, *New Tracks in North America* (2d ed., London, 1870); J. H. Beadle, *The Undeveloped West, or Five Years in the Territories* (Phila., 1873).

The classic account of traffic on the plains is Josiah Gregg, *Commerce of the Prairies, or the Journal of a Santa Fé Trader* (many editions, and reprinted in Thwaites); H. M. Chittenden, *History of Steamboat Navigation on the Missouri River* (N.Y., 1903), and *The American Fur Trade of the Far West* (N.Y, 1902), are the best modern accounts. A brilliant sketch is C. F. Lummis, *Pioneer Transportation in America, Its Curiosities and Romance* (*McClure's Magazine*, 1905). Other works of use are Henry Inman, *The Old Santa Fé Trail* (N.Y., 1898); Henry Inman and William F. Cody, *The Great Salt Lake Trail* (N.Y., 1898); F. A. Root and W. E. Connelley, *The Overland Stage to California* (Topeka, 1901); F. G. Young, *The Oregon Trail*, in *Oregon Hist. Soc. Quarterly*, Vol. I; F. Parkman, *The Oregon Trail*.

Railway transportation in the Far West yet awaits its historian. Some useful antiquarian data are to be found in C. F. Carter, *When Railroads were New* (N.Y., 1909), and there are a few histories of single roads, the most valuable being J. P. Davis, *The Union Pacific Railway* (Chicago, 1894), and E. V. Smalley, *History of the Northern Pacific Railroad* (N.Y., 1883). L. H. Haney, *A Congressional History of Railways in the United States to 1850;* J. B. Sanborn, *Congressional Grants of Lands in Aid of Railways*, and B. H. Meyer, *The Northern Securities Case*, all in the *Bulletins* of the University of Wisconsin, contain much information and useful bibliographies. The local historical societies have published many brief articles on single lines. There is a bibliography of the continental railways in F. L. Paxson, *The Pacific Railroads and the Disappearance of the Frontier in America*, in *Ann. Rep. of the Am. Hist. Assn.*, 1907. Their social and political aspects may be traced in J. B. Crawford, *The*

Credit Mobilier of America (Boston, 1880) and E. W. Martin, *History of the Granger Movement* (1874). The sources, which are as yet uncollected, are largely in the government documents and the files of the economic and railroad periodicals.

For half a century, during which the Indian problem reached and passed its most difficult places, the United States was negligent in publishing compilations of Indian laws and treaties. In 1837 the Commissioner of Indian Affairs published in Washington, *Treaties between the United States of America and the Several Indian Tribes, from 1778 to 1837: with a copious Table of Contents.* After this date, documents and correspondence were to be found only in the intricate sessional papers and the *Annual Reports of the Commissioner of Indian Affairs,* which accompanied the reports of the Secretary of War, 1832–1849, and those of the Secretary of the Interior after 1849. In 1902 Congress published C. J. Kappler, *Indian Affairs, Laws, and Treaties* (57th Cong., 1st sess., Sen. Doc. 452). Few historians have made serious use of these compilations or reports. Two other government documents of great value in the history of Indian negotiations are, Thomas Donaldson, *The Public Domain* (47th Cong., 2d sess., H. Misc. Doc. 45, Pt. 4), and C. C. Royce, *Indian Land Cessions in the United States* (with many charts, in 18th *Ann. Rep. of the Bureau of Am. Ethnology*, Pt. 2, 1896–1897). Most special works on the Indians are partisan, spectacular, or ill informed; occasionally they have all these qualities. A few of the most accessible are: A. H. Abel, *History of the Events resulting in Indian Consolidation West of the Mississippi* (in *Ann. Rep. of the Am. Hist. Assn.,* 1906, an elaborate and scholarly work); J. P. Dunn, *Massacres of the Mountains, a History of the Indian Wars of the Far West* (N.Y., 1886; a relatively critical work, with some bibliography); R. I. Dodge, *Our Wild Indians . . .* (Hartford, 1883); G. E. Edwards, *The Red Man and the White Man in North America from its Discovery to the Present Time* (Boston, 1882; a series of Lowell Institute lectures, by no means so valuable as the pretentious title would indicate); I. V. D.

Heard, *History of the Sioux War and Massacres of 1862 and 1863* (N.Y., 1863; a contemporary and useful narrative); O. O. Howard, *Nez Perce Joseph, an Account of his Ancestors, his Lands, his Confederates, his Enemies, his Murders, his War, his Pursuit and Capture* (Boston, 1881; this is General Howard's personal vindication); Mrs. Helen Hunt Jackson, *A Century of Dishonor, a Sketch of the United States Government's Dealings with Some of the Indian Tribes* (N.Y., 1881; highly colored and partisan); G. W. Manypenny, *Our Indian Wards* (Cincinnati, 1880; by a former Indian Commissioner); L. E. Textor, *Official Relations between the United States and the Sioux Indians* (Palo Alto, 1896; one of the few scholarly and dispassionate works on the Indians); F. A. Walker, *The Indian Question* (Boston, 1874; three essays by a former Indian Commissioner); C. T. Brady, *Indian Fights and Fighters* and *Northwestern Fights and Fighters* (N.Y., 1907; two volumes in his series of *American Fights and Fighters*, prepared for consumers of popular sensational literature, but containing much valuable detail, and some critical judgments).

Nearly every incident in the history of Indian relations has been made the subject of investigations by the War and Interior departments. The resulting collections of papers are to be found in the congressional documents, through the indexes. They are too numerous to be listed here. The searcher should look for reports from the Secretary of War, the Secretary of the Interior, or the Postmaster-general, for court-martial proceedings, and for reports of special committees of Congress. Dunn gives some classified lists in his *Massacres of the Mountains*.

There is a rapidly increasing mass of individual biography and reminiscence for the West during this period. Some works of this class which have been found useful here are: W. M. Meigs, *Thomas Hart Benton* (Phila., 1904); C. W. Upham, *Life, Explorations, and Public Services of John Charles Frémont* (40th thousand, Boston, 1856); S. B. Harding, *Life of George B. Smith, Founder of Sedalia, Missouri* (Sedalia, 1907); P. H. Burnett, *Recollections and Opinions of an Old Pioneer* (N.Y., 1880; by one who had followed

the Oregon trail and had later become governor of California);
A. Johnson, *S. A. Douglas* (N.Y., 1908; one of the most significant biographies of recent years); H. Stevens, *Life of Isaac
Ingalls Stevens* (Boston, 1900); R. S. Thorndike, *The Sherman
Letters* (N.Y., 1894; full of references to frontier conditions in the
sixties); P. H. Sheridan, *Personal Memoirs* (London, 1888; with
a good map of the Indian war of 1867–1868, which the later
edition has dropped); E. P. Oberholtzer, *Jay Cooke, Financier
of the Civil War* (Phila., 1907; with details of Northern Pacific
railway finance); H. Villard, *Memoirs* (Boston, 1904; the life of
an active railway financier); Alexander Majors, *Seventy Years on
the Frontier* (N.Y., 1893; the reminiscences of one who had belonged to the great firm of Russell, Majors, and Waddell); G. R.
Brown, *Reminiscences of William M. Stewart of Nevada* (1908).

Miscellaneous works indicating various types of materials
which have been drawn upon are: O. J. Hollister, *The Mines of
Colorado* (Springfield, 1867; a miners' handbook); S. Mowry,
Arizona and Sonora (3d ed., 1864; written in the spirit of a mining
prospectus); T. B. H. Stenhouse, *The Rocky Mountain Saints*
(London, 1874; a credible account from a Mormon missionary
who had recanted without bitterness); W. A. Linn, *The Story
of the Mormons* (N.Y., 1902; the only critical history of the
Mormons, but having a strong Gentile bias); T. J. Dimsdale, *The
Vigilantes of Montana, or Popular Justice in the Rocky Mountains* (2d ed., Virginia City, 1882; a good description of the
social order of the mining camp).

INDEX

DATE DUE

Please remember that this is a library book,
and that it belongs only temporarily to each
person who uses it. Be considerate. Do
not write in this, or any, library book.